The Gardener's Guide
to Growing
CLEMATIS

The Gardener's Guide to Growing
CLEMATIS

Raymond J. Evison

David & Charles
Newton Abbot

TIMBER PRESS
Portland, Oregon

PICTURE ACKNOWLEDGEMENTS
Karl Adamson 24, 31,44, 62, 66, 82, 86, 108, 116; John De Garis 6;
all other photographs © Raymond J. Evison

Illustrations on pages 12 and 14 by Coral Mula

NOTE: Throughout the book the time of year is given as a season to make the reference
applicable to readers all over the world. In the northern hemisphere the seasons may be
translated into months as follows:

Early winter	December	*Early spring*	March	*Early summer*	June	*Early autumn*	September
Midwinter	January	*Mid-spring*	April	*Midsummer*	July	*Mid-autumn*	October
Late winter	February	*Late spring*	May	*Late summer*	August	*Late autumn*	November

First published in the UK in 1998 by David & Charles Publishers,
Brunel House, Newton Abbot, Devon
ISBN 0 7153 0639 1

First published in North America in 1998 by Timber Press Inc.,
133 SW Second Avenue, Suite 450, Portland, Oregon 97204, USA
ISBN 0-88192-423-7
Cataloguing-in-Publication Data is on file with the Library of Congress

Typeset by ACE
and printed in Italy by Lego SpA

♈ The Award of Garden Merit (AGM) is given by the Royal Horticultural Society to recognize plants
of outstanding excellence for garden use, whether grown in the open or under glass. The AGM is of practical value for gardeners
in that it highlights exceptional plants among the tens of thousands currently offered in the international horticultural trade.

The Ⓝ symbol stands for a variety that is protected either by
Plant Breeders' Rights or Plant Patent.

ACKNOWLEDGEMENT
The author wishes to thank Diana Rowland for her help with the preparation of this text
and David & Jane Russell for the use of their garden, Mille Fleurs, Guernsey.

Photographs page 1 C. 'Burma Star'; page 2 C. 'Walter Pennell'; page 3 C. 'Proteus'

CONTENTS

INTRODUCTION

For the plant collector, plant breeder and gardener, the genus *Clematis* encompasses some of the most fascinating of flowering plants. The flower form and colour, foliage and seedheads are so variable among the 200 or so species recorded that they seem too diverse to be considered a single genus. Even as a group of plants, the variation seems inexplicable if the pitcher-shaped red flowers of *C. texensis* from the USA are compared with the pale blue hyacinth-like flowers of *C. heracleifolia* from China, or the flat white flowers of *C. florida* from China with those of the thick yellow-tepalled flowers of *C. tibetana* spp. *vernayi* L & S 13342 from Tibet. Some of the species perhaps have no garden value except for a collector or for reference in a botanic garden. Others have become household names, such as *C. armandii*, with its swags of scented white flowers and large handsome evergreen leaves, and *C. montana* and its botanical variants and cultivars, which can rampage to great heights, delivering a waterfall of white or pink flowers in late spring.

Some species grow to 15 m (50 ft) high; others creep at ground level, like *C. columbiana* var. *tenuiloba* from northwest USA or the evergreen *C. marmoraria*, which reaches only 10–12.5 cm (4–5 in) high and looks like dwarf parsley. Some, such as *C. integrifolia* from Europe, are perennials. The scent produced by some species, such as *C. recta* from central Europe and *C. flammula* from Southern Europe, is outstanding. Sadly, this strength of scent has not been bred into the large-flowered cultivars as yet.

The large-flowered cultivars, which began to appear from the 1850s onwards, either from Japanese gardens or from British and European breeders, have given the genus an even larger range of flower shape and colour. They bloom at different times from the species and over a longer period, thus extending the clematis flowering season. Today, with the use of a conservatory or cold glasshouse and a mild climate, it is possible to have clematis flowering the whole year through. As I write this on a sunny January day in Guernsey, *C. florida*, *C. f.* 'Plena', *C. f.* 'Sieboldii' and *C. viticella* 'Venosa Violacea' are still in full flower in my cold glasshouse.

Needless to say, there is a drawback. Most of the hardy gardenworthy species and their small-flowered hybrids can establish themselves quite easily and can then be guaranteed to produce flowers for many years. Sadly, this is not the case with the large-flowered cultivars, as some succumb to clematis wilt before they become established. However, most plants do overcome wilt; even if they do not, gardeners do persevere. My guess is that this is because clematis have a special mystique. They are sometimes not easy to establish, so they provide a challenge; but once they are established, their beauty, elegance and sheer volume of outstanding flowers offer the greatest reward a gardener can wish for.

My own fascination with the genus began when I was 16, and I subsequently had the good fortune to attend the Chelsea Flower Show to help Percy Picton and his son Paul on their alpine exhibit. Percy Picton, a great plantsman, introduced many plants to British gardens, including some clematis – notably *C.* 'Silver Moon' and *C.* 'Hagley Hybrid'. As a younger man, Percy worked for the great old gentleman of British gardening, William Robinson, at Gravetye Manor in Sussex, under the head gardener, Ernest Markham. I believe his stories of clematis growing and breeding were responsible for my great respect for this astonishing genus.

C. JOSEPHINE™ 'Evijohill' Ⓝ, discovered by Mrs Josephine Hill and introduced in 1998 by the author.

1

HABITAT, CLASSIFICATION & BOTANY

This chapter is perhaps one of the most important in the book, as it explains the classification of clematis into groups. The system of grouping is intended to help the gardener in a practical way, giving a guide to cultivation conditions, garden use and, very importantly, pruning requirements. With such a very diverse genus, which includes over 200 species and well over 1000 cultivars, understanding the groups into which the plants fall is invaluable. Necessarily, with such a huge genus, only the best-known plants and those of gardenworthy merit can be discussed in this book.

Though clematis species are native to many parts of the world, the majority of the species grown in European and North American gardens are natives of the northern hemisphere. While such charming species as the evergreen Australasians can be grown with care in milder gardens the clematis of the southern hemisphere are generally of botanical interest only, and are for use in heated conservatories where they give the gardener a challenge to grow them successfully to a flowering state.

The European species are very variable and grow in very different habitats. *C. vitalba*, the only species native to the British Isles, grows particularly rampantly on the chalk downs in southern England, where it seeds itself most freely, scrambling to 6–9 m (20–30 ft). It can also be found on wasteland in many areas and soil types where it has naturalized. *C. alpina* of the mountains of Austria, Germany and Switzerland is seen in low-growing trees on the mountainsides or scrambling over rocks. The perennials *C. integrifolia* and *C. recta* can be

found in meadows in central Europe, the former growing on the banks of the Danube in Hungary, while *C. viticella* can be found in the drier regions of southern Europe, from Italy through to Turkey. *C. flammula* grows in southern Europe in Spain and the Balearic Islands in very dry, sunny locations, where it enjoys the poor, free-draining soil. *C. cirrhosa*, an evergreen species, can be found on the coastline throughout southern Europe to Israel, especially enjoying the Balearic Islands, where it is at its most variable. In these hot climates it generally goes into a summer dormancy and loses its foliage, only slowly coming into growth as the temperature drops to about 25°C (77°F) and the moisture of early rain encourages the production of leaves and autumn flowers.

The Himalayas and North America have an interesting range of species, the various pitcher-shaped species being found in the lower half of the eastern and central states of the USA while the Himalayas produce many clematis belonging to the Meclatis Section. However, it is to China that we turn to find the most exciting range of clematis species. China boasts at least 108 species and they vary considerably from *C. armandii*, with large evergreen leaves, to the exciting *C. florida* and the most important species of all, *C. patens*, with its large, flat, open flowers that have given us the many large-flowered clematis for our gardens today. It would take too long to describe the different habitats in which clematis can be found as they are quite variable, but when I have been searching for clematis species in the wild I have found that in most cases they have established themselves firmly in moist places, especially in China where their root system has found a cool spot, very often in a limestone area. In Japan, I have found

C. *viticella* 'Carmencita', a colourful and free-flowering viticella cultivar that was raised in Sweden by Magnus Johnson in 1952 (shown twice normal size).

C. japonica on the edge of a small forest under shade, *C. patens* in thick grass in a meadow, *C. stans* in small cracks in walls with very little moisture at all and *C. terniflora* in thick grassland on banks and roadsides with good moisture levels.

As a generalization, species that are similar in habit grow in similar habitats. *C. vitalba* of Europe and *C. ligusticifolia* and *C. virginiana* of the western and eastern parts of North America all grow in the same type of locations. The Atragene subgenus – *C. alpina* var. *alpina* of Europe, *C. alpina* var. *sibirica* of northern Europe and *C. columbiana* var. *columbiana* and *C. occidentalis* var. *occidentalis* of the USA and Canada – can all be found in mountain habitats. The pitcher-shaped North American species of the Viorna Section are found in the USA only, but in variable locations, while *C. orientalis* and *C. tibetana* of the Meclatis Section are natives of Turkey, the Himalayas and China – not of North America, though they have naturalized there. *C. patens* is found only in northern China and Korea and in Japan, where it has naturalized. *Clematopsis scabiosifolia* (formerly *Clematis stanleyi*) is found only in South Africa, growing best in savannah where its growth has been burned by fire the previous season. It will only grow in very poor soil and hates fertilizer and rich soils.

Clematis species in the wild are scramblers and climbers, though if no support is at hand they will form small clumps or even large mounds. Most plants of climbing habit do find support but in their native environment they do not perform the same when they are grown under cultivation. For example, in the wild in China, *C. chrysocoma* produces a short, stocky plant perhaps 45 cm (18 in) high, but under cultivation it will grow to 2 m (6½ ft) or so.

Some clematis species breed quite freely with each other in the wild. In New Zealand, several species produce hybrids, most notably *C. paniculata*. In South Africa, *C. brachiata* hybridizes freely with *Clematopsis scabiosifolia* (formerly *Clematis stanleyii*) in and around Johannesburg, producing some interesting variants.

CLASSIFICATION

Clematis belong to the *Ranunculaceae* family. Other members of this very large and diverse family include the buttercup (*Ranunculus*) of the meadows, the kingcups (*Caltha*) of moist places, columbines (*Aquilegia*), thalic-

trums, delphiniums, aconitums and hellebores. While the spurs of columbines do resemble those of *Clematis koreana* and thalictrums look like some of the starry white-flowered clematis species found in China, it is hard to see the relationship with delphiniums and hellebores except that the latter, like clematis, enjoy deep alluvial soils which can be acidic. Most of these close cousins of clematis are generally perennial in habit, while a few clematis species, such as *C. integrifolia*, are truly perennials, some being sub-shrubs as in *C. heracleifolia* or climbers having semi-woody to woody stems. The majority of clematis are deciduous but some are evergreen, especially the Australasian species. Because of the vast diversification of the species from short-growing herbaceous perennials to scandent or trailing shrubs and climbers reaching 9–15 m (30–50 ft) in height, the leaf formation is very variable; the leaves may be opposite or alternate, hairy or hairless, simple or pinnate, and with entire or irregular margins. The leaf stalk (petiole) clings on to other objects to assist the plant to climb.

The root system of clematis is also variable. Generally, the small-flowered species have fine fibrous rootlets, especially *C. alpina* and *C. macropetala* of the Atragene subgenus, *C. montana* and the Meclatis Section, making the job of replanting established plants extremely difficult. *C. viticella* has large, more fleshy roots, as does *C. florida*, aligning it closer to the large-flowered cultivars which are probably all descendants of *C. patens* and *C. florida*.

CLASSIFICATION SECTIONS

The clematis species and cultivars listed below in sections are given in order of their flowering period rather than in a systematic classification. In a book such as this, which is intended to be a practical guide for gardeners as opposed to a more detailed reference book, such an approach will help the gardener understand the genus and its cultivation in a logical way. I have followed the classification used by Magnus Johnson in his book *Släktet Klematis*, published by Magnus Johnson, Plantskola AB, Södertälje, Sweden 1997, as the basis for my own classification and the splitting of clematis species into sections.

Evergreen Species & Their Cultivars

These are generally natives of the southern hemisphere, with the exception of *C. cirrhosa* from southern

Europe and evergreen species from China such as *C. armandii*. They produce evergreen leaves in various sizes and forms and flower in nearly all cases from the previous season's ripened stems, during late autumn, early to late winter and early spring. The flowers are produced in racemes as in *C. meyeniana* or fascicles as in *C. cirrhosa* var. *balearica*. They can be bell-shaped and nodding as in *C. cirrhosa* var. *cirrhosa*, or flat and open as in *C. armandii*. The number of tepals vary from four as in *C. napaulensis* to six as in *C. paniculata*. They can be dioecious, that is having male (staminate) and female (pistillate) flowers on different plants as in *C. paniculata*, or hermaphrodite (bisexual), having stamens and pistils in the same flower as in *C. armandii* and *C. cirrhosa*. They produce a range of different types of seedheads, from *C. cirrhosa* with full seedheads which become fluffy as the plumose seed tails age to the sparsely produced seeds of *C. armandii* which are also plumose, the seedheads having no garden value.

The hardiness of this group varies and this is detailed within the A–Z of Species & Cultivars. They must not be thought of as totally winter hardy or plants to be used in a garden location to give dense evergreen cover; rather they should be grown with other plants to provide added interest.

Members of the evergreen group include the following species and their respective cultivars:

The New Zealand evergreen species: *C. afoliata*, *C. australis*, *C. forsteri*, *C. marmoraria*, *C. paniculata*.

Section Aspidantera: *C. aristata*, *C. gentianoides*, *C. glycinoides*, *C. microphylla*.

Section Cheiropsis Subsection Cheiropsis: *C. cirrhosa*, *C. napaulensis*, *C. williamsii*.

Section Flammula Subsection Meyenianae: *C. armandii*, *C. finetiana*, *C. meyeniana*.

Section Flammula Subsection Fasciculiflorae: *C. fasciculiflora*.

The Atragene Section

This section, often recognized as subgenus Atragene, comprises *C. alpina* var. *alpina*, *C. a.* var. *ochotensis*, *C. a.* var. *sibirica*, *C. occidentalis* var. *occidentalis*, *C. o.* var. *grosseserrata*, *C. columbiana* var. *columbiana*, *C. c.* var. *tenuiloba*, *C. macropetala*, *C. koreana* and *C. chiisanensis*, together with their respective cultivars. These species from Europe, North America, China, Mongolia and Korea are deciduous and have ternately compound

C. armandii, a strong-growing Chinese species with evergreen foliage and scented flowers.

leaves, divided into leaflets, some being entire, others having coarse teeth. The flowers are produced on long pedicels from the ripened leaf axil buds from the previous year. They are generally solitary, or occasionally in groups, being bell-shaped at first, opening almost flat with age. They normally have four longer outer tepals with a cluster of petaloid stamens inside as in *C. alpina*, these being more pronounced, larger and longer in *C. macropetala*, giving the appearance of a fully double flower or inner skirt. The flowering period is mid- to late spring, with occasional summer flowers. The seed tails are plumose and produce large attractive seedheads which are sphere-shaped on the top, becoming pointed at the base. All clematis in this section are hermaphrodite and produce seeds freely. *C. alpina* and *C. macropetala* are fully inter-fertile. No hybrids have been

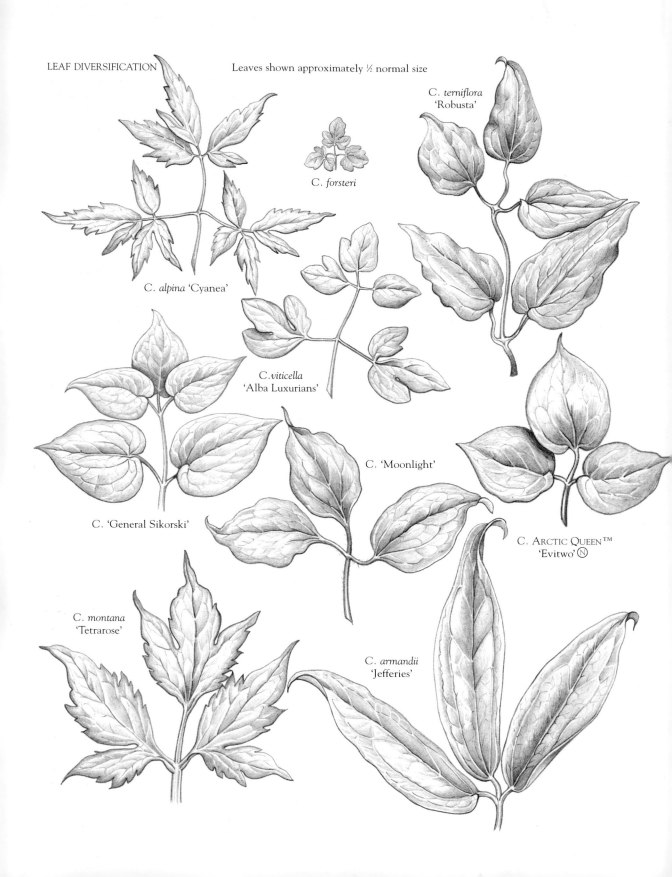

LEAF DIVERSIFICATION   Leaves shown approximately ½ normal size

C. terniflora
'Robusta'

C. forsteri

C. alpina 'Cyanea'

C.viticella
'Alba Luxurians'

C. 'Moonlight'

C. 'General Sikorski'

C. Arctic Queen™
'Evitwo' Ⓝ

C. montana
'Tetrarose'

C. armandii
'Jefferies'

reported between species of this subgenus and species of other subgenera or sections. The clematis within this subgenus are all fully winter hardy to at least −35°C (−31°F) and flower freely after severe winters.

There are some outstanding cultivars in this subgenus, notably of C. *alpina* and C. *macropetala* (see the A–Z of Species & Cultivars).

The Bebaeanthera Section

C. *japonica*, the only species in this section, is akin to the plants in the Atragene Section in habit, but its flowers differ in having only four thick, waxy tepals and no petaloid stamens.

The Cheiropsis Section
Montanae Subsection

Natives of the Himalayas, China and Tibet, these clematis are deciduous and have trifoliate leaves, some with entire leaflets, others toothed. The flowers are produced singly or in clusters on short flower stalks (pedicels) from the ripened leaf axil buds produced the previous year. The flowers have four tepals and are flat open in shape. The seedheads are of little garden value, the seeds being produced rather sparsely, the plumose seed tails becoming fluffy with age. The flowers are borne in late spring to early summer, with occasional summer flowers, with the exception of C. *montana* 'Wilsonii', which flowers in midsummer. They are not fully winter hardy, being hardy to Zones 7–9.

The species which belong to this group include C. *montana* var. *montana*, C. *m.* var. *rubens*, C. *chrysocoma* var. *chrysocoma* and C. *gracilifolia* var. *gracilifolia*. Their cultivars, especially those from C. *montana*, include semi-double and double forms such as C. *montana* 'Broughton Star'.

The evergreen species, the Atragene Section and Montanae Subsection all flower from the ripened previous season's stems, so any pruning which is to be undertaken must be left until they have produced their main crop of flowers between winter and early summer. All belong to pruning group one (see page 46).

The Early Large-flowered Cultivars

These large-flowered flat open-shaped clematis have been derived from C. *patens*, a species native to northern China and Korea, though it has also naturalized in

Japan. The cultivars were produced first in Japan but since 1860 have also originated in Europe and North America. The species patens belongs to Section Viticella Subsection Patens and has been the parent of many of the large-flowered cultivars grown today.

The cultivars are deciduous, with mostly trifoliate leaves, the leaflets lanceolate, entire to occasionally serrate. The single flowers are borne solitarily on stems of varying length directly from the leaf axil buds ripened the previous season. They are flat open in form and 10–20 cm (4–8 in) in diameter with six to eight tepals in a range of bright colours, generally with yellow or red anthers. The seedheads are most attractive, usually spherical, and the seed tails change from green to golden-brown to dark brown. The flowers are produced between late spring and early autumn, the main crop of early flowers appearing from late spring to early summer. Some are almost continuously flowering, while others repeat flower during late summer to early autumn. The later flowers are always smaller than the first crop of flowers.

Cultivars which belong to this section include C. 'Miss Bateman', C. 'Nelly Moser' and C. ANNA LOUISE™ 'Evithree' Ⓡ.

The Semi-double &
Double Large-flowered Cultivars

The clematis within this section grow in a very similar way to those in the previous section, differing in having semi-double or fully double flowers. It is difficult to establish exactly where these clematis were derived from, but they most probably originated as sports from C. *patens* or its cultivars. Some cultivars, for example C. ARCTIC QUEEN™ 'Evitwo' Ⓡ and C. 'Belle of Woking', always produce double flowers, both from the previous season's ripened stems and from the current season's growth. The flowers from the former can be 12 cm (4¾ in) across or larger, those from the current season's growth being smaller. Other cultivars, such as C. 'Daniel Deronda', bear semi-double flowers from stems produced the previous season and single flowers from the current season's stems. These cultivars have the same cultivation requirements as those in the previous section. The flowering period is slightly later, beginning in early summer and continuing on until early autumn. The cultivars in this section produce attractive seedheads.

C. 'Nelly Moser', a cultivar dating from 1897 which is best planted out of direct sun to avoid the flowers fading.

The Mid-season Large-flowered Cultivars

These clematis have been derived from C. *lanuginosa* and crosses with C. *patens*. C. *lanuginosa* belongs to Section Viticella Subsection Lanuginosae and although it is thought by some authorities to be a species, others believe it to be a form of C. *patens*. Whatever its origin, it has been useful to hybridists to create the mid-season flowering large-flowered cultivars. As with the two cultivar sections above, clematis in this section produce their first flowers from the leaf axil buds which were ripened the previous year. However, the new stems produced by this section grow much longer before they bear their solitary flowers, which are 15 cm (6 in) or larger. This group then continues to produce new growth after flowering, bearing further crops of flowers until early autumn. The second and later crops of flowers are produced along the flowering stem towards its apex, from each of the last three to five pairs of leaf axil buds. This section also produces attractive seedheads. Cultivars in this section include C. 'Henryi', C. 'Marie Boisselot', and C. 'W. E. Gladstone'.

All clematis cultivars that belong to the early large flowered section, the semi-double and double large-flowered section and the mid-season large-flowered section require light pruning in late winter to early spring (see page 46). All are winter-hardy to Zone 4–9.

The Late Large-flowered Cultivars

The clematis belonging to this section have been raised from crosses between C. *lanuginosa* and C. *viticella*, and between cultivars of these two species. They all flower on the current season's stems, with some such as C. 'Gipsy Queen' producing occasional early flowers from the previous season's ripened stems. They are deciduous, producing mostly trifoliate leaves with leaflets being entire or occasionally serrated. The flowers are produced along the terminal ends of the current season's stems from midsummer until early or late autumn. The flowers are flat open, with four to six tepals, and are 12 cm (4¾ in) in diameter or larger. The flowers produced towards the autumn are smaller. This group does not produce interesting seedheads. They are fully winter hardy to Zones 3–9 and are extremely useful plants in cold climates. The clematis which belong to this section include C. 'Jackmanii', C. 'Comtesse de Bouchaud' and C. 'Ascotiensis'.

The Viticella Section

C. *viticella*, a native of southern Europe to Turkey, has given rise to a good range of larger-flowered cultivars. These are extremely valuable garden plants for their free-flowering habit. They are deciduous, with pinnate, semi-bipinnate to trifoliate leaves, some leaflets entire, others toothed, with wavy margins. The flowers range from bell-shaped and nodding to open flat or fully double, as are those of C. *v.* 'Purpurea Plena' and C. *v.* 'Purpurea Plena Elegans'. The tepals vary from four to six to numerous in the double cultivars. The seedheads are of little garden value, the seeds being very large, 1 cm (⅜ in) across, and without plumose seed tails. The flowers are borne on new growth only, from midsummer to early autumn. All are fully winter-hardy to Zones 3–9.

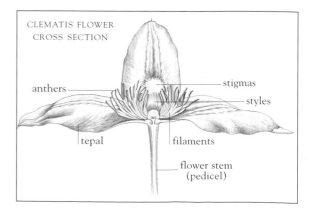

CLEMATIS FLOWER CROSS SECTION

anthers

stigmas

styles

tepal

filaments

flower stem (pedicel)

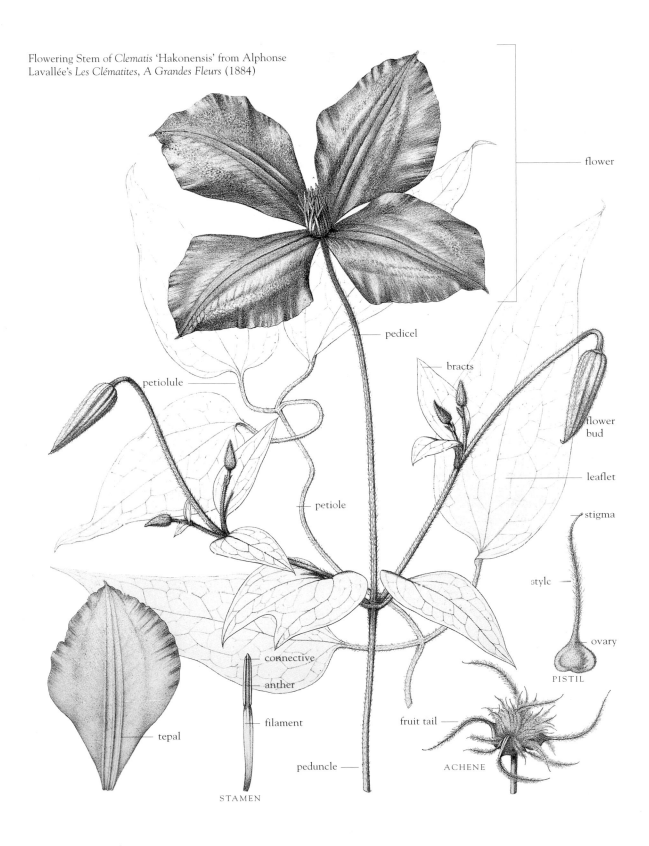

Flowering Stem of *Clematis* 'Hakonensis' from Alphonse
Lavallée's *Les Clématites, A Grandes Fleurs* (1884)

flower

pedicel

petiolule

bracts

flower
bud

leaflet

stigma

petiole

style

ovary

connective

PISTIL

anther

fruit tail

filament

tepal

peduncle

ACHENE

STAMEN

The clematis in this group include *C. campaniflora*, *C. viticella* 'Alba Luxurians', *C. v.* 'Royal Velours' and *C. v.* 'Venosa Violacea'.

The Late-flowering Species & Their Small-flowered Cultivars

This group includes a very wide range of clematis species from many geographical areas, such as Europe, North America, the Himalayas, China and Japan. Their habit is almost entirely deciduous in northern Europe, some, such as *C. flammula*, being semi-evergreen in mild locations where temperatures rarely drop below 0°C (32°F). They all flower from the current season's growth, the flowers varying considerably (see the A–Z of Species & Cultivars). Some have exceptionally attractive seedheads, such as those belonging to the Meclatis Section (for example *C. tangutica* 'Bill Mackenzie'). Their winter hardiness is variable, details being given in the A–Z of Species & Cultivars.

This group includes the following sections:

Section Aethusifoliae: *C. aethusifolia*.

Section Clematis Subsection Clematis: *C. apiifolia*, *C. brachiata*, *C. brevicaudata*, *C. gouriana*, *C. grata*, *C. ligusticifolia*, *C. peterae*, *C. potaninii*, *C. virginiana*, *C. vitalba*.

Section Connatae: *C. buchananiana*, *C. connata*, *C. grewiiflora*, *C. lasiandra*, *C. ranunculoides*, *C. rehderiana*.

Section Flammula Subsection Flammula: *C. flammula*, *C. recta*, *C. terniflora*.

Section Flammula Subsection Chinensis: *C. chinensis*.

Section Flammula Subsection Uncinatae: *C. uncinata*.

Section Fruticella Subsection Fruticella: *C. fruticosa*.

Section Fruticella Subsection Phlebanthae: *C. phlebantha*.

Section Fruticella Subsection Songaricae: *C. songarica*.

Section Lasiantha: *C. lasiantha*, *C. pauciflora*.

Section Meclatis: *C. akebioides*, *C. graveolens*, *C. ladakhiana*, *C. orientalis*, *C. tangutica*, *C. tibetana*, *C. serratifolia*.

Section Pterocarpa: *C. brachyura*.

Section Tubulosae: *C. heracleifolia*, *C. stans*.

Section Viorna Subsection Crispae: *C. crispa*.

Section Viorna Subsection Fuscae: *C. fusca*.

Section Viorna Subsection Hirsutissimae: *C. hirsutissima*.

Section Viorna Subsection Integrifoliae: *C. integrifolia*.

Section Viorna Subsection Viorna: *C. addisonii*, *C. pitcheri*, *C. texensis*, *C. viorna*.

Section Viticella Subsection Floridae: *C. florida*.

C. terniflora, a Japanese species which is ideal for sunny locations in North America.

All the clematis in the late large-flowered section, the Viticella Section and the late-flowering species and their cultivars produce their flowers on the current season's stems. They need to be pruned each year, when all the previous season's growth should be removed (see page 46).

BOTANY

THE FLOWERS

The flowers of clematis are occasionally unisexual but they are mostly bisexual and are borne singly or in panicles or cymes. Clematis do not have petals or sepals as in, for example, roses, but tepals. The number of tepals per flower varies greatly from four to ten and many more are produced on the double- and semi-double large-flowered cultivars, such as C. *viticella* 'Purpurea Plena Elegans'.

The flower shape varies enormously throughout the species from tubular, bell-shaped, open-bell-shaped, star-shaped, saucer-shaped and open-and-flat-shaped to the large, flat, open upward-facing flowers of C. *florida* and C. *patens*. In the large-flowered cultivars the tepals are usually elliptical in shape.

The most dramatic part of the clematis flower is generally the tepals, though in some, for example C. *florida* 'Sieboldii', the petaloid stamens, or 'inner skirt' are a considerable attraction. The tepals, particularly in the large-flowered cultivars, are colourful shades from pale pastel pinks and blues to dramatic deep purple-reds and deep blues and purples. The whites are sometimes pure white while others are creamy, almost yellow. The deep yellow of a buttercup is not seen in the large-flowered cultivars but only in the members of the Meclatis Section. Many of the large-flowered cultivars have stripes or bars down the centre of the tepal, giving added colour and interest.

THE REPRODUCTIVE ORGANS

The ovary is hypogynous, with the tepals and stamens being below it. The stamens (the male part of the flower), which produce the pollen for fertilization, consist of a filament connected to the receptacle with, at its apex, an anther which holds the pollen. They are very numerous, there being over 100 in some large-flowered clematis. The stamens are very prominent and are usually of a different colour from the tepals; in the large-flowered cultivars, the filament sometimes takes on the base colour of the tepals. Occasionally the styles are particularly prominent in the large-flowered single cultivars, for example C. 'Myojo', and in C. *napaulensis*, a species from southwest China and northern India. The base of the style is connected to the ovary, while the top holds the stigma, the whole making up the female part of the flower. The styles are also numerous – sometimes over 100 in number.

As the flower tepals open, the stamens unfold from the centre of the flower, revealing the styles and stigmas. When pollen is released from the anther soon after the flower opens, the stigmas are normally receptive. The pollen is generally white or cream in colour. As the flower matures, the outer stamens fold back against the tepal allowing younger stamens to unfold, releasing their pollen. At this time the styles become more prominent and are fully ready for fertilization. Once the ovules have been fertilized the ovaries begin to swell, producing the seed. The styles begin to mature and become plumose, first turning yellow, then light golden brown and silky.

At this point, the ovary has swollen and any remaining tepals and stamens fall away. The seeds swell and become green, while the seed tails become more yellowish as the hairs on the seed tails mature. As the seeds mature they become light brown and then dark brown in colour, the seed tails becoming golden brown. Once the seeds are fully ripe, they are easily detached from the receptacle. By this time the seed tails have become fluffy with age and are ready to be wind-blown for dispersal. With some early large-flowered cultivars, there can be up to 40–50 seeds per flower.

The seedheads are very decorative in some clematis and are an added bonus to the plant, bringing further interest and form to the garden. Due to the variation between the species and the large-flowered cultivars, the seedheads vary considerably, the best being produced by Section Atragene, the early large-flowered cultivars, the double and semi-double large-flowered cultivars and the early flowers from the mid-season large-flowered cultivars. The late-flowering species and their cultivars also produce some outstanding seedheads, the best belonging to plants in Section Meclatis, Section Clematis Subsection Clematis, Section Viorna Subsection Fuscae and Subsection Hirsutissimae and Section Flammula Subsection Flammula. The seedheads can be used in flower arrangements during the summer or dried for winter decoration (see page 77).

SCENTED CLEMATIS

Very few of the large-flowered cultivars have scent at all, and in those that do it is rather faint. However, with the species and the small-flowered cultivars the gardener is much more fortunate.

Some winter- and spring-flowering evergreen species have a good fragrance, especially some of the clones of the New Zealand species, such as C. *forsteri*, which has a strong scent of lemon verbena. C. *armandii* also has scented clones, for example C. *armandii* 'Apple Blossom', which is hawthorn-scented. The Atragene Section does not usually have scented flowers, although the Swedish clematis breeder Magnus Johnson reported an almost yellow clone of C. *turkestanica* which had a perfume.

The Montana Section has some of the best scented flowers, their scent being generally of vanilla. C. *montana* 'Mayleen' and C. *m.* 'Vera' are two of the most recommendable in this respect.

Of the large-flowered cultivars, in Thomas Moore and George Jackman's book *The Clematis as a Garden Flower* (1877) the Japanese introduction C. 'Fortunei' is described as having scent. Unfortunately this clematis now appears to be lost to cultivation. Moore and Jackman also list as scented several cultivars they created, these being C. 'Fair Rosamond', C. 'Edith Jackman', C. 'Maiden Blush', C. 'The Queen', C. 'Stella' and C. 'Vesta'. Only C. 'Fair Rosamond' is still in cultivation as far as I am aware, although I do remember that 25 years ago I grew C. 'The Queen', which was similar in habit to C. 'Sir Garnet Wolseley'. The habit of C. 'Fair Rosamond' is rather weak and its pale off-white flowers with a pinkish central bar are not outstanding. The scent is best appreciated on a warm evening, and is that of violets.

Other early large-flowered cultivars to have a slight scent are C. 'Miss Bateman', C. 'Lady Londesborough', C. 'Moonlight', C. 'Sir Garnet Wolseley', C. 'Souvenir du Capitaine Thuilleaux' and C. 'Wada's Primrose'. Again, these are violet-scented. From the double and semi-double large-flowered cultivars only C. 'Veronica's Choice' has a scent, also of violets; although C. 'Duchess of Edinburgh' is reputed to be scented, I have not found it so. The late-flowering large-flowered cultivars have no scented clematis to offer, while the Viticella group has just one, C. *viticella* 'Betty Corning'.

Among the later-flowering species and their cultivars there are quite a few with very good perfume. From the following sections the most notable are listed:

Section Aethusifoliae: C. *aethusifolia*.
Section Connatae: C. *rehderiana*.
Section Flammula Subsection Flammula: C. × *aromatica*, C. *flammula*, C. *recta* and C. × *triternata* 'Rubromarginata'.
Section Flammula Subsection Chinensis: C. *chinensis*.
Section Tubulosae: C. *heracleifolia* var. *davidiana*.
Section Viorna Subsection Crispae: C. *crispa*.
Section Viorna Subsection Integrifoliae: C. *integrifolia* 'Alba' and C. *i.* 'Rosea'.

It is to be hoped that in time the scent of the small-flowered clematis can be transferred through hybridization to the large-flowered cultivars, or at least to the clematis belonging to the Viticella Section.

One clematis has scented leaves – C. *heracleifolia* var. *davidiana*. When they begin to die back in the autumn they take on a strong, slightly woody aroma as they dry.

NOMENCLATURE

The two authoritative documents on nomenclature are the International Code of Botanical Nomenclature, which deals with botanical names, and the International Code of Nomenclature for Cultivated Plants, which is concerned with the correct naming of cultivated plants. In recent years botanists have made some necessary name changes to clematis and they will continue to do so, frustrating though this may be for the gardener and nurseryman. However, some outdated names persist for generations; in the USA and Canada C. *terniflora* is still referred to as C. *paniculata* by both gardeners and nurseries, years after it was discovered to be incorrectly named. The name C. *paniculata* properly belongs to the New Zealand species which had been known under the name of C. *indivisa*. Unfortunately, C. *terniflora* went from C. *paniculata* to C. *maximowicziana* before it arrived at its present name, so the confusion is understandable.

Some large-flowered cultivars have also been incorrectly named, going under the same name as old and lost cultivars. However, with International Clematis Registration now in the hands of the Royal Horticultural Society in the British Isles, such errors can henceforth be avoided.

SEEDHEADS

C. *alpina* 'Frankie'
(Atragene Section)

C. 'Guernsey Cream'
(early large-flowered cultivar)

C. *tangutica*
(late-flowering species)

C. *gentianoides*
(evergreen)

C. 'Beauty of Richmond'
(mid-season large-flowered
cultivar)

C. 'Warsaw Nike'
(early large-flowered cultivar)

C. *campaniflora* 'Lisboa'
(Viticella Section)

C. 'Blue Boy'
(late-flowering small-flowered cultivar)

C. *viticella* 'Venosa Violacea'
(Viticella Section)

2

THE HISTORY OF CLEMATIS

The name 'clematis' is derived from the Greek word *klema*, meaning vine branch or vine-like. It is possible that even before the use of the word 'Klema-tis' the whole genus was known as atragene, meaning 'firecracker' in Greek. Apparently, when large dry stems of *C. vitalba* are placed in a fire, the heat causes them to split, making a noise like firecrackers. Although the Atragene group now embraces *C. alpina*, *C. macropetala* and similar North American species, atragene was at one time used as a name for *C. vitalba*.

In the 1870s, Thomas Moore and George Jackman published their book *The Clematis as a Garden Flower*, in which they stated that the genus was at that time split into four different sections. They defined them thus:

'(i) *C. flammula*, in which the flowers are without involucre or petals and the achenes or seed-like fruits are lengthened out into a bearded, feathery tail – represented by *C. flammula*.

(ii) *C. viticella*, in which the flowers are as in *C. flammula*, but the achenes have only a short, and not a plumose, tail – represented by *C. viticella*.

(iii) Cheiropsis, in which there are two bracted calyx-like involucres at the top of the pedicels, no petals and a bearded plumose tail to the achenes – represented by *C. calycina* [now *C. cirrhosa*].

(iv) Atragene, in which there is no involucre, the outer stamens passing gradually into the petaloid staminodes and the achenes having a bearded plumose tail – represented by *C. alpina*.'

Moore and Jackman also recorded that in 1877 scientific records showed that some 230 clematis species had

C. macropetala, a Chinese species which is very hardy and therefore ideal for exposed sites (shown twice normal size).

George Jackman of the famous nursery in Woking, Surrey, where C. 'Jackmanii' was bred.

been identified. Of these, some 17 were European, chiefly occurring in the southern and eastern regions; 43 were of Indian origin; 9 were Javanese; approximately 30, comprising some of the finest species, came from China and Japan (we now know that 108 species are native to China); 11 were from the Siberian regions;

2 were from the Fiji Islands; 24 were from South America; 9 species were from Central America and the West Indies; 35 species were North American; 14 species came from tropical Africa; 4 were from South Africa; 6 species were from the Mascarene Islands and Madagascar; 15 species were recorded as coming from New Holland (Australia) and 5 from New Zealand. Many of these species have lost favour and are obviously not now in cultivation. However it would be marvellous to collect them again.

THE 16TH-CENTURY INTRODUCTIONS

The early records show us that some of the European species started to find their way to British gardens as early as 1569. When C. *viticella* was introduced, the only clematis found in British gardens up until then was the native C. *vitalba*, a rampant scrambler and climber that reaches 9–12m (30–40ft). C. *vitalba*'s greatest contribution to the British countryside is, of course, its marvellous fluffy seedheads, which are outstanding on a frosty winter's day. C. *viticella* was to become a most important species in the early breeding work and can still help improve today's clematis, especially when one remembers that neither it nor its small-flowered cultivars succumb to clematis wilt. Its other great asset is its very free-flowering habit.

By the end of the 16th century, other European clematis had arrived on English shores: C. *cirrhosa*, C. *flammula*, C. *integrifolia* and C. *recta*. Because it is only semi-hardy C. *cirrhosa* has not established in English gardens other than in milder climates, which is a great shame as it has attractive winter flowers and evergreen foliage. A larger-flowered cultivar, C. *cirrhosa* 'Freckles', which I introduced in 1989, appears more winter hardy and its flowers are borne in late autumn and early winter in England.

C. *flammula* is a very variable species (as is C. *cirrhosa*) and again it has not established widely in British gardens, perhaps because of its preference for dry, free-draining soils. It is to be hoped that its variable habit will allow a form to be found that will establish well in the British Isles and countries of similar climatic conditions.

C. *integrifolia* is a most useful mixed border plant, together with some of the more recent introductions of good blue, pink and white forms, as well as the marvellous cultivar C. *integrifolia* 'Pangbourne Pink'. I trust this species will be much more widely used in the future.

C. *recta* is another very variable species, varying in flower size, form and height from plants that grow only to 90 cm (3 ft) to those reaching 1.8–2.1 m (6–7 ft). Again, good selected forms of C. *recta* should be found to enhance gardens both in Europe and in North America.

THE 18TH- & 19TH-CENTURY INTRODUCTIONS

There were no introductions to the British Isles in the 17th century, but in the first quarter of the 18th century two useful American species, C. *crispa* and C. *viorna*, were introduced. Both should have been used more extensively in breeding work than they have been. C. *crispa* has scent to offer and the most delightful nodding flowers, and one of its progeny, C. *viticella* 'Betty Corning', has retained the scent. C. *viorna*, which is extremely free-flowering and has delightful seedheads, is a must for future breeding work.

Over a period of time various species came to the British Isles, but it was the introduction to Sweden from Japan of the Chinese species C. *florida* by Carl Peter Thunberg in 1776 that caused great excitement. As far as I am aware, C. *florida* did not become really established in gardens and was lost to cultivation. The herbarium type sheet held by Uppsala University is not typical of C. *florida*, but rather similar to an unnamed poor form of C. *florida* 'Sieboldii', a variant introduced in 1837 by Dr Phillipp von Siebold into the Leiden Botanic Garden in Holland, where he was director. It sported almost immediately to produce C. *florida* 'Plena', and both were introduced from Holland to the British Isles. Dr von Siebold was also responsible for bringing the Chinese species C. *patens* to the British Isles, together with cultivars which are now lost, their names being C. 'Sophia', C. 'Monstrosa', C. 'Amalia' and C. 'Louisa'. It would appear the Japanese breeders have been developing cultivars of C. *patens* for perhaps 300 years. The possible relationship between C. *florida* and C. *viticella* and whether C. *patens* is in fact native to Japan or if the plants found in the wild in Japan have just naturalized are some queries yet to be answered definitively. There is also speculation as to whether C. *lanuginosa* is a species or is just a form of C. *patens*. The Dutch taxonomist Dr Willem Brandenburg is particularly interested in this group of species and it is to be hoped that one day he will discover the history of their origin.

CLEMATIS FLORIDA

I believe my own practical experience of some of these species is of interest in this section of the history of clematis. It is my opinion that no-one in recent times has found or reintroduced the true *C. florida* from China. Both Barry Fretwell and Ruth Gooch have fine photographs of *C. florida* in their clematis books (*Clematis*, William Collins 1989 and *Clematis, the Complete Guide*, Crowood Press 1995 respectively), but Ruth Gooch's *C. florida* came about as a sport, like mine, except that her plant came from *C. florida* 'Sieboldii'. She, too, has been able to propagate from her sport and it appears stable.

As all who grow it are aware, *C. florida* 'Sieboldii' is rather unstable. It constantly sports to produce *C. f.* 'Plena' or plants with rather strange flowers; sometimes half the flower is 'Sieboldii' and the other half 'Plena'. *C. f.* 'Plena' will revert back to *C. f.* 'Sieboldii' quite often so it is rather unstable also. In about 1990, three or four of my stock plants of *C. f.* 'Plena' started to produce sports. Usually, one stem would have *C. f.* 'Plena' on one side of the stem, and what I believe to be the true species of *C. florida* on the other side. Eventually, the length of stem grew until both leaf axil buds on the same node of the stem had flowers of *C. florida*. We then rooted cuttings from this section. The plants we produced varied in flower size, some reverting further to produce another sport.

The best large-flowered form from these sports was selected and named *C. florida* 'Evison' for use within our nursery production business. The plants under the 'Evison' name which were selected from one clone only have remained true to type. They are being used in our breeding programme and are not yet released, although I believe them to be of historical importance. *C. florida* 'Evison' produces seeds quite freely and the resultant seedlings are usually similar to the type specimen *C. florida*, though some revert to *C. florida* 'Plena'. Some seedlings have been selected that have foliage very similar to *C. patens*, although they do retain some of the foliage characteristics of *C. florida* 'Evison'.

Two very interesting plants have emerged from a batch of *C. florida* 'Evison' seedlings. One of these is extremely similar to a line drawing of *C.* 'Hakonensis' on plate IV in Alphonse Lavallée's book *Les Clematites, A Grandes Fleurs* of 1884. The other seedling has produced a long flowering stem in which the foliage is more

like that of *C. patens*, the flower being most similar in shape to *C. patens* on plate III of the same publication. The flowers produced in January 1997 were pale in

C. florida 'Plena', an excellent cultivar for growing through wall-trained evergreen shrubs.

PLATE I

VITICELLA SECTION
All flowers are shown at
approximately ½ size

C. *viticella* 'Royal Velours'

C. *viticella* 'Venosa Violacea'

C. *viticella* 'Polish Spirit'

C. *viticella* 'Abundance'

C. *viticella*
'Margot Koster'

C. *viticella* 'Minuet'

C. *viticella* 'Purpurea Plena
Elegans'

C. *viticella* 'Etoile Violette'

C. *viticella* 'Alba Luxurians'

C. *viticella* 'Betty Corning'

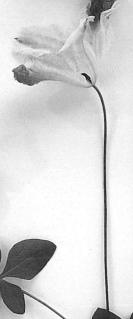

colour due to light levels but those that appeared in July of the same year were a violet-purple. Although similar in size to forms of C. *patens*, the flower has many characterists of C. *florida*.

If one assumes these seedlings are just chance reversions or 'throwbacks', much of the history of clematis could be explained. However, as they were grown from seed produced by C. *florida* 'Evison' where pollen could have been transposed onto the flowers of C. *florida* 'Evison' from other clematis, these seedlings may be of no historical value at all. Only time will tell.

CLEMATIS VITICELLA

C. *viticella* is important in the evolution of clematis species. Its flowers are as near as any other species to the flat open flowers of C. *florida* and C. *patens*, and it could well be that C. *viticella* of Europe is closely related to C. *florida* from China. Certainly, C. *viticella* and C. *florida* were used in early hybridization programmes, being most compatible. C. *viticella* 'Venosa Violacea' is proof of this, together with C. *florida* (Thunb.) var. 'Venosa' (possibly lost to cultivation now) featured on plate VI in Lavallée's book. It looks very similar to C. *viticella* 'Venosa Violacea' in many characteristics. The fruits of both C. *viticella* and C. *florida* are without plumose seed tails. C. 'Hakonensis' is reported as being introduced from Japan as a species and could have been a plant raised with C. *florida* as its parent, or one of its parents. I believe the original and true C. 'Hakonensis' has been lost to cultivation. However, from Lavallée's line drawing of the seedheads of C. 'Hakonensis', they do have semi-plumose seed tails, which my seedling also has. From my C. *florida* and C. *patens* type seedlings, it could also be that C. *patens* was somehow involved with the evolution of C. *florida*. Logically, it would be a natural progression.

As to where the double flowers originate, this too may come back to C. *viticella*. It is believed C. *viticella* 'Purpurea Plena Elegans' is an old European cultivar, possibly from the 16th century or maybe before. I have always asked myself how a double-flowered clematis such as this could have been produced in cultivation so long ago, and what its parentage was. Our nursery could hold an explanation to this also. During 1996, several thousand seedlings of C. *viticella* cultivars were allowed to scramble wild so we could assess their flowers, hoping to find something new and distinct. To my surprise, we pro-

duced two or three plants with double flowers in exactly the same shape and flower colour as C. *viticella* 'Purpurea Plena Elegans', another throwback of nature – a historical one, I believe. The cultivar and my double C. *viticella* seedling are both sadly sterile, as is C. *florida* 'Plena'.

Another historical plant lost to cultivation is the dwarf C. *viticella nana*, a plant reported by Moore and Jackman in 1877 to have been raised in the Jardin des Plantes Museum National d'Histoire Naturelle in Paris, which grew to only 60cm (2ft) in height. Fortunately, I also have a C. *viticella* which is dwarf and stunted in growth, reaching only 45–60 cm (1½–2 ft). Its habit and flower is very similar to those described by Moore and Jackman, who wrote, 'differing from the type in not being of climbing habit but producing short erect stems and forming a compact bush of from one to two feet, which becomes covered with continuous masses of flowers of a rosy-lilac colour, larger than those of the

Sports of C. *florida*, top to bottom: C. *f.* 'Evison', C. *f.* PISTACHIO™ 'Evirida' ⑤, C. *f.* 'Sieboldii' and C. *f.* 'Plena'.

type, but corresponding with them in form'. My seedling appeared by chance in the crack between two old paving slabs in a garden of mine in England. Fortunately, it was spotted and I was able to propagate it, although with difficulty due to its very short internodes. This is not being released but is used in my breeding programme. I believe this shows the importance of C. *viticella* as a species with great historical and modern-day value and it is maybe the key to producing large-flowered clematis which do not suffer from clematis wilt. It copes with the cold climates of northern Europe and northern USA and also enjoys the summer heat of mainland Europe and North America.

FURTHER 19TH-CENTURY INTRODUCTIONS

During the 19th century various species were introduced into the British Isles from many areas around the world. C. *florida* 'Sieboldii' was introduced in the 1830s, but as it is sterile it was not possible to use it in breeding. However, the most important introductions during the 19th century which gave the breeders the greatest opportunity of all time to create new cultivars were C. *patens* and its cultivars in the 1830s, the amazing C. *lanuginosa* in 1851 and C. 'Fortunei' and C. 'Standishii' in 1863. After the arrival of these species and cultivars from Japan, the breeders of the British Isles, France, Belgium and Germany embarked upon a race to produce the best, most colourful cultivars.

THE DEVELOPMENT OF CULTIVARS

One of the earliest clematis cultivars ever raised – possibly the first – was C. 'Eriostemon', though according to the Swedish nurseryman Magnus Johnson its origin is not known exactly. It was probably raised in Belgium or the Netherlands before 1830. It was described and pictured by Decaisne in *Revue Horticole* in about 1852, C. 'Eriostemon' being the result of a cross between C. *viticella* and C. *integrifolia*.

The next cultivar raised was C. 'Hendersonii' in 1835, produced also from crossing C. *viticella* with C. *integrifolia*. It was raised by Mr J. A. Henderson in the Pine Apple Place Nursery, London. It was flowered for the first time by Mr Chandler of Vauxhall, London, and has sometimes been called C. *chandlerii*. In the nursery trade, C. 'Eriostemon' and C. 'Hendersonii' are frequently sold incorrectly under the same name of C. × *eriostemon* 'Hendersonii', although they are two distinct plants.

Although these two plants are very similar, coming from the same parentage, there are differences. Magnus Johnson describes the main difference as follows. Stem leaves near to the base of C. 'Eriostemon' are entire, broadly ovate or three to five-lobed; in C. 'Hendersonii', the stem leaves are entire, narrowly ovate or three-lobed. In C. 'Eriostemon', the upper stem leaves are pinnate with generally five acutely elliptic segments and in C. 'Hendersonii' the upper stem leaves are pinnate with five to seven lanceolate segments. The flowers are virtually the same in form, with tepal size slightly larger in C. 'Eriostemon'. The colour varies and is as follows. C. 'Eriostemon' is lobelia blue RHS Colour Code HCC 41/1 with a bar of a slight shade of violet purple. With C. 'Hendersonii', the colour is spectrum violet RHS Colour Code HCCC 735–735/1 and a shade of amethyst violet on the central bar. The flower buds differ slightly also, with C. 'Eriostemon' having nodding, comparatively short conical buds, while C. 'Hendersonii' has long conical buds. The other flower components vary only slightly. These are fully described in *The International Clematis Society's Newsletter* Vol. 4 No. 1 Winter, 1987.

The Large-flowered Cultivars

The most important step towards producing the very large-flowered clematis of today was made by Isaac Anderson-Henry of Edinburgh, Scotland, in 1855, when it is recorded that he crossed C. *patens azurea grandiflora* with C. *lanuginosa*. The resulting cultivar was C. 'Reginae', which was described as a handsome lavender-coloured cultivar of intermediate character. It was shown in London in 1862 and gained a Certificate of Merit. Shortly afterwards, Anderson-Henry bred the world-famous C. 'Henryi' and C. 'Lawsoniana'. His detailed account of these later cultivars appeared in the Moore and Jackman book of 1877, where he described the crosses as coming from C. *lanuginosa* as the female or seed-bearer and C. 'Fortunei' as the male parent. C. *lanuginosa* and C. 'Fortunei' have long since been lost to cultivation but fortunately C. 'Lawsoniana' is still in commerce, although not grown widely, and C. 'Henryi' is sold in large quantities. Anderson-Henry recounts with excitement that 'Lawsoniana' had flowers which could reach up to 24 cm (9½ in) across and describes his disbelief in the blue of this cultivar being considerably darker than either parent. C. *lanuginosa* is described as pale lilac and C. 'Fortunei' as having pure white semi-double flowers. He points out that C. 'Fortunei' is probably a seedling from C. 'John Gould Veitch', a plant introduced from Japan in 1862 by Robert Fortune to the nursery of John Standish, later to be transferred to the Veitch Nursery. C. 'John Gould Veitch' is still alive and growing well in my collection thanks to Magnus Johnson, who gave it to me some years ago.

I believe that even in the mid-1860s Anderson-Henry had reached the conclusion that most of the large-flowered introductions from Japan were of cultivar status rather than species and these early introductions were probably already well inbred and perhaps weak in constitution. As a result of the intense breeding programme that then evolved they were responsible for the introduction of the 'weak link' in the chain, letting in the dreaded clematis wilt (*Phoma clematidina*) in the late 1800s. Certainly, the C. *patens* which I imported from Japan (from a wild source) in the late 1960s and

early 1970s were full of this fungal problem. Although C. *lanuginosa* is reported to be a species, I believe this may not be so. If my assumption is correct it too may have contributed to the genetic susceptibility of later cultivars. When C. *lanuginosa* was introduced in 1851 by Robert Fortune from Ningpo, China, it was reported that the plant was found growing in a churchyard. Another report tells us that it was found on a hillside. Whatever the origin of this plant, it has not been found in this area since. C. *lanuginosa* could well be a form/sport of C. *patens*, though it has larger flowers and produces them along the stem, while the true C. *patens* normally produces terminal flowers. However, it appears to be similar in habit to C. 'Moonlight' (syn. 'Yellow Queen') which I believe to be a plant of wild origin and belonging to C. *patens*. The true C. *patens*, as

C. 'John Gould Veitch', an old cultivar introduced from Japan by Robert Fortune in 1862.

I know it and as per Lavallée's book featured in plate VII, has the typical, more star-like flowers with pointed tepals, typical of the plants I have seen growing in the wild in Japan. However, comparing C. *lanuginosa* in plate 1 of Lavallée's book and plate III of C. *patens*, I believe there is a great likeness in the flower formation, although there is a distinct difference between the leaves, C. *patens* having three leaflets, while C. *lanuginosa* normally has a large simple leaf.

In cultivation, I have seen cultivars with the C. *lanuginosa* type of habit produce flowers that have sported. One of these was C. 'Blue Gem', which should normally have pale lilac blue flowers with red anthers. On one particular plant I grew, there was a group of six flowers on the growing tip; five had the correct red anthers, while the remaining one had yellow anthers. My point is that perhaps C. *lanuginosa* itself may have been a variation of C. *patens*, perhaps a sport occurring in the wild. Then again, if C. *lanuginosa* was found in a churchyard, by the time it was collected by Robert Fortune it may have already been a cultivated variety which had been planted in the churchyard. Further research needs to be done in this area.

THE 19TH-CENTURY NURSERIES & BREEDERS

Next in order of the new cultivars of the 19th century came the Woking hybrids, raised by Messrs George Jackman and Sons. These were the result of using C. *lanuginosa* with C. 'Hendersonii' and C. *viticella atrorubens* during the summer of 1858. The first plants reported to have bloomed were those named C. 'Jackmanii' and C. *rubroviolacea* in 1862. These were shown in 1863 in Kensington, presumably to the Royal Horticultural Society, receiving Certificates of Merit in the first class. C. 'Jackmanii' was, of course, to become one of the most outstanding clematis ever raised. Its free-flowering habit and masses of flowers of a deep, intense violet-purple are easily recognizable on archways and porches throughout Europe and North America, where it is particularly winter hardy.

Other notable English nurserymen who were responsible for the progression of some of the early cultivars were Messrs Cripps & Sons of Tunbridge Wells and Charles Noble of Sunningdale. They introduced clematis cultivars which are still grown today. In 1866 Cripps produced C. 'Lady Caroline Nevill' and in 1867

came C. 'Star of India', which is similar in habit to C. 'Jackmanii'. Two of the Noble cultivars were C. 'Lady Londesborough' and C. 'Miss Bateman', the latter being a popular commercial plant that is produced in many thousands annually.

In Europe, great work on producing new cultivars was also well underway. The British often criticized their European counterparts for producing clematis with gappy flowers, but the Europeans did rather well with the depth of colour. The most successful European breeders were the Moser family, who gave us C. 'Nelly Moser' in 1897 which, along with C. 'Jackmanii', is perhaps still one of the best-known clematis in the world. C. 'Marcel Moser' was introduced in 1896 but, overshadowed by the colour and impact of 'Nelly Moser', it is somewhat forgotten today.

According to Moore and Jackman, M. Briolay-Goiffon of Orleans was one of the earliest European breeders. He too was using C. *lanuginosa* and C. *patens*, but sadly it appears his cultivars did not stand the test of time. Victor Lemoine of Nancy produced cultivars such as C. *lanuginosa* 'Candida' (1862) which is still catalogued today in the USA. However, the plants I have seen look very much like C. 'Marie Boisselot'. His C. *lanuginosa nivea* has been lost but C. 'Otto Froebel' is still listed by some growers. Lemoine's C. 'Lucie Lemoine' is a plant I once grew but it did not survive; it is similar in growth and habit to C. 'Duchess of Edinburgh', but of a weaker constitution. Lemoine also produced a double form of C. *recta*, the European scented white herbaceous clematis. I believe it too has been lost. I have been fortunate enough, however, to raise seedlings from C. *recta* that have produced semi-double flowers. Hopefully, some may provide double flowers in the future.

Other notable European contributors to clematis breeding during the latter half of the 19th century were M. Simon-Louis of Metz, M. Rinz of Frankfurt, M. Carre of Troyes, M. Dauvesse of Orleans, M. Modeste-Guérin and M. Bonamy Frères. Sadly, none of their early cultivars survive today.

Moore and Jackman report that in the British Isles Messrs G. Baker & Son of Bagshot were also crossing C. *lanuginosa* and C. 'Standishii', producing C. 'Gem', which was very similar to C. 'Reginae' produced by Anderson-Henry some years earlier. Messrs George Jackman and Sons and the other hybridists of that time continued the breeding programme and by the turn of the century some 500 clematis cultivars were listed. Most of these have since been lost to cultivation. However, it must have been one of the most exciting times ever in any plant's development, especially the period 1855–77. Moore and Jackman listed over 250 cultivars in their book of 1877 – an explosion of new clematis.

Some 40 or so of those early cultivars are still listed by today's nurseries and sold in garden centres around the world. Included among them is C. 'Fair Rosamond', raised in 1881, which is still one of the few large-flowered cultivars to have slight scent. During the 1880s, further cultivars were raised but some of the excitement had died down. One good clematis, C. 'Beauty of Worcester', raised by Messrs Smiths of Worcester around 1890, is still in cultivation. Its stunning double purple-blue flowers must have caused a sensation when it was introduced.

CLEMATIS TEXENSIS

The introduction of C. texensis (syn. C. coccinea) from the USA caused further excitement when it was used to cross with some of the C. 'Jackmanii' cultivars. A cross made between C. texensis and C. 'Star of India' produced the miniature tulip-shaped cultivar C. 'Countess of Onslow' in 1894, now lost to cultivation. Jackmans of Woking continued these crosses, producing five other cultivars which were known as the Wokingensis hybrids. These were C. texensis 'Duchess of Albany', C. t. 'Duchess of York', C. t. 'Grace Darling', C. t. 'Admiration' and C. t. 'Sir Trevor Lawrence', named after the one-time President of the Royal Horticultural Society. Unfortunately, only C. t. 'Duchess of Albany' and C. t. 'Sir Trevor Lawrence' are currently in cultivation.

M. André and M. Morel of France also produced C. texensis cultivars but most of these have disappeared. Otto Froebel of Zurich produced some 15 cultivars which have also been lost. However, one of M. Morel's cultivars, C. texensis 'Gravetye Beauty', which was introduced to England by William Robinson in 1914, is still widely grown. Its flowers open more than the Wokingensis hybrids and are a most dramatic ruby red colour. One of the prettiest C. texensis cultivars, C. texensis 'Etoile Rose', raised by Lemoine in France about 1903, is delightful. It has nodding open bell-shaped flowers of a lovely soft pink colouring and a central pale scarlet bar.

NORTH AMERICA

In the United States and Canada very little breeding work is recorded. The native clematis species also seemed of little interest to gardeners and were, in fact, more highly thought of by the Europeans. However, through plant collectors such as Ernest Wilson, the Arnold Arboretum introduced several new species from China. Luther Burbank raised several cultivars including C. 'Snowdrift' (not C. armandii 'Snowdrift'), C. 'Ostrich Plume' and C. 'Waverly'. He also raised some unnamed C. texensis hybrids which were distributed by J. C. Vaughan of Chicago in 1903–5. All of these seem to be lost to cultivation, except C. 'Waverly', which my friend Brewster Rogerson, a keen clematis collector, grows in his collection in Portland, Oregon.

There is controversy about the history of one of the earliest American cultivars, C. 'Ramona'. In some of Lemoine's catalogues of 1890, it is ascribed to the Storrs and Harrison Company of Painesville, Ohio. However, it was first described and illustrated in 1888 in the American publication The Horticultural Art Journal, where it was called 'An American Production' and was said to have been raised by the Jackson and Perkins Company. At the time, J. & P., as they are now known in the USA, said that they were the originators of C. 'Ramona', although some time later the company said the plant came to them without a name and they called it C. 'Ramona' – probably adopting the title of a contemporaneous American novel of the same name – and distributed it in 1888.

As early as 1893, C. 'Ramona' was regarded as being synonymous with the Dutch cultivar C. 'Hybrida Sieboldii', which was raised by B. Droog, a nurseryman from Boskoop, Holland, in 1874 by crossing C. lanuginosa and C. patens. Even today, C. 'Hybrida Sieboldii' (not to be confused with C. florida 'Sieboldii') is thought to be synonymous with C. 'Ramona'. In 1885, Peter Henderson & Co. of New York listed C. 'Hybrida Sieboldii' (Boskoop seedling). As there is confusion between several clematis which look very similar to C. 'Hybrida Sieboldii' and C. 'Ramona' (which I believe are distinct), Ronald Sidwell, a horticultural lecturer in Worcestershire, and I undertook the identification of a group of clematis which included C. 'Hybrida Sieboldii', C. 'Ramona', C. 'Mrs Hope', C. 'Mrs Melville', C. 'Princess of Wales', C. 'Sensation'

PLATE II

C. TEXENSIS CULTIVARS
All flowers are shown at
approximately ½ size

C. texensis
'Etoile Rose'

C. texensis
'Pagoda'

C. texensis
'The Princess of Wales'

C. texensis
'Duchess of Albany'

C. texensis
'Sir Trevor Lawrence'

and C. 'Blue Gem'. We were able to see distinct differences in their filaments. Sometimes the apex of the filament was the colour of the anther (generally red) and the base of the filament was very often the colour of the pale blue tepals. What we could not decide was which cultivar was which, as the old records and descriptions of these cultivars were so vague. However, I still have many of these clematis in my collection in Guernsey – probably all under the wrong names!

Although the North Americans did not raise their own cultivars in the early years, they showed considerable interest in the introduction of clematis from Europe or Asia. As early as 1838, C. *florida* was exhibited at the Massachusetts Horticultural Society by the Winship Nursery. C. *florida* 'Sieboldii' was flowered for the first time that year by John Lowell in Roxbury, Massachusetts, and exhibited by Robert Buist of Philadelphia at the Pennsylvania Horticultural Society in 1840. C. *patens* was exhibited in Boston in 1841, and C. *lanuginosa* in 1856. In 1864, Eugene Bauman, a nurseryman in New York, raised several thousand seedlings of crosses between C. *lanuginosa* and C. *patens*. The historian Francis Parkman exhibited C. 'Jackmanii' in Boston in 1866, and in 1869, C. 'Fortunei' and C. 'Standishii' were also being cultivated in the USA. In 1873, Elbert S. Carman, creator of the Carman Potatoes, imported C. 'Henryi' and so the European cultivars began to be introduced. Today, both C. 'Jackmanii' and C. 'Henryi' are bestsellers to gardeners in the USA and Canada, proving that they have more than stood the test of time.

THE 20TH CENTURY

By the turn of the century clematis wilt had started to appear and A. E. Jackman gave a lecture on the 'sickness', as it was called, to the Royal Horticultural Society. The interest in breeding subsided considerably as the sickness caused by clematis wilt (*Phoma clematidina*) became a serious threat to clematis nurserymen. I believe the introduction of the various cultivars of C. *patens* from Japan and the inbreeding that subsequently took place of what was probably already inbred stock certainly would not have increased the plants' vigour. By this time, nurserymen were using C. *vitalba* or C. *viticella* as understock for grafting clematis, but using these, and particularly C. *vitalba*, did not help the sickness problem. The grafts were successful but I think the former species and the

large-flowered cultivars would not have been compatible in the long term and C. *viticella* would have been a much more compatible understock.

Plant collectors such as George Forrest and Ernest Wilson continued to bring back clematis species from China, increasing the range available until just before the First World War. Some of the most useful garden clematis brought back at that time were C. *armandii* and C. *montana* var. *rubens* in 1900, C. *rehderiana* in 1908, C. *chrysocoma* in 1910, C. *fargesii* (now known as C. *potaninii* var. *fargesii*) in 1911 and C. *macropetala* in 1912.

This was a period in which three men in particular made a notable contribution to the development of clematis as a garden flower: William Robinson, Ernest Markham and Percy Picton, proprietor, head gardener and under-gardener respectively at Gravetye Manor in Sussex. From the time when I was 15 or so until his death, Percy was certainly my mentor as far as interesting plants and clematis were concerned.

In his book *The Virgin's Bower*, published by John Murray in 1912, William Robinson describes the clematis at Gravetye Manor and advises his readers to grow their clematis plants through trees and shrubs. Many of us propound this today as if it were the latest fashion; 85 years is a long time for a practical idea to become fashionable but at last it is, and clematis are being grown through other plants more and more rather than against bare walls.

Ernest Markham tells us in his book *Clematis*, published in 1935, that he has vivid memories of the robust seedlings raised by Morel at Lyons, France, which he planted at Gravetye in 1914. C. 'Huldine', which received an Award of Merit from the Royal Horticultural Society in 1934, may have been one of these. Markham's other well-known introduction was C. *macropetala* 'Markham's Pink', originally known as C. *macropetala* var. 'Markham'. It received the Royal Horticultural Society's Award of Merit on 5 March, 1935, demonstrating how early the macropetala clematis flowered in Sussex.

The plant named after Markham, C. 'Ernest Markham', is a bestseller worldwide. Grown and introduced by Jackmans of Woking from seedlings raised at Gravetye after Markham's death in 1937, it has recently been awarded the RHS Award of Garden Merit.

Percy Picton moved away from Gravetye Manor and spent some time at Hagley Hall, where he raised and

C. *chrysocoma*, the white-flowered clone of the Chinese species, reintroduced by Roy Lancaster in the early 1980s.

named yet another famous clematis, C. 'Hagley Hybrid', introduced by Fisk's Clematis Nursery in 1956. He raised many other fine clematis, including C. 'Silver Moon', which is still the only clematis with a lovely silver-grey colouring. C. 'Joan Picton' was named after his wife. He was also responsible for finding and reintroducing C. 'Eriostemon' to commerce (having found it in a garden in Worcestershire), together with the true form of C. *armandii* 'Apple Blossom' and the very fine C. *montana*, which my company distributes under the name of C. *montana* f. *grandiflora*. Another of his stunning small-flowered cultivars is C. *m.* var. *rubens* 'Picton's Variety', which is more compact in habit than most types of C. *montana*, making it ideal for a small garden.

In the British Isles the major resurgence of interest in clematis was stimulated by Jim Fisk through his exhibits at the Chelsea Flower Show and other flower shows around England. He introduced plants from his friends and customers around the world and also seedlings raised in his own nursery in Saxmundham, Suffolk.

Among his long list of introductions, I believe two of the most outstanding are C. 'Dr Ruppel' from Argentina and C. 'Gillian Blades', a seedling from C. 'Lasurstern'.

However, it is the Pennell family and Walter Pennell in particular whom we must thank for all their work in the breeding and development of the large-flowered hybrid clematis. The history of the Pennells of Lincoln Nursery is well documented in *The International Clematis Society's Newsletter* No.1, Spring, 1984, by the present owner of the company, Richard Pennell. Pennells was established as long ago as 1846, when it listed seven clematis for sale. The intensive breeding programme undertaken by Walter Pennell in the 1950s ended in 1962 but his great contribution to clematis had produced 26 large-flowered cultivars, including famous names such as C. 'Vyvyan Pennell', C. 'Mrs N. Thompson', C. 'H. F. Young', C. 'Richard Pennell', C. 'Walter Pennell' and C. 'Will Goodwin'. I remember very clearly the meetings between Pennell, Fisk and Treasures of Tenbury Ltd, of which I was a junior partner in the later 1960s and early 1970s. It was great to be part of that resurgence of clematis interest at the Chelsea Flower Show each year.

NORTH AMERICA

One of the earliest recorded successful breeders of clematis in the USA was Dr Frank L. Skinner, who moved from Scotland to Manitoba, Canada, in the late 1890s. He concentrated on producing very hardy clematis for the severe winters of North America, working mostly with C. *alpina* and C. *macropetala*. Two of his cultivars, C. *m.* 'Blue Bird' and C. *m.* 'Rosy O'Grady', have been offered by nurseries for some years, though in my view both have rather open and gappy flowers with poor pale colouring. However, his C. *m.* 'White Swan' is a clematis with a very attractively formed flower, albeit rather slow to grow and become established in gardens. Dr Skinner's C. 'Blue Boy', a cross between C. *integrifolia* and C. *viticella* raised in approximately 1947, is a fine plant but it is still hardly known. This plant is non-clinging, as are the similar cultivars C. 'Eriostemon' and C. 'Hendersonii'. I am trialling variations of pale and dark blue, purple, pink, mauve and white in the hope of selecting and introducing a 'Blue Boy' range.

Arthur Steffen of Fairport, New York, the leading American nursery of the 1960s, 1970s and 1980s, were responsible for introducing many more modern clematis to the USA and Canada and helped tremendously in publicizing the genus. Many of their plants were distributed by the Park Seed Company and Wayside Gardens of South Carolina. From the late 1960s until their large nursery closed down I worked closely with both Mr Steffen senior and his son, Bing. I introduced into Europe two of the very fine cultivars they raised, C. 'Perrins Pride' and C. 'Sunset', the latter being an outstanding very free-flowering plant.

EUROPE

In Europe, the main flyer of the clematis flag was the nurseryman Jan Fopma of Boskoop, Holland. Jan collected clematis from many countries and distributed them through his nursery to other countries, helping considerably with the distribution of a great range of old and modern cultivars. However, to me the grand old

C. 'Gillian Blades', a delightful early-flowering cultivar with frilly edges to the tepals.

man of clematis is my dear friend from Sweden, Magnus Johnson, who celebrated his ninetieth birthday on 6 February, 1997. Magnus's nursery has been a mecca for clematis nurserymen and collectors of clematis for many years. His book, for which we have all been waiting for 15 years, has at last been published in Swedish under the title *Släktet Klematis*. Magnus's nursery is just south of Stockholm in the village of Södertälje, though for a period he left it to be head gardener at the Gothenburg Botanical Gardens. He has always been more than generous in sharing his knowledge and his collection of clematis plants, especially his many new creations, with me. He also obtained clematis plants and seed from people all over the world.

One of Magnus Johnson's greatest contacts was Mrs Anne (C. W.) Harvey from Kitchener, Ontario, Canada, who was responsible for the distribution by seed of many of the North American clematis species to her friends around the world and became a great personal friend of mine also. Through friends such as Magnus Johnson, Anne Harvey, Tage Lundell (who raised

and introduced many fine clematis from Sweden), and Vince and Sylvia Denny (for whom I introduced C. 'Sylvia Denny' at the Chelsea Flower Show), I have been fortunate enough to introduce over 50 clematis species and cultivars into commercial cultivation in the British Isles. These include Japanese cultivars, such as C. 'Pink Champagne' (syn. 'Kakio'), C. 'Asao' and C. 'Wada's Primrose', C. 'Edith' of my own raising, and C. 'Dawn', C. Serenata' and C. 'Corona' from Tage Lundell.

The great work undertaken by breeders in Latvia and Estonia in the 1950s was almost unknown to us until about 14 years ago. Renewed interest in the genus took place when plants were imported from Magnus Johnson's nursery. Between 1958 and 1982, 130 new clematis cultivars were produced in the Soviet Union, some of which are now finding their way into British catalogues. One of the most widely grown of these is C. × fargesioides 'Summer Snow' (syn. C. × f. 'Paul Farges'), which was raised in 1964 by A. N. Volosenko-Valenis. M. Orlov, M. A. Beskaravaingaja and A. N. Volosenko-Velenis were most successful breeders in the 1960s and in 1963 the latter two raised C. 'Aljonushka', a non-clinging plant which grows to 1 m (3¼ ft). It is now being produced in good numbers for sale in the British Isles. The lilac-purple flowers resemble a large-flowered form of C. integrifolia, which was one of its parents. However, it is Uno Kivistik who has been the most prolific of all, producing some 58 cultivars between 1979 and 1982 and still continuing his work today.

JAPAN

Once more, the interest in clematis in Japan is at fever pitch with a great resurgence of breeding and development work. My friend Yoskiaki Aihara has one of the largest collections of clematis in Japan. He has been responsible for the distribution of many fine Japanese cultivars to the West, including C. 'Pink Champagne' (syn. 'Kakio'), and C. 'Asao'. He is a most active member of the International Clematis Society and provides all the latest information from Japan on the developments of Japanese breeders such as Hirashi Hayakawa, thereby keeping the Western world fully informed.

TOWARDS THE MILLENIUM

Little work is being done in the USA or Canada today, although C. 'Blue Ravine' was recently introduced from the Royal Botanic Gardens in Vancouver and Brian Bixley in Ontario is concentrating on the hardy alpina and macropetala types. In the southern hemisphere, very little is being introduced except for the fine cultivars Alister Keay is sending to us from New Zealand, including C. 'Allanah', C. 'Prince Charles' and the gorgeous white, C. 'Snow Queen'. In Japan, many new cultivars are being produced by nurserymen and keen hobby breeders. In Poland, Brother Stefan Franczak has already produced some fine cultivars, including C. viticella 'Polish Spirit', which he gave me in 1984. This clematis is grown in many thousands around the world. C. 'John Paul II' is also well known. Many more fine clematis are on their way from this most productive of plant breeders.

In the British Isles, Vince Denny is still producing interesting cultivars, including C. montana 'Broughton Star', a lovely double montana, and Barry Fretwell has raised fine selections of some of the species and large-flowered cultivars such as C. 'James Mason', C. 'Mrs James Mason', C. texensis 'The Princess of Wales' and C. viticella 'Tango'. Since 1993 I have introduced a range of clematis from the Evison/ Poulsen breeding programme, namely C. VINO™ 'Poulvo'®, C. ALABAST™ 'Poulala'®, C. SUGAR CANDY™ 'Evione'®, C. ARCTIC QUEEN™ 'Evitwo'®, C. ANNA LOUISE™ 'Evithree'®, C. Royal Velvet™ 'Evifour'® , C. LIBERATION™ 'Evifive'®, C. PETIT FAUCON™ 'Evisix'®, C. EVENING STAR™ 'Evista'®, C. BLUE MOON™ 'Evirin'® and C. JOSEPHINE™ 'Evijohill'®.

I believe we are again in one of the most exciting periods of the development of clematis, coming almost 150 years since the introduction of those first large-flowered species and cultivars from China and Japan. In my breeding house in Guernsey last year, we undertook some 2,400 crosses, generating some 30,000 or more seeds. However, I believe we all have a most important role to play in the breeding, development and introduction of clematis. We must breed selectively, rather than producing another new clematis – that is easy. It is our duty to be most selective as to which cultivars are named and marketed. Only the best will do.

If only I could produce the first C. 'Jackmanii' or the first large white C. 'Henryi'; or discover C. florida in the wild or maybe the buttercup-yellow form of C. patens in the wild in China. Yes, gardeners and plant breeders are, and must be, dreamers. Without the dreams, there is no reality, no action, no development. The breeders of the 1850s and 1860s knew that. They were the pioneers.

3

CULTIVATION

In the wild, clematis seed themselves in cracks between rocks, in open ground or wherever the seeds are blown by the wind. However, it would appear that the most successful are those which find themselves a spot where there is some shade from direct sun or where there is sufficient moisture to survive. From observations in large-scale clematis production, we know that if the soil temperatures reach above 27°C (80°F) the roots stop developing and therefore top growth becomes very woody and rather stunted, with short internodes.

Clematis do not seem to require high light levels to grow, and in the garden they will tolerate semi-shade as they do in the wild. However, they do need long days to grow well. As days shorten in mid-autumn, clematis start to go into dormancy in central Europe. This happens earlier further north and, naturally, later further south in the northern hemisphere. In a Mediterranean climate clematis will start into growth much earlier as a result of warmer temperatures and higher light levels and some of the species from such a climate will go into a summer dormancy, reserving their energy until the autumn rains come when they grow again. Some even flower during the late autumn or early winter, for example C. *cirrhosa* 'Freckles'.

The ideal garden location is in a deep loam or prepared site where the clematis root system can grow in some moisture with shade to its root system, allowing its top growth to enjoy the sunlight. However, with careful cultivation, extra watering and feeding, clematis can be grown in more difficult locations and certain species

and cultivars may be grown very successfully in containers for the patio or a small terraced garden. If the entire range of plants currently available is taken into account, you can plant clematis so as to have one in flower from late autumn (as with C. *cirrhosa* 'Freckles'), right through the winter (in mild locations) into spring, summer and mid-autumn.

CHOOSING YOUR CLEMATIS

Choosing a good plant is important. Small, weak and cheap plants are not a good buy. Strong, well-branched and healthy young plants growing in a 11.5 cm (4½ in) (about 1 litre) pot are ideal and should establish easily. Larger plants in 14 or 17 cm (5½ or 7 in) (about 2 or 3 litre) pots will establish themselves and make a strong showing faster, but the larger the plant, the higher the cost. The height of the plant is not important. Plants on short supports of 38–45 cm (15–18 in) are perfectly adequate as long as the plants are well-branched, strong and healthy. The most important part of a clematis for planting is a strong root system and healthy basal stems. Only 8–10 cm (3¼–4 in) of stem is required if it is well-developed.

Whether you are planting clematis against a wall or fence, over a pergola, into a tree or as ground cover, the basic rules for the correct preparation of the site and planting generally remain the same. It is advisable to plant the clematis as far away as possible from the base of a wall as the soil there is generally extremely dry and hot in the height of the summer, especially on south-facing walls. Always choose the shadiest position possible for the planting site; for example, if you are planting a clematis to grow up into a large evergreen tree, choose the shady side of the tree as the planting site.

C. *cirrhosa* 'Freckles', a late autumn and early winter-flowering evergreen clematis for mild locations.

PLANTING OUT

Most clematis are bought today as container-grown plants, so with some extra care and extra watering the season for planting can be all year round. The natural and most logical planting time is during the period from late summer (unless the weather is still hot) right through until late autumn or the early winter. The ideal moment is while the soil is still warm from the summer sunshine, before it becomes too damp and wet. (Obviously, on heavy wet clay soils, early planting will be essential.) Planting at this time of the year allows the clematis the chance to establish some new roots before the onset of winter. During mid-autumn, clematis can produce a considerable amount of new roots, thus giving the plant a chance to establish well in the new site before the following spring and summer. This planting period will also save you from doing a good deal of watering while it is establishes.

Today however, many people are fine-weather gardeners and planting is mainly carried out in the spring or very early summer when gardening is much more pleasant than during a rainy autumn day. Even if soil conditions are favourable it is not advisable to plant in the depths of winter, but depending on weather and soil conditions planting can resume once that season is over, early to mid-spring being ideal. Planting until early summer is also possible, but the later you plant the more watering will be required to help the plant become established.

The preparation of the planting site is most important. Clematis will be expected to adorn their host or support for many years and you should regard the time spent in preparing the planting site as an important investment that will truly be rewarded in the future. Dig a hole of 45 × 45 cm (18 × 18 in) and discard the soil unless it is a good loam. Break up the base and sides of the hole with a garden fork, especially on clay or compacted soil, as otherwise the hole will become like a large clay pot where the clematis root system may not penetrate. Add well-rotted farmyard manure or garden compost to the base of the hole to a depth of 7–10 cm (3–4 in) and fork it well in. It is important that this is kept well away from the new clematis root system. Back fill the hole with good loam or old potting compost mixed with two or more bucketfuls of peat or peat substitute, which should have two handfuls of bone-meal or the appropriate amount of general fertilizer

added. Tread the soil down so that shrinkage will be at a minimum.

Before planting, it is important to 'condition' the clematis plant. Submerge it in its container in a bucket of water for at least 20 minutes so that the compost is thoroughly wetted and the roots have had time to take up water. This is necessary because, once planted, the roots will take time to re-establish and be able to take up moisture. After the plant has taken up water, remove it carefully from its container. The roots at the very bottom can be gently loosened to help them re-establish, but the main rootball must be left intact.

A garden trowel can then be used to remove enough soil from the prepared site to accommodate the clematis rootball. Plant the rootball at an extra depth of 6 cm (2½ in) below the soil level in its container to help the clematis establish a basal root crown of buds below soil level. Once the basal buds become established most will lie dormant, waiting there just in case of need. They will be forced into growth if the top growth becomes damaged in cultivation or, in the case of a large-flowered cultivar, the plant succumbs to clematis wilt. If the disease does strike, the plant has a much better chance of survival and regrowth if it has been planted at this depth. Although Ernest Markham recommended this deep planting as long ago as 1935, many old clematis growers that I met in the 1960s mounded soil over the root crown to achieve the same result. However, deep planting looks much better and, of course, the main roots of the clematis will be cooler if planted deeper.

After planting, carefully firm in the rootball with your open hands and fists. The clematis stems will need a firm support to the host plant or structure; the existing cane can be removed gently from the clematis stems or another cane can be used. The cane should be pushed into the ground outside the clematis stems at an angle sloping towards the host. This will also give protection from damage to the clematis root crown and basal stems during cultivation. At the time of planting or a little later, a low-growing plant or shrub should be planted near to the clematis rootball to give added shade to the root system. Stone slabs can also be used to give coolness and shade, but plant material looks much more natural. However, the shade plant should be shallow-rooting so that it does not take too much moisture away from the clematis plant's root system. Some of the best clematis my father grew in his garden in South

C. montana 'Elizabeth', a vanilla-scented, vigorous climber belonging to the Montana section.

Shropshire were planted to grow against a wall through other wall-trained shrubs, such as ceanothus and pyracantha. The clematis root systems found their way from the border to grow underneath a wide concrete pathway, and once they reached the moisture and coolness of the rubble there they romped away. Such cool conditions for the root systems of clematis are ideal.

After planting, the most important job is to water the clematis. They will require constant attention in this respect after planting. Immediately the clematis has been planted, it should receive at least 4.5 litres (1 gallon) of clear water. This should be repeated within two days if the weather conditions are hot and dry. If you have planted the clematis in early summer almost daily watering will be required until the clematis has established a new root system that has started to take up moisture. This will be signified by substantial new growth. If clematis are planted to grow up into large trees or shrubs or at the base of a dry sunny wall, daily watering will be needed to help them establish.

REPLANTING

If a clematis is to be replanted from an existing site, the late winter before bud break is the time to do this. However, it is only the large-flowered cultivars or the *C. viticella* cultivars that generally can be replanted from an open ground position due to their large fleshy roots. The clematis species and their cultivated forms have a very fibrous root system that usually breaks up when it is being dug up. The montana types and the Meclatis Section are also extremely difficult to replant once they have been established for more than two or three years. If a clematis is to be relocated, it is advisable to prune down the top growth to a pair of strong leaf axil buds on each stem to within 60 cm (2 ft) of the soil level. Place a strong bamboo cane or stick firmly into the soil near the base of the stems (not too close or you will cause damage to the base of the main roots) and tie all remaining stems carefully to the support provided. It may be tempting to leave longer stems, but remember that a very large percentage of the plant's root system will be destroyed and the remainder will be unable to provide enough moisture to support the top growth if a large amount is left on the plant.

The digging up of the clematis is also an operation that requires care. First dig a circle around the rootball as deeply as possible (at least a spade depth), leaving a rootball with a diameter of approximately 45 cm (18 in). It may be necessary to go around the rootball several times to ensure that all the roots have been cleanly cut. Then get the spade well under the rootball to at least a spade depth from all angles to ensure that all the roots are cut. Enlist the help of another person if possible, so that two spades can be used to remove the clematis rootball from its site. Place the root onto a large piece of strong polythene or sacking and keep it moist until it can be replanted – ideally, the new planting site will be prepared and ready. It is important that the rootball be planted an extra 5–8 cm (2–3¼ in) deeper than the previous soil level. The remaining stems should be carefully tied and trained to the new support or host plant. It is essential for the replanted clematis to be watered during the coming spring and summer, together with the following spring and summer if the season is at all hot and dry.

As new growth appears during the spring, it should be tied and trained to its support. If the growth is at all weak and spindly, it is advisable to pinch out the soft tip growth to help the plant develop a good bushy stem structure. If the clematis belongs to the early large-flowered group (pruning group two, see page 46), do not expect large flowers during the first or maybe even the second season after replanting. This is because these clematis flower from the previous season's ripened stems and with the hard pruning that took place before removing it from its previous site nearly all the flowering stems will have been removed.

Whichever group the clematis belongs to, all top growth should be cut back to just above the base of the previous season's stems during the second spring after replanting. This will encourage the plant to become bushy and well furnished towards its base. During the third spring onwards, the clematis can be pruned following the pruning recommendations for its pruning group (see page 46).

CONTAINER PLANTING

Late summer to early autumn is the best time for container planting as the clematis will start to establish itself during mid- to late autumn and be in a position to produce some flowers the following summer. The choice of container is vital for the successful cultivation of clematis. Although clematis need a moist, cool root run they do not like cold wet feet in winter, so a free-draining compost is important. This rules out the use of thin plastic containers as in the summer the soil in the container would become far too hot and in the winter no protection would be given to the thick fleshy roots of the large-flowered clematis, so they would freeze and then decay. The ideal container is one made out of stone, or reconstituted stone, with a 5 cm (2 in) side wall, or an old cider or beer barrel made out of thick wood. Specially made wooden boxes that have been treated against rotting are also ideal, particularly if they have an inner skin, maybe of tin, to help preserve the wood. Thick-walled frost-resistant terracotta pots and urns and large strawberry pots look most effective with a healthy clematis growing out of them, but terracotta does not give the same amount of protection against the sun in summer or the frost in winter.

The size of the container is also important. A container with a diameter and depth of about 38 cm (15 in)

is the smallest size that should be used, and this will only suffice for about two years before the clematis will need to be upgraded to a larger container. Moving a clematis up in such a way involves extra work, but it is worth doing as clematis dislike being put in too large a pot at the outset. Generally, I recommend that the smallest container for long-term growing be no less than 45 × 45 cm (18 × 18 in). However, the larger the better because it is then possible to plant other shallow-rooting plants within the container to help keep the clematis root system cool in summer – 60 × 60 × 60 cm (2 × 2 × 2 ft) is ideal.

The container must have adequate drainage holes. These depend upon the size of the container. A container measuring 45 × 45 cm (18 × 18 in) should have at least three drainage holes measuring 2.5 cm (1 in) across. To ensure the drainage is effective, raise the container off the ground by placing bricks beneath it.

Before placing the compost in the container, put a layer of broken crocks, stones or pebbles over the drainage holes to stop the compost from clogging up the holes. Lay large pieces first and then place smaller stones, large pebbles and then small pebbles or pea-gravel on top of these. If available, rotted turf can be placed upside down on top of the small pebbles or pea-gravel. If not, well-rotted farmyard manure or garden compost can be used in its place but these materials must be kept away from the newly planted clematis roots. Then fill the container with John Innes Potting Compost No. 2, or an equivalent. A loam-based compost is best because loam-free composts sometimes dry out too quickly and can then be very difficult to re-wet even if they do have a polymer mixed with the compost. Once the compost has been placed into the container, firm it well to avoid sinkage – it should be 5 cm (2 in) below the rim of the container, allowing sufficient depth for watering.

Use a small garden trowel to dig out enough compost to make room for the clematis rootball. Planting in a container should be done under the same guidelines as planting into the garden soil, which is to say drench the rootball before planting, plant an extra 5 cm (2 in) deep and water well after planting. The aftercare for a clematis in a container is of course much more than that required for one in open ground as it will require extra training, tying and feeding and attention to watering is a must, especially in dry weather.

TRAINING

A clematis growing in a container obviously needs some support. The type of support very much depends upon where the container is placed. If it is alongside a wall so that the clematis will grow up and through other wall-trained shrubs, a strong bamboo cane or thick stake can be placed at an angle between the container and the wall or limb of the host tree or shrub. The clematis stems may then be tied to the cane or stake and up into the host plant.

If the container is to stand in the open, some form of more elegant support will be required – how elegant depends upon the location in the garden. A simple wigwam made out of thick bamboo, pea-sticks or thick hazel poles is an inexpensive solution. Alternatively, there are attractive iron or plastic-covered steel supports available. These are freestanding and can be placed securely within the container.

The training of a clematis in a container is important, the aim being to produce a bushy, well-furnished plant with plenty of foliage and flowers at the base of the support as well as up it, rather than a bunch of foliage and flowers at the top of the support as is so often seen. After planting, train the stems horizontally around the support as low down as possible. I use string, raffia or stem ties with a central thin wire to tie in the existing clematis stems and new growth. The aim is to produce a well-furnished plant and build up the framework of stems for future years. If the clematis has been planted during the late summer or early autumn, any dead or weak stems should be removed to a pair of strong leaf axil buds during the following late winter/early spring. Train in the remaining stems. If these are weak or thin, they too should be reduced. As new growth appears during mid- and late spring, this too should be tied in horizontally to help cover the base of the support as well as the top.

If the planting time is mid- to late spring and the clematis has not been pruned before it was purchased from the nursery or garden centre, remove any weak stems and possibly reduce others to a pair of strong leaf axil buds. As new growth appears, gently pinch the top growth with thumb and finger after two or three nodes have been produced on each stem to encourage new growth from the leaf axil buds, which will produce a bushy plant. The best clematis for growing in containers are the small-flowered mid-spring flowering types and the late spring and early summer-flowering large-

A range of clematis growing in Uno Kivistik's clematis trial garden in Estonia, from which numerous good cultivars have been introduced.

flowered clematis. These clematis produce their main crop of flowers from the growth ripened the previous season and this pruning and pinching back means that very little flower can be expected during the first season. However, some flowers can be expected later during the summer months and as these clematis are more compact in their habit and will produce more flowers in a given space than other types it is worth being patient.

Adding other plants to the containers is advisable, partly to provide shade for the clematis root system but also to give extra foliage, flowers and form. If such plants are added, they should be of a shallow rooting habit and, if possible, be allowed to flop over the sides of the container, giving a natural effect. Summer bedding plants are an easy choice in the summer; in the winter some carefully selected winter-flowering heathers would be ideal. A few spring-flowering bulbs, for example tulips, daffodils or shorter growing bulbs such as *Iris reticulata* will give added interest and colour, perhaps with a selection of wallflowers and forget-me-nots. The bulbs will die down once they have finished flowering, and the other spring-flowering plants can be removed to allow replanting with summer bedding plants.

WINTER PROTECTION

When growing clematis in containers you must consider the type of clematis and the winter protection it will need in your area. In mild locations, with night temperatures dropping only to about –7°C (19°F), the top growth of the small-flowered mid-spring flowering types and the late spring and early summer-flowering large-flowered clematis will not be damaged or destroyed. It is vital to retain the top growth in order to obtain the early large flowers of the large-flowered cultivars. If the night temperatures drop below those figures for two or three weeks at a time bud damage may occur, depending upon the wind chill factor and the amount of desiccation caused by the winds. The very hardy *C. alpina* and *C. macropetala* types will withstand open garden temperatures as low as –35°C (–31°F) and still flower the following year, so they will only need winter protection in very exposed cold climates. For safety, a fleece material can be wrapped around the top growth to give added protection. This can also be used in cold locations with the large-flowered cultivars, but only as a short-term protection; if the winter is expected to be severe, any large-flowered cultivars should be removed to a shed, outbuilding or garage where the temperatures are not expected to drop below –7°C (19°F) for any length of time. The fleece may be removed from outdoor clematis as soon as the weather improves and when spring has almost arrived – before the weather becomes too warm, as the extra protection may cause the plant to come into growth too early and the growth will be damaged when the fleece is removed.

Clematis containers wintered inside a building may be brought out once the worst of the cold weather is over. Again, it is important that the plants are not forced into growth prematurely by rising indoor temperatures. Any plants which have been over-wintered under cover must be well watered as soon as you have placed them in their spring and summer locations, choosing a mild day to do so. Early-morning watering is preferable so that the compost within the container can drain well before nightfall.

FEEDING

Clematis are generally hungry feeders and will take whatever is offered. In the open ground, feeding during the growing period and annual mulching must be considered for the continued well-being of the plant; feeding will encourage better growth, more flowers and a much healthier plant. A spring-planted clematis will benefit from additional feeding. This can be carried out at the time of watering by the use of liquid fertilizer. There are many of these available, or any good general feed can be used instead. Those which can be used as a foliage feed can be most beneficial and green up the foliage. A simple liquid feed used for roses is quite sufficient. The amount of feed and the frequency of feeding will depend upon the type used and careful attention should be paid to the manufacturer's recommendations. However, through experience, I have found it advisable to start feeding once new growth commences in mid-spring, continuing until just before flowering. Resuming after flowering will encourage further growth and, with luck, another crop of flowers. If feeding commences during flowering, the flowering period will be ended prematurely.

An annual mulch in late winter or early spring will help feed the plant in later months and a thick mulch will also give added shade to the root system. A 7.5 cm (3 in) layer of well-rotted farmyard manure, spent hop waste or well-rotted garden compost is ideal. Do not place the mulch close to the base of the stem of the clematis – leave a gap of 10–13 cm (4–5 in) diameter or harmful gasses may cause burning to the new stems and growth that may appear from below soil level. A frosty day when the garden soil is frozen is an ideal time to do this rather than damaging wet winter soil by walking on it. If none of the above materials are available, a mulch of peat or peat substitute mixed with two handfuls of bonemeal per bucket of peat will suffice. However, peat should be lightly forked in otherwise it will become dry in early summer and be blown away. Any general garden fertilizer can also be used according to the manufacturer's recommendations.

Clematis growing in containers will need regular feeding. For newly planted clematis, liquid feeding is best. This can be carried out at the time of watering. Again, any general soluble feed can be used – rose feed is ideal. A feed of Phostrogen is also most beneficial for container-grown clematis.

For established plants growing in containers, it is important to renew the topsoil in the container each spring, ideally in the middle of the season. This can be done when any winter- or spring-flowering plants have finished flowering and are to be removed to make room for new plantings. Replace the top 5–7.5 cm (2–3 in) of the soil with a good potting compost to give a fresh start to the clematis and additional feed for the summer bedding plants. When removing the old soil, take care not to damage the clematis plant's root system or that of any other permanent plant in the container.

PRUNING

Many people regard the pruning of clematis as a complicated area, but in fact as long as the gardener understands the flowering habit of clematis it is perfectly simple. Clematis are basically old- or new-wood flowering. I admit that as clematis do not do the same things at the same time each year this becomes something of a grey area, but as long as the plant's name is known it can be looked up in catalogues or reference books, where the relevant information will be available. I also have a simple rule for gardeners in the British Isles – if they have lost the label for their clematis and it cannot be easily identified, they should take heed of the saying 'If it flowers before the end of June, don't prune', as it must be an old-wood flowering clematis.

The confusion about clematis pruning that has arisen was engendered by the original breeding carried out in the 1850s and 1860s. The breeders referred to clematis as evergreen, C. *alpina* types, C. *patens* types, C. *lanuginosa* types, C. *jackmanii* types, C. *viticella* types large or small-flowering and, of course, the miscellaneous later-flowering species and their cultivars. This system of putting clematis in these old groups was continued into the 20th century and was still in practice when I became involved with clematis in the 1960s. I and a few other breeders started the system that is used by most people today – that of pruning groups one, two and three.

Although I still see authors referring to the original groups, because of the inbreeding between all types and groups the clear lines between the groups have become less firm and I believe it is the date of flowering that is the most important aspect of pruning.

Pruning should be carried out with the aim of producing the maximum amount of flowers on the clematis plant. Therefore, once the main flowering period of the clematis species or cultivar is known, the question of pruning becomes very simple. If you prune an old-wood flowering clematis hard, no harm is done; the first main crop of flowers will be lost but these will be replaced by a later batch of flowers which will be smaller but possibly more profusely borne. The growers of the old-wood flowering clematis in Northern Europe and colder areas of North America sometimes have no choice – their clematis top growth is killed right down to soil level by the frosts and winter desiccation. The clematis then regrow each year from ground level, producing flowers in late rather than early summer.

During mild winters, especially in warmer parts of Europe, some clematis may continue to grow slowly, or new growth may appear too early. It is tempting to get underway with pruning early, but this may encourage fresh new growth that will sometimes be killed by severe late spring frosts. The best growth may thus be destroyed, so it is advisable always to wait until the correct pruning time.

PRUNING GROUPS

Group one consists of all the early-flowering evergreen species and their cultivated forms, the C. *alpina* and C. *macropetala* types, the C. *montana* groups and any other early and mid-spring flowering species. The clematis species and cultivars that fall into this group produce their flowers either singly or in clusters on 5–13 cm (2–5 in) flower stalks (peduncles) from the leaf axil buds produced and ripened the previous season. Therefore, no pruning should be carried out until the main flowering period has been completed. Some clematis from this group will produce occasional summer flowers from new growth, especially the C. *alpina* and C. *macropetala* types.

Group two consists of all the old-wood flowering clematis, the early large-flowered cultivars, the double and semi-double large-flowered cultivars and the mid-season large-flowered cultivars. The clematis cultivars that belong to this group also produce their main crop of

PLATE III

ATRAGENE
SECTION

All flowers
are shown at
approximately
½ size

C. alpina
'Pink Flamingo'

C. macropetala
'Jan Lindmark'

C. macropetala
'Markham's Pink'

C. macropetala

C. alpina
'Albiflora'

C. alpina var. ochotensis
'Frances Rivis'

C. alpina
'Constance'

C. alpina
'Jacqueline du Pré'

C. alpina
'Cyanea'

C. alpina
'Blue Dancer'

C. alpina
'Burford White'

flowers from leaf axil buds which were produced and ripened the previous season. The length of new growth produced before their solitary flower is borne on each new stem varies from cultivar to cultivar, but basically the earlier the cultivar flowers the shorter the flower stem. This may be a stem with only two or three sets (pairs) of leaf axil buds at perhaps 15 cm (6 in) as in cultivars such as C. 'Miss Bateman' or C. 'Lady Londesborough', or C. 'Nelly Moser', which will produce stems perhaps 30 cm (12 in) long before the large cartwheel-type flowers open. The mid-season large-flowered cultivars also produce their crop of solitary terminal flowers on the new growth from the ripened previous season's growth. This may be up to 60–90 cm (2–3 ft) in length. These include C. 'Henryi', C. 'Marie Boisselot' and C. 'Elsa Späth'. This group will produce a later crop of flowers on new growth, with the number varying per cultivar.

Group three consists of the late large-flowered cultivars, the C. *viticella* types and all late-flowering species and the cultivated forms that flower on the current season's growth. Generally, these bloom profusely, producing many flowers per stem, some in panicles as in C. *recta*, some at tip growth along the flowering stems as in C. 'Jackmanii'.

HOW TO PRUNE

Group one All dead and weak stems can be removed after flowering, generally in early summer, and any growth that has spread beyond its allotted space should be removed or shortened. After pruning, new growth will be produced by all clematis in this group. This new growth will ripen as the season progresses and will produce flowers the next spring or early summer.

Group two All dead and weak stems should be removed in late winter or early spring and remaining stems should be reduced down to the highest pair of strong leaf axil buds. All old leaves, be they dead or green, should also be removed at this time. It is the fat leaf axil buds, easily visible by early spring, which will produce the large spring or early summer flowers. The remaining stems should be carefully trained and tied into their host or support, spaced out evenly to allow enough room for the full development of the foliage and flowers. The aim is to ensure that the lower part of the plant is well covered. If not, some stems can be trained

downwards to cover gaps. As new growth appears in mid-spring, this too should be trained carefully.

Group three This group requires major pruning, with all stems being removed in late winter to early spring. All top growth can be cut down to where strong new leaf axil buds appear at a point just above the base of the previous season's stems, at approximately 30–75 cm (1–2½ ft) from soil level. Any old dead leaves should also be removed at this time. As new growth appears in mid-spring, tie it in carefully, spacing it evenly to ensure that the support or host plant has an evenly balanced amount of clematis growth.

Pruning group three clematis growing through evergreen trees or shrubs can be reduced in growth during

C. 'Jackmanii', one of the most popular clematis in the world, in full flower gracing a cottage doorway.

late autumn. About two-thirds of their top growth may be removed; not only does this reduce wind damage to these usually leafy clematis, but the host tree or shrub looks much more attractive during the winter months without a covering of dormant clematis stems and wet leaves. The final annual pruning can then be carried out at the correct time in late winter to early spring.

Newly Planted Clematis

All newly planted clematis require hard pruning during the first spring after planting, regardless of which group they belong to, unless they are extremely strong with plenty of stems growing from the base. All top growth should be reduced down to approximately 30–45 cm (12–18 in) so that young growth will be produced from the base of the plant.

Pruning of Clematis on Groundcover Plants

Clematis scrambling over evergreen groundcover plants such as heathers should be cut back by two-thirds in late autumn. With clematis belonging to the Viticella Section growing on or through winter-flowering heathers, all top growth should be removed back to within 30 cm (12 in) of ground level at this time.

Pruning to Change the Flowering Period

If a clematis cultivar from pruning group two has been selected for its flower colour to blend with, for example, a rose, it may be pruned as for group three clematis. Although the early flowers will be lost, flowers will be produced to coincide with the blooming of the rose. The clematis to select here are the repeat-flowering cultivars from group two such as C. 'Elsa Späth', C. 'General Sikorski' or C. 'Niobe'. The A–Z of Species & Cultivars lists the full range of repeat-flowering clematis.

Mid-season Large-flowered Cultivars

Certain large-flowered cultivars which produce their first flowers in early summer on long stems that have grown from the previous season's ripened leaf axil buds can, if required, be pruned as per group three, rather than group two. This will cause the loss of some early flowers but the plants will benefit, growing vigorously and producing flowers over a long period from early summer to mid-autumn. These clematis, bred from the old C. lanuginosa types, do not quite fit into group two

or group three, so with experience they can be pruned either way. In northern Europe or northern North America, these clematis generally lose their top growth in severe winters in any case.

Summer Pruning & Deadheading

Some clematis growers prefer to remove spent flowerheads to encourage further crops of flowers, especially with the early large-flowered single, double and semi-double clematis. Certainly, if the old flowers are removed with a length of stem with 2–3 nodes, new growth will appear and a further crop of flowers will be produced. When this is done, it is important to keep the clematis well watered and fed. The only drawback to this is that the attractive seedheads on this group of clematis will be lost. A compromise can be achieved by removing only 50 per cent of the spent flowerheads, retaining the remainder to develop into the fluffy flowerheads which are also important. This is particularly to be recommended when clematis are cultivated in containers.

Pruning Mixed Groups of Clematis

Many people like to grow clematis belonging to all three pruning groups together to obtain a long flowering period. Unless your eyesight is extremely good, you have a lot of patience and a very, very even temperament at pruning time I do not recommend this; even with all these attributes, I feel it is an almost impossible task to sort out the stems belonging to the different clematis and carry out appropriate pruning. However, growing clematis which belong to pruning groups two and three together is quite feasible. If the wrong stems are cut or damaged, all is not lost for the following season – it just causes a delay in flowering.

I am very much in favour of growing clematis together to achieve interesting colour combinations. Growing the pink, blue and white C. alpina and C. macropetala types together does not cause any problems at pruning time. In containers, planting two or even three cultivars belonging to group two can be very effective and if they have slightly different flowering periods so much the better.

PEST & DISEASE CONTROL

Fortunately, there are very few pests or diseases that affect clematis on a regular basis – though every gardener dreads the appearance of clematis wilt. The other troublesome problems are those that affect other plants such as roses – aphids (greenfly), whitefly, red spider mite and mildew. All can be avoided or controlled very easily.

PESTS

Aphids and Whitefly

Aphids can be troublesome in the late spring or early summer, causing damage to the soft young top growth and marking foliage. Spray the plants with a proprietary pesticide – one recommended for roses will be perfectly adequate. Whitefly is normally less troublesome and generally only affects plants grown under glasshouse conditions. Again, use a proprietary pesticide.

Birds

In the spring small birds such as bullfinches often damage the swollen flower buds of the C. montana group and the leaf axil buds of large-flowered cultivars can also be attacked on occasion. The bird-scarers used in fruit orchards are not suitable for the small garden as the noise would not go down well with the neighbours. Though it is frustrating when the buds of a C. montana are totally destroyed, the problem is not generally a great one.

Earwigs

These can be quite troublesome, especially if the clematis is growing near to old buildings with brickwork or timbers that have cracks in them, offering ideal places for the earwigs to hide during the daytime. They will emerge at night to chew holes in the leaves of clematis or to attack young growth and bore holes into flower buds, often destroying the flower before it has opened.

Chemical sprays are available but there is an old-fashioned method of control that works perfectly well. Stuff a small flower pot with moss or similar dry material and stand it upturned on a stick near to where the damage occurs. The earwigs will hide in the moss and you can then shake them out and destroy them by treading on them.

Mice

Mice have a habit of biting off pieces of stem at ground level to use for nesting material. The only notice the

gardener generally gets of this is in the early spring when clematis stems are found collapsing for no apparent cause until the stems are found to be without their connection to the root system. To avoid permanent damage to the clematis, the extra-deep planting described on page 38 is a must as the plants will then regrow from below the soil level. Clematis which are being grown through other groundcover plants, such as dense heather, are more likely to be attacked by mice looking for nesting material during the winter months or early spring. If there are no cats to keep mouse numbers down, mousetraps placed in drainpipes among the heathers are one solution but in a large garden in the countryside this becomes a difficult job. However, if the C. viticella types are used as suggested to grow through winter-flowering heathers, they are extremely vigorous, producing plenty of stems from below ground level. Once the stems become thick, they are less interesting to the mice. If the mice do carry out some unintended pruning for you, there are benefits – the clematis will become more bushy and well-furnished at the base.

Rabbits

Rabbits destroy top growth, so preventative action is certainly needed if they are known to be in the locality. There are two ways to protect plants. Land drainpipes made of clay blend in reasonably well with foliage and if lengths of about 45 cm (18 in) are upturned over the root crown the clematis stems will grow up through them. If rabbits do cause any damage it will be above the top of the pipe and the clematis will regrow from this point.

Another form of protection is fine-mesh chicken wire. This can be cut to form a collar 23 cm (9 in) in diameter and about 60 cm (2 ft) high. Once it has become weathered, the chicken wire will blend in with the background and be less obtrusive than clay drainpipes or any of the rather obvious tree guards which I prefer not to use, except in a woodland setting.

Red Spider Mite

Red spider mite normally affects clematis when the soil conditions are dry and red spider is having a good year. A severe infestation can be recognized by the top surface of the leaves becoming blotchy and paler in colour; when the leaf is turned upwards the lower surface is generally found to be covered with pinkish-red spider mites. As the foliage and flower buds will become totally distorted, the clematis must be checked immediately if red spider mite is found on other plants. The most efficient control is by prevention rather than cure; use a pesticide recommended for roses.

Slugs and Snails

These pests generally cause trouble during mild winters and early spring. They tend to graze on new growth and the fat leaf axil buds, sometimes removing them altogether. Use proprietary brands of slug destroyers or try the old remedy of placing a shallow tray or container filled with beer near the plants. Surrounding the plants with abrasive material such as coal ashes does deter slugs and snails to some extent.

DISEASES

Clematis Wilt

This is the biggest problem that clematis growers face, though fortunately it attacks only the large-flowered clematis cultivars and not the species or their small-flowered cultivars. Clematis wilt is caused by a fungus called *Phoma clematidina*. Normally, the point where the fungus attacks the clematis is at or just above the soil level. The fungus appears to enter the clematis stem through a crack or at the point of some previous damage or weakness. Once it starts to grow it destroys the cells of the stem and blocks the sap from reaching any area above the infection, thus causing the stem to collapse, becoming black and then brown as it wilts. What may have appeared a perfectly healthy plant the day before can suffer total collapse literally overnight, though sometimes only one or two stems will be affected. Clematis wilt normally attacks plants in early summer, very often just when they are at the point of flowering, causing maximum disappointment to the gardener.

Once wilt on a plant is discovered, the affected stems must be removed and burnt. The fungus may have been present in the soil before the attack and been splashed on to the plant by rain or during watering. Therefore, when the top growth has been removed, it is advisable to drench the base of any remaining stems and the soil area to a diameter of at least 60 cm (2 ft) around the plant. The fungicide to use is a Bio Supercarb (carbendazim) solution. This should help prevent the fungus spreading and reduce the risk of further attacks.

If the clematis has been planted 6 cm (2½ in) below soil level (see page 38) and has built up a root crown of growth buds below the soil, in most cases the plant will recover and grow away. When new growth appears, a programme of drenching should continue using the Bio Supercarb solution as described on the container to destroy any remaining spores of *Phoma clematidina*. When new growth has reached two to three nodes, say 23–30 cm (9–12 in) tall, the tip growth should be removed, encouraging it to break and produce more side shoots. It is important to get the new stems as woody as possible. They too should be carefully tied into their support so they are not damaged by wind or rain. As it recovers, the clematis should be treated as if it were newly planted from the point of view of pruning, feeding, watering and training.

If a clematis persistently succumbs to clematis wilt it is best to dig it up, remove most of its soil, drench it in a solution of Bio Supercarb and replant it in a less important planting site. The plant will show you that it can perform and you will be rewarded with marvellous flowers where you did not really want them. The old clematis planting site can be replanted but it is advisable that the site is also drenched with the solution of Bio Supercarb to clean up any remaining fungal spores. The soil should be replaced with new soil or compost as described on page 39. If your garden seems prone to clematis wilt, replant with the *C. viticella* cultivars, such as *C. viticella* 'Blue Belle' which has masses of flowers (as do all the *C. viticella* types) but larger, at 8 cm (3¼ in) or more in diameter. The *C. viticella* types do not suffer from clematis wilt.

Mildew

Mildew generally affects the later large-flowering cultivars, such as *C.* 'Jackmanii' and some of its group. Of these, *C.* 'Perle d'Azur' can be badly affected some summers, as can *C.* 'Madame Edouard André'. In some years *C. texensis* cultivars, particularly 'Etoile Rose' and 'Pagoda', can be covered in powdery mildew. As a preventative action – and it should be prevented as there is no cure once the mildew has taken hold – use the same spray as is recommended for roses. Only the later large-flowered clematis and the *C. texensis* types should be sprayed, as other late-flowering clematis such as the Meclatis Section and *C. viticella* and its cultivars are not normally affected.

4

PROPAGATION

The propagation of clematis can be carried out by various means: seed, division, layering, cuttings or grafting. I consider the latter to be an inferior method of propagation, but it may be used as a last resort if cuttings or layering fail for some reason.

Clematis species grown from seed may be slightly variable but are normally found to be acceptable within the species range and invariably come 'true' from seed. However, if a batch of clematis are germinated from seed, it is always worth watching out for poor-performing forms – and, of course, improved forms. A good keen eye is needed.

If any large- or small-flowered cultivars or species are closely planted with a compatible species (such as the New Zealand and some American pitcher-shaped species), the resultant seedlings will be variable and generally not at all like the seed parent. These botanical variants or hybrid seedlings may be poor or a great improvement on the parent. To reproduce a good form of a species exactly, or any large- and small-flowered cultivars, the plants must be vegetatively propagated by division (with perennial types), layering or cuttings.

SEEDS

While some authorities state it is advantageous to place seeds in a cold store, or stratify them, I firmly believe that all seeds should be sown as soon as they have become ripe and have been cleaned for sowing. The early-flowering species such as *C. alpina*, *C. macropetala* and *C. montana* will produce ripened seeds by mid-summer, while the midsummer- and autumn-flowering clematis will have ripened seed by mid-autumn. Some may need help to dry off, especially the autumn-flowering species. If the autumn is damp, rainy or cold, cut off

a length of stem of about 60 cm (2 ft) once the seeds have become large and swollen. This can then be hung upside down in a dry room or a boiler room where the atmosphere is always dry but not too hot, otherwise the seeds will become dried out.

When the seed is left on the plant to dry off and ripen, care must be taken that it is not dispersed by the wind. Those fluffy seed tails are so designed that once they are ripened and the wind blows, they will take flight. For this reason it is always advisable to place a muslin bag over the seeds before they are completely ripe.

Once the seeds have ripened, they may be detached from the old flower stalks (pedicels). They break away in the hand easily. The seed should then be detached from the seed tail which again should break away easily in the fingers, though some may need a sharp pair of scissors or small secateurs. Take care not to damage the seeds in the process.

Sow the seed in large or small pots or seed trays, depending upon the amount. The container should have good drainage and crocks, small stones or pea-gravel should be placed in the bottom to assist with the drainage. Then fill the container with a good seed compost to within 2.5 cm (1 in) of the rim and firm it gently, first with your fingers and then with a piece of wood or the base of a small flower pot to flatten it. Water the compost and allow it to dry off before sowing the seeds.

Place the seeds evenly on the compost surface – do not sow them too densely as some species will germinate like mustard and cress and then become difficult to

C. alpina 'Pink Flamingo', a free-flowering alpina belonging to the Atragene section (shown twice normal size).

prick out. Cover the seeds with a thin layer of finely sieved compost so that they are only just covered and water them lightly. The seeds of most clematis will take some time to germinate; though seeds of plants in the Meclatis Section will germinate in about two weeks, other seeds may not germinate until the following spring. Some species, for example C. *campaniflora*, may produce a few seeds that will germinate the first spring after planting but the main batch may take a further year. Consequently, the decision as to where the seed container should be placed is an important one as otherwise it may have to be moved many times before germination occurs. It must not be a place where it will dry out quickly, so a cool site under a bench in a glasshouse or perhaps in a cold frame would be ideal. The most important aspect is that it should be placed in an area where it can be protected against mice, as they adore clematis seeds and will destroy the whole lot if not prevented. The old method of placing large sheets of glass over the seed container not only keeps mice at bay but also helps to warm up the soil, assisting with germination. Cover the glass with brown paper or newspaper to protect the seeds from being overheated by the sun.

The seed container must be inspected on a regular basis to check the moisture level. Do not let the seeds become dried out. I prefer a loam-based compost as this gives more flexibility regarding watering and feeding. As the seedlings germinate and mature, the seed container can be watered with a light liquid feed to help the seedlings become established more easily.

When the seedlings have produced two to three pairs of properly formed leaves they may be pricked out into a 7.5 cm (3 in) pot. Handle the seedlings by the leaf with thumb and finger and avoid touching the stem as this may become bruised and damaged, leading to damping off after pricking out. If only a few seeds have germinated and you decide to prick out the most advanced seedlings, use a dibber to ease the root system out of the seed container, tugging the leaves of the seedling very gently with the thumb and finger. Take care – these seedlings are delicate. The compost used for pricking out the seedlings can be either loam-based or peat-based. If the weather conditions are hot, the pricked-out seedlings must be shaded from the sun until they become established and have started to put on new root growth.

C. 'Ken Donson' produces some of the most attractive and perfectly formed seedheads of any of the large-flowered clematis cultivars.

As new top growth appears, it is advisable to pinch out the growing tips at about 10 cm (4 in) to encourage the plant to become more bushy. Tie the new growth to a split cane about 45 cm (18 in) tall. When the young clematis plant has become well rooted inside the base of the pot, it can be potted up into another pot of about 23 cm (9 in) in diameter, using a John Innes No. 2 Potting Compost or equivalent. Once the plant has re-established itself and grown away it can be planted out in the garden – or allowed to flower first to see if it has sufficient merits to be grown as a garden plant. Plant out as described on page 38.

Although the small- and large-flowered cultivars will not come true from seed, this can of course be used to advantage. If you are looking to produce new cultivars from seed, follow exactly the same procedure as for the species. However, more patience is needed as most of the small and large clematis cultivars take 9–12 months or perhaps even longer to germinate. Obviously, it is advisable to flower the plants to see what merit they have before going to the hard work of preparing a planting site and planting them out.

DIVISION

It is generally only the herbaceous clematis such as *C. recta* and *C. integrifolia* that are propagated by division. It is easy to remove their top growth and then lift them from the garden as with any other perennial plant. The method is as follows. The root and crown of the plant can be dug up with the use of a garden spade. Dig a circle around the plant of a diameter of about 45–60 cm (18–24 in) for large established plants and to at least a spade depth. By sliding the spade underneath the plant's root system you will be able to remove the root and crown from the ground. Then, with the use of two garden forks – or hand forks if the rootball is small – divide the root up by placing the forks back-to-back into the centre of the root crown and splitting it. It may be necessary to use a sharp knife to cut through the top of the root crown before the roots can finally be split apart.

Division should be carried out from mid-autumn to early spring during mild weather. The autumn is preferable so that the new plant can become established before late spring. Replant as described on page 39.

Some of the climbing forms of clematis, both species and small- and large-flowered cultivars, can be split by division but the success rate is not high. It would be impossible with the fibrous-rooted species such as *C. alpina*, *C. montana* and *C. tibetana* as their roots would just fall away and the original plant would be destroyed. Therefore, although it has been done successfully, I would not advise the division of the root system of the climbing clematis.

LAYERING

The layering of species (with the exception of the perennial clematis) and small- and large-flowered clematis cultivars is a rewarding but somewhat lengthy way of reproducing clematis true to type. Layering is generally done in early spring as soon as the worst of the winter weather has passed.

C. tibetana var. *vernayi* L & S 13342, a clone of the species with delightfully thick tepals and dainty foliage.

C. *alpina* 'Foxy' is a very free-flowering plant from the Atragene section which also produces pretty seedheads.

good drainage given by a layer of crocks or pebbles and preferably be filled with John Innes Potting Compost No. 1 or equivalent to within 2.5 cm (1 in) of the rim of the pot. Firm in to avoid sinkage. Remove the remaining leaves from the previous season on the chosen stem with a pair of secateurs. As you bend the stem towards the sunken pot, choose a suitable node that has active leaf axil buds to use for the layer. Using a sharp knife or razor blade, cut a sliver towards the base of the node from about 2.5 cm (1 in) below it, cutting into the node. Dipping it in some rooting hormone powder will assist in the faster rooting of the layer. Peg the cut node into the surface of the compost in the pot with a bent piece of wire, then cover it with compost and place a stone on top to ensure the layered stem does not spring up from the soil and dry out. It is a good idea also to secure the stem of the clematis by tying it to a bamboo cane pushed into the soil. The length of stem that remains above the node that has been layered can be reduced to about 45 cm (18 in). This can also be tied to a bamboo cane placed in the compost of the sunken flower pot.

The layered stem will of course receive some rainwater, but the compost in the sunken flowerpot will become dry unless it is checked and watered regularly. An early spring-layered clematis will have become a fully integrated plant before the autumn. It can then be detached from the 'mother plant' by cutting the stem before the layered part. The pot can be lifted once any new top growth has been reduced down to about 45–60 cm (18–24 in) and tied carefully to the bamboo cane that was placed into the flower pot. The new clematis can then be planted as described on page 38.

During early spring, the leaf axil buds will be visible on the clematis stems and just starting to swell. It is important to use a stem that has active leaf axil buds as this will usually be a stem produced within the last 12 months. Older stems will be less flexible and therefore more difficult to bend down to ground level and will also probably have less active leaf axil buds which will most likely take longer to root once layered. Generally, older stems can be recognized by their darker brownish-grey stems as opposed to the light brown stems belonging to the previous year's growth.

To layer the stem, sink a plastic flowerpot of approximately 15 cm (6 in) in diameter into the soil to a depth such that the rim is just visible. The pot should have

CUTTINGS

The rooting of clematis by the use of internodal cuttings is sometimes extremely successful but very often frustrating and difficult. Some clematis species, for example C. *alpina*, C. *macropetala*, C. *montana*, C. *tangutica*, C. *tibetana* and C. *viticella* and its cultivars, are usually fairly easy to propagate from internodal cuttings. However, other species such as C. *armandii* and the American pitcher-shaped species and the cultivar C. *florida* 'Sieboldii' are exceedingly difficult. The small- and large-flowered cultivars can be successfully rooted on the whole, but as a general rule the larger the flowers are of the large-flowered clematis cultivars the more difficult the job of rooting the cuttings seems to become.

If it is possible to obtain cutting material from plants grown under glasshouse conditions the rooting of internodal cuttings becomes that much easier. Material from garden-grown clematis is generally more susceptible to failure, sometimes due to botrytis caused by damage which has usually been inflicted before the cutting material was removed from the 'mother plant'.

Internodal cuttings from clematis grown under glasshouse conditions can be taken from mid-spring to midsummer; from garden-grown plants the period is shorter, from late spring until the later part of early summer. It is the semi-ripened fleshy green new growth that is used. The ideal cutting is an internodal piece that includes a leaf axil node which has not become too ripened but also is not too soft. Therefore, an ideal cutting will come from the middle part of a 60 cm (2 ft) length of stem. The cutting should be about 5 cm (2 in) long, with 1 cm (½ in) of stem above the node and 3.5 cm (1½ in) below it. One leaf from a pair near to the leaf axil bud can be removed and the remaining leaf or leaflets reduced by 50 per cent, thus minimizing the loss of moisture from the leaves by transpiration.

Insert the prepared cuttings into deep seed trays or suitably sized flower pots, depending upon their number. Only one species or cultivar should be inserted into each container as otherwise it is easy to lose track of which plant is which. All the cuttings should be labelled with their name and the date they were inserted.

The containers should have good drainage material, such as broken crocks or pea-gravel, placed into the bottom to assist with drainage, with a thin layer of John Innes Potting Compost No. 1 on top. This should not be within reach of the base of the cuttings. The aim of this layer of compost containing a little fertilizer is to help feed the cuttings once they have become rooted, helping them to establish more quickly. The container can then be filled with cutting compost which can be purchased or made up with equal parts of loam, peat and sand. Shake it through a sieve with 6 mm (¼ in) mesh to provide a fine compost for the cuttings to be struck into. A thin layer of fine sand over the top of the compost will help to keep the surface free of botrytis; flatten the compost with a board before adding the sand.

Dip the bottom 1 cm (½ in) of each cutting into rooting hormone for semi-ripe cuttings, handling them by the node – not the stem, leaf-stalk or stalk, thus avoiding damage to these delicate areas – and then push them directly into the compost with finger and thumb. (If you wish, you can use a dibber instead.) The node should be just below the surface of the sand.

Place the containers in a cold frame or propagation unit for rooting to take place – or, as a simple alternative, cover each container with a polythene bag secured with a rubber band. The warmer the environment the faster the rooting, although temperatures above 27°C (80°F) should be avoided. High humidity also assists with better and faster rooting. The cuttings will require shading from the direct rays of the sun and unless they are in a mist or fog unit or enclosed by a polythene bag they will need to be damped over with a fine rose on a watering can several times a day to keep the humidity levels up and prevent the cuttings from becoming dehydrated or even dried out. Rooting will take place in 3½–5 weeks, depending upon the growing conditions of the cuttings; those in a cold frame will take up to eight weeks, depending on weather conditions. The time will also vary according to the species or cultivars being propagated.

As the cuttings become rooted the propagation unit, glasshouse or cold-frame conditions can be changed, allowing more sunlight and ventilation into the area. It is important to air the cuttings for an hour daily, unless they are being rooted by the polythene bag method. Botrytis and moulds are the biggest enemies of rooting cuttings and a careful watch should be kept throughout the propagation period. An appropriate programme of prevention and control treatments should be carried out, using approved products. Good cultural practices before and after taking the cuttings, a fungicide drench after the cuttings have been inserted and 'watered in', together with further fungicide applications as indicated, should lead to healthy plants.

When top growth appears from one of the leaf axil buds and develops to approximately 2.5 cm (1 in) in height, the rooted cutting can be potted up. However, if this occurs later than midsummer, it is best to leave the cuttings in the container until early in the following spring, when new growth will start to appear. If they are overwintered in the container, all leaves on the rooted cuttings should be removed by early winter to avoid botrytis and mould attacking them as they die back.

To pot up the rooted cuttings, remove them from the compost by gently tugging with thumb and finger either side of the node. Separate the new roots very carefully from the compost and the adjoining rooted cuttings.

The rooted cuttings can be potted up individually into 7.5 cm (3 in) pots containing John Innes Potting Compost No. 2 or equivalent. Plant the node of the rooted cutting so that it is just 1 cm (½ in) below the compost level in the container. Grow the cuttings on in conditions of shade, high humidity and warmth to assist with easy establishment of the root system. Avoid air temperatures above 27°C (80°F) until the roots are taking up moisture and new growth is starting to develop as high temperatures may cause damage by dehydration and eventually death to the newly potted rooted cuttings.

Once the young plant has become established and approximately 10–12.5 cm (4–5 in) of top growth has been attained, pinch out the growing tip to encourage the plant to become bushy at its base. At this stage, a 45 cm (18 in) split cane can be pushed into the compost near the clematis stem and the top growth tied into the cane. A fully established young plant may be potted on further into a larger pot of 11 cm (4½ in) diameter before being planted in the garden.

BREEDING

It is quite easy to develop new clematis cultivars just by collecting the seeds of the cultivars, sowing them, and waiting to see what comes up. With an intentional breeding programme using the small- or large-flowered cultivars, the end result is almost the same – the cultivars that we grow today are so inbred that the result of any cross is a bit of a guessing game as to the flower colour. However, it is possible to predict in more detail the habit of a plant.

If the parents are of the same habit, for example if two C. *viticella* small-flowered cultivars are crossed together, it can be expected that a new C. *viticella* cultivar will be produced (though this is not inevitable, as a throwback may result). Likewise, if two early large-flowered types are crossed together, the likelihood of the same type of

C. *viticella* 'Little Nell', raised in France by Morel and introduced by Ernest Markham in 1915, bears masses of flowers from midsummer to early autumn.

habit being produced would be very high. The same applies when *C. alpina* and *C. montana* are crossed with cultivars from within their own group or type. Species of some countries, particularly New Zealand, are very compatible and produce interspecies hybrids in the wild. However, if two species are not compatible (because their chromosome numbers are different) then the likelihood of the pollination being successful is very slim indeed. Added to this, a breeding programme is obviously limited by the flowering period of the clematis.

Therefore, to plan a careful breeding programme, you need to study what crosses should be attempted – but first you need to have a clear objective as to what sort of clematis you are aiming to produce. For your early attempts it is best to start with crosses where a good result can be reliably anticipated; if *C. alpina* types, *C. macropetala* types, *C. montana* types or early large-flowered types are used and crosses are attempted within these groups, seed should be produced. After some success with these groups of clematis, you can embark upon more interesting crosses.

MAKING THE CROSS

To make a successful cross you will require only minimal tools: small label tags to record the crosses, a sharp razorblade and a small artist's paintbrush. Having chosen your female flower (the seed parent) you will need to prepare it to receive pollen from the male flower by removing the tepals very carefully from the base. Then remove the stamens (the filaments and anthers – the male part of the clematis flower), leaving just the ovaries and styles. The styles may be pollinated as soon as the stigmas are receptive (slightly sticky) by gently brushing pollen from the anthers of the selected male flower over it, using a paintbrush to effect the transfer. If the pollen of the donor is not yet visible on the anthers, cover the styles for a few days with a muslin bag to avoid accidental pollination by another plant.

If the pollination has been successful seeds will slowly be produced, swelling gently, and after 6–10 weeks the seed tails will begin to develop. If it has been unsuccessful, the seed tails will be produced in a stunted form with no viable seed. They will become fluffy but will be very small compared to those with seeds that develop fully. Harvest the seeds as soon as they have ripened fully (see page 50).

Obviously, it is most important that none of these potentially valuable seeds are dispersed by the wind or just fall off the plant. To avoid this, while the seeds are still green the seedhead should be covered with a muslin bag which allows air to the seed but protects them from being lost or destroyed unintentionally.

REGISTERING A NEW CLEMATIS

The hybridization of clematis can be very rewarding, though only the very best of new clematis cultivars should be named and put into the commercial marketplace; there is room for only a certain number of new introductions each year, and these should be something special. However, if you do produce an exciting new clematis that has an outstanding flower colour or shape, growth formation or flowering habit, it should certainly be named and made available to gardeners.

The naming of new clematis is most important if large volumes of plants are expected to be sold around the world. There are two codes that have rules for the naming of plants: the International Code of Botanical Nomenclature, which deals with botanical names, and the International Code of Nomenclature for Cultivated Plants, which advises on the naming of garden forms or new cultivars. A simple, easy-to-remember name is best, most probably derived from the appearance of the flower or the whole plant, or the name of a person or place connected with its breeding. Contact the Registrar of the International Clematis Registration Authority (see page 154) to see if your proposed name has been used previously for clematis; if it has it cannot be used again, even if the clematis is no longer in existence. Once the name has been approved by the Registrar it can be entered on the International Clematis Register.

If the new clematis cultivar is of exceptional interest to commercial nurserymen it can be protected in Europe by Plant Breeders' Rights and in the USA and Canada by Plant Patents. All other countries around the world recognize this protection and offer their own systems of protection; once a clematis is protected in Europe, it is easier to protect it in other countries too. When the plants have been registered and given protection, licensed growers only can propagate the new clematis with the permission of the person or company owning the Plant Patents or Plant Breeders' Rights. Royalties can then be collected from the licensed growers, providing revenue for the breeder.

5

GARDEN USES &
PLANT ASSOCIATIONS

Clematis account for perhaps the most diverse groups of plants from within one genus, so they are very versatile as to where they will grow and the plants they will associate well with. I believe they should always be grown in association with other plants, shrubs and trees as they can be found doing in the wild; in cultivation they thrive much better in the micro-climate thus achieved.

For many years, clematis have been thought of as climbers that needed to be grown up a wall, their only support being that of a bare trellis – generally a sunny south-facing wall with little, if any, shade for their root system. In his book *The Virgin's Bower*, published in 1912, William Robinson wrote about growing clematis through shrubs. Ernest Markham did likewise in his book *Clematis*, first published in 1935, going into detail of growing clematis with other plants and shrubs and in beds. Somehow, gardeners lost sight of that advice from very knowledgeable clematis growers and instead planted clematis in the most unnatural ways. Fortunately, the trend has now shifted away from these bad practices and clematis can be seen in many gardens growing in a much more natural environment.

While clematis are very easygoing about their planting location, some are undoubtedly better suited to certain sites than others. The plants you can associate with them will also depend upon the site you have chosen.

WALLS

Clematis are very useful for covering walls with interesting foliage, colourful flowers and often attractive

seedheads. Extensive walled areas over 3.6–4.5 m (12–15 ft) in height and large gable ends of buildings are best served by *C. montana* types, due to their vigour. They will soon romp over such areas, covering them with foliage and, on an established plant, thousands of 5 cm (2 in) wide white or pink flowers. They are also excellent for disguising garden sheds.

Clematis do not cling onto walls as do ivy (*Hedera* spp.) or Virginia creeper (*Parthenocissus henryana*), for example. You will need to hammer in wall nails and then stretch wires 45 cm (18 in) apart between them, giving the clematis plenty of opportunity to wind their leaf tendrils around them. *Clematis montana* and its clan do not require annual pruning, so they are quite happy to be left alone smothering the wall or buildings until you feel they have outgrown their allotted space. Some of the best for this purpose are *C. m.* f. *grandiflora* (white) and *C. m.* 'Elizabeth' (scented pink flowers).

Alternative choices for walls and small buildings can be found in *C. tangutica* and *C. tibetana* (Meclatis Section). Again, wall nails and wire will be required. In theory, plants in this group need hard pruning but in such locations they can generally be trimmed with garden shears during the autumn or early spring to reduce some of their top growth, allowing fresh growth to develop and attach itself to the remaining old stems. Clematis such as *C. tangutica* 'Bill Mackenzie' are great value for money in such locations, producing their lovely yellow open cowbell-like flowers from midsummer onwards to late autumn. Once the first flowers have finished, the gorgeous fluffy seedheads are produced. This clematis therefore produces its own plant association of attractive foliage, flowers and seedheads for approximately 4–5 months.

C. ROYAL VELVET™ 'Evifour' Ⓝ is an ideal plant for growing with shrubs such as helichrysum.

C. *tangutica*, a vigorous species that needs a large wall area or tree to accommodate its growth.

Walls of less than 3.6 m (12 ft) should have a range of other plants, either climbers or wall-trained shrubs, which clematis can be allowed to grow up and trail from in a natural way with, of course, a little direction from the gardener. Nearly all groups of clematis can be grown in association with other wall-grown plants, but it is worth taking time to select the clematis that will give the best effect. There are several things that should be taken into consideration, the first being whether the host and clematis should flower at the same time. If so, you must work out which colour association you want – a matter of personal taste.

I also believe that the foliage of the host and the clematis should be complementary. The foliage of most clematis species is made up of tiny leaflets, so the overall appearance is that of a delicate climber, one exception being C. *armandii*, which has large pointed evergreen leaves and a vigorous habit that would swamp a ceanothus, for example. The C. *montana* group

are also far too vigorous to grow through other wall-trained shrubs or climbers.

The large-flowered clematis cultivars including the early and double and semi-double types, the midsummer and later summer-flowering cultivars would all be suitable for growing with other wall-trained plants. The early and double and semi-double large-flowered cultivars would all benefit from protection from the wind or heavy rain given by shrubs such as ceanothus, pyracantha, winter-flowering jasmine, forsythia and *Garrya elliptica*. A number of evergreen shrubs are ideal, giving spring or summer flowers, some winter fruit, and year-round foliage cover.

Another aspect to bear in mind is that some clematis flowers fade in strong sunlight faster than others. If the plant association is for a south-facing wall, strong, deep colours must be chosen rather than the paler-coloured clematis such as the pink/mauve striped C. 'Nelly Moser', or C. 'Hagley Hybrid' with its pale shell-pink flowers. Generally, the pinks and the paler striped clematis, such as C. 'Barbara Jackman', will also disappoint on a south-facing aspect. The pale blues usually retain their colour, and deep blues and purples are also good; the deep reds, such as C. 'Niobe' and C. 'Ernest Markham', do not fade and in fact the latter is best suited to a sunny south-facing aspect, where its wood ripens better and it is more free-flowering. The pale mauve/pink striped and pink clematis are better grown on north-facing walls, where their flowers will not fade prematurely.

If you want the clematis to flower before the host, or perhaps afterwards, a range of choices becomes available. If the host plant does not require pruning, choose a light-pruning clematis. For example, C. *alpina* and C. *macropetala* types would be ideal, although the host would need to be 3–3.6 m (10–12 ft) high and of reasonable vigour or the rather dense foliage of the clematis would swamp it totally. These two groups of clematis have a great range of coloured forms, through blue, mauve, pink and white. Although they are quite happy on a wall facing any direction, they are ideal for an exposed location facing north, northeast or northwest because of their very winter-hardy nature. They are also ideal growing by themselves on low walls or fences, where they will completely cover their allotted areas.

If clematis are required to flower after a spring- or early summer-flowering host, the later flowers such as

C. 'Jackmanii', C. 'Victoria', C. 'Comtesse de Bouchaud' and C. 'Madame Edouard André' can be used. The C. *viticella* types are also suitable, producing plenty of small to medium-sized flowers in a range of colours from white to pink, mauve, red and purple. The clematis belonging to the C. 'Jackmanii' and C. *viticella* groups are most useful for growing through deciduous or evergreen host plants as their stems and foliage can be removed in late autumn so that the host looks at its best without being cluttered by untidy and soggy clematis leaves. The final pruning can be done in late winter (see page 46). Both the C. 'Jackmanii' and C. *viticella* types are ideal for growing with wall-trained roses, giving additional colour when the roses are flowering.

The best time for planning the association is when the host is flowering or in fruit, followed by autumn or very early spring planting for the clematis.

Visit other gardens to find inspiration for planting ideas. At Bodnant Garden in North Wales, for example, I saw a most effective use for C. *montana* types; they were tightly clipped and trained on a balustrade-type wall only 1 m (3¼ ft) high. The effect at flowering time must have been stunning.

PERGOLAS & ARCHWAYS

Clematis are ideal for growing up pergolas and archways. The less rampant species, such as C. *alpina*, C. *macropetala*, the large-flowered cultivars and the C. *viticella* types, would beautify the supports and lower parts of a pergola, but you would need the more vigorous C. *montana* types or C. *tangutica* or C. *tibetana* to clothe the top of a pergola or large archway and give shade beneath. The vigorous C. 'Huldine' would do well in such a situation and its flowers, which have semi-transparent tepals of pearly white with three mauve ribs on the underside, are best appreciated from below. Another choice would be C. *viticella* 'Polish Spirit', which has deep purple flowers.

A pergola should not be given over entirely to clematis as it would be very dull during the winter months. Combine the clematis with evergreen plants that will give interest in winter and allow the clematis to take over in summer. Late spring large-flowered cultivars can be planted to grow through the lower stems of ceanothus or pyracantha. On the supports, clematis of the pruning group three category can be planted to grow with roses. C. *viticella* types such as the red-flowered

C. Petit Faucon™ 'Evisix' Ⓝ, a non-clinging clematis that is ideal with roses or in a mixed border.

C. *v.* 'Madame Julia Correvon' will give startling colour during mid- and late summer. The green-tipped white flowers of C. *v.* 'Alba Luxurians' are nodding and blow around in the breeze just like butterflies, and the plant will grow to 3.6 m (12 ft). Another relatively new clematis, C. Petit Faucon™ 'Evisix' Ⓝ, is a very free-flowering plant reaching only about 1 m (3¼ ft) in height. Its deep blue nodding flowers are produced for three months non-stop from early summer onwards, making it ideal for clothing the lower part of the support poles to a pergola. A near relative, C. 'Erio-stemon', which grows to about 2 m (6½ ft), would also be effective here. Both of these clematis need to be tied into their support or host as they are of a non-clinging nature.

LARGE TREES & CONIFERS

Large trees such as pines can be clothed in flowers each spring if a C. *montana* in white or pink is planted to grow up into their branches. A well-established C. *montana* var. *rubens* growing up into a large old Corsican pine with large limbs, for instance, makes a perfect combination.

PLATE IV

LATE LARGE-FLOWERED CULTIVARS
All flowers are shown at approximately ¾ size

C. 'Dorothy Walton'

C. 'Gipsy Queen'

C. 'Cardinal Wyszynski'

C. 'Victoria'

C. 'Jackmanii Superba'

C. 'Madame Edouard
André'

C. 'Pink Fantasy'

C. 'Ascotiensis'

C. 'Hagley Hybrid'

When an established plant is in full flower in late spring it really can look like a pink waterfall cascading down the branches of such a majestic tree. *C. montana* types are also ideal for growing into established conifers such as *Thuja*, giving interest each spring. However, the host tree needs to be of an open habit and at least 7.6–9 m (25–30 ft) in height. Smaller, more densely foliaged conifers would become overwhelmed and their foliage spoiled by the density of the clematis's growth.

Two of the less vigorous cultivars of *C. montana* are *C. m.* 'Tetrarose' and *C. m.* 'Freda'. The former has most attractive bronze-green leaves with serrated edges and its saucer-shaped deep mauve pink flowers are the largest of the *C. montana* group. It blends perfectly with golden-foliaged conifers. *C. montana* 'Freda' has the deepest coloured mauve/pink flowers of all the group. It is ideal for growing into small conifers of only 4.5–6 m

C. × fargesioides 'Summer Snow' (syn. *C. × f.* 'Paul Farges'), a vigorous climber with slightly scented flowers that was raised in the Crimea in 1964.

(15–20 ft) in height, and again will blend beautifully with the golden-foliaged forms.

Deciduous trees such as elm, beech and oak have such attractive skeletons in winter that they should not be used as a host for clematis. However, many of the fir trees, for example Douglas fir and Scottish pine, often have very bare trunks, especially when old, and this is not such a pleasing sight. The *C. montana* group can be used to disguise this, but other interesting clematis, such as *C. tangutica* and its forms and *C. tibetana* ssp. *vernayi* L&S 13342, will give added interest, flower form, colour and, of course, their delightful fluffy seed-heads which will stay on the plant right into the winter.

A fairly new plant to Western gardens is the Russian clematis *C. × fargesioides* 'Summer Snow' (syn. *C. × f.* 'Paul Farges'). This rampant clematis will easily reach 6 m (20 ft). It has attractive foliage and 2.5 cm (1 in) wide slightly scented creamy-white flowers which are borne from midsummer onwards, attracting bees which then produce rather good honey. Due to its vigour and habit, it too can be used to grow up into large trees.

SMALL TREES & LARGE SHRUBS

To achieve added interest later in the season, some of the C. *viticella* group can be used. They offer a good range of colours and look delightful flowering in moderate to small trees, such as *Prunus* (cherry), *Sorbus*, *Syringa* (lilac) and *Crataegus* (hawthorn). The delicate pink/mauve-veined flowers of C. *v.* 'Minuet' look absolutely charming as they tumble down from a lilac tree. C. *v.* 'Alba Luxurians' growing into a sorbus with grey foliage makes a delightful picture in mid-late summer, while the pink-flowered C. *v.* 'Södertälje' raised by Magnus Johnson in Sweden is particularly stunning grown into young pine trees.

Holly trees (*Ilex*) also make great hosts for clematis. The almond-scented starry white flowers of C. *flammula* are a great sight in late summer growing through *I. aquifolium*. Its close cousin, C. × *triternata* 'Rubromarginata', also with tiny scented flowers which have reddish pink margins to the tepals, can be planted to grow through silver- or golden-variegated hollies.

Some of the columnar trees, such as *Prunus* 'Amanogawa' or fastigiate oaks (*Quercus robur* f. *fastigiata*), make good host trees for clematis belonging to the C. 'Jackmanii' group. As these are group three pruning types they need hard pruning each spring, but some of their top growth can be removed in late autumn so that these trees with elegant winter shapes do not look cluttered and their form can be enjoyed. Clematis such as C. 'Comtesse de Bouchaud', C. 'Victoria' and C. 'John Huxtable' can be used to great effect, along with any of the C. *viticella* group.

Magnolias are marvellous small trees and their open framework of branches offer ideal sites for some of the mid-season large-flowered cultivars, such as C. 'Marie Boisselot', C. 'Henryi' (both white), C. 'General Sikorski' and C. 'Will Goodwin' (both blues). The magnolias are variable in habit and I prefer to use *Magnolia* × *soulangeana* and its cultivars as host trees for clematis.

Large evergreens such as rhododendrons can be used most successfully as hosts for clematis. Rhododendrons generally have a limited flowering period, mostly in the mid- and late spring, and need to be given added interest during the summer months and early autumn, so decorate them with the later flowering clematis that belong to group three (hard) pruning types to give an extra splash of summer colour. There is a wide choice even from within this group and it is important to be selective. Old

and straggly rhododendrons with bare lower limbs can be graced with any of the C. *viticella* group. Some of the glaucous-foliage rhododendrons will make ideal backgrounds for the white and pink/mauve C. *viticella* cultivars but darker-flowered cultivars, such as C. *viticella* 'Royal Velours' and C. *viticella* 'Polish Spirit', would be lost against the dark evergreen leaves of such a host.

Other small-flowered cultivars or somewhat distinct species, such as C. *aethusifolia* with its delicately cut foliage and charming tiny yellow bell-like flowers, look most attractive against the large leaves of rhododendrons. C. *campaniflora*, a close relative of C. *viticella* with small bluish-white flowers, and C. *flammula* would also be most attractive on such an evergreen, as would the compact C. *tangutica* 'Helios', which reaches only about 2 m (6½ ft) and bears open lantern-shaped yellow flowers.

The dark foliage of English yew trees (*Taxus baccata*) makes a splendid background for a range of white- or pale-flowered clematis. If the clematis are planted to grow into the outer branches, which on an old tree may be almost lying on the ground, a strong stake tied to the branches will give something for the clematis to anchor itself to, allowing it to get up into the tree. Only the hard-pruning type (group three) should be used so that the yew looks uncluttered during the winter months. Choose from the following clematis to achieve the best effect: C. *aethusifolia* (tiny yellow bell-shaped flowers), C. *campaniflora* (nodding white flowers), C. × *fargesioides* 'Summer Snow' (syn. C. *f.* 'Paul Farges') (clusters of white open flowers, suitable only on large, old trees), C. *flammula* (masses of tiny white star-shaped flowers), C. *florida* 'Plena' (unusual fully double creamy white flowers), C. 'Huldine' (8 cm/3¼ in wide saucer-shaped flowers), C. *rehderiana* (scented cowslip-shaped yellow flowers), C. *serratifolia* (nodding yellow lantern-shaped flowers), C. *tangutica* 'Bill Mackenzie' (yellow open bell-shaped flowers, only for large trees), C. *terniflora* (masses of white star-shaped flowers, for sunny areas only, as otherwise it is shy flowering) and C. *vitalba* (insignificant cream flowers but good for old unshapely trees where its much-prized fluffy seedheads will adorn the tree until mid-winter if left unpruned until late winter). If common ivy (*Hedera helix*) is covering the lower part of a large tree, its foliage can also be used as a host for any of the same clematis.

Large shrubs such as shrubby lilac trees (*Syringa*), *Deutzia*, *Philadelphus*, *Viburnum rhytidophyllum* and also

PLATE V

MID-SEASON
LARGE-FLOWERED CULTIVARS
All flowers are shown at approximately ¾ size

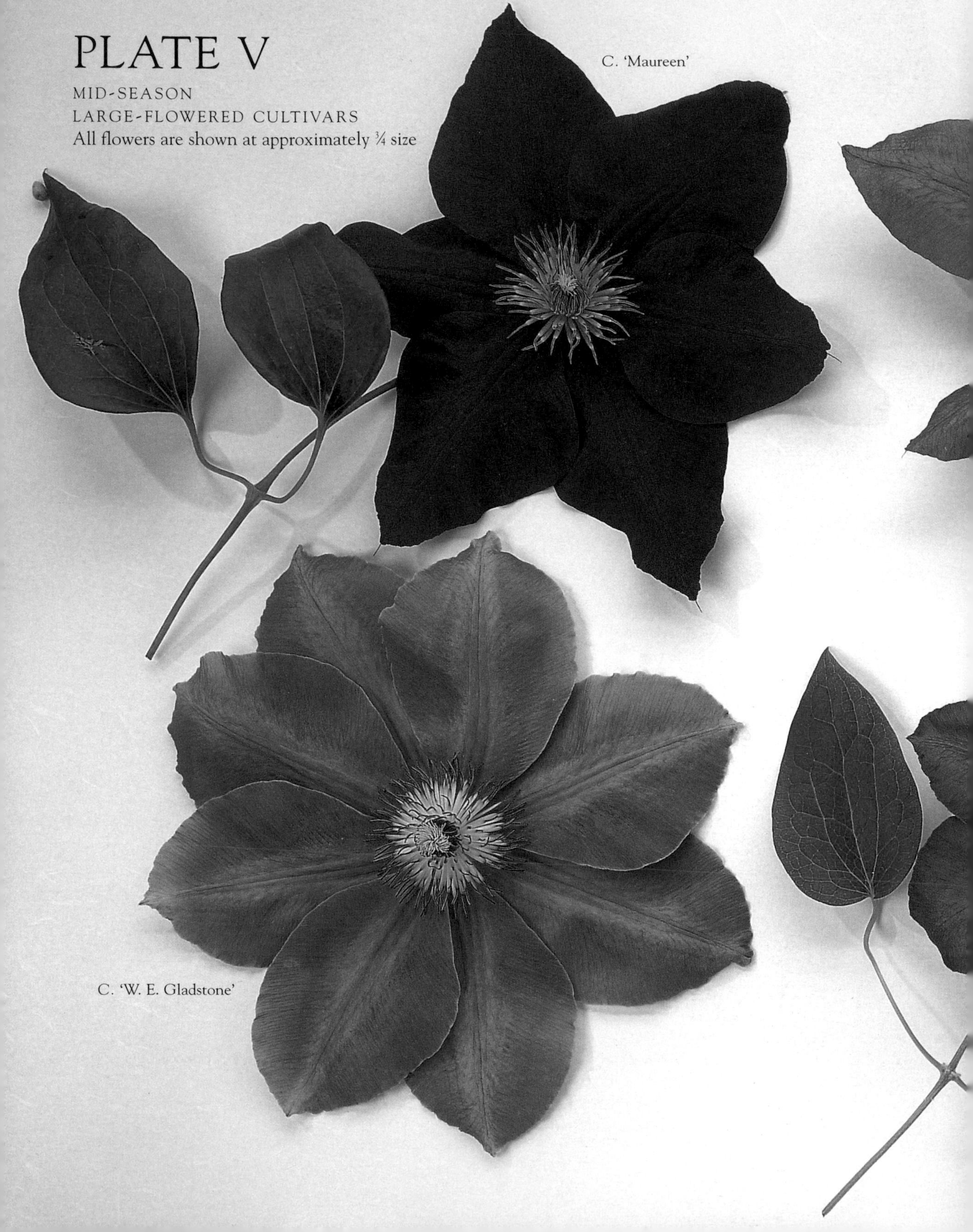

C. 'Maureen'

C. 'W. E. Gladstone'

C. 'Violet Charm'

C. 'Lawsoniana'

C. 'Henryi'

C. 'General Sikorski'

C. 'Henryi'

C. 'John Huxtable', a valuable large-flowered clematis similar in growth and habit to C. 'Jackmanii'.

the winter-flowering viburnums V. × bodnantense 'Dawn', V. × burkwoodii, V. × carlcephalum, V. farreri, V. juddii and V. tinus make useful hosts for the later-flowering clematis of pruning group three. The selection should generally be taken from the C. 'Jackmanii' group using C. 'Comtesse de Bouchaud', C. 'Victoria', C. 'Star of India' or C. 'John Huxtable', or from any of the C. viticella group. Free-standing Escallonia and Elaeagnus offer other good choices, again from the pruning group three clematis. These are only suggestions for initial inspiration; the possible combinations for clematis with trees or large to medium-sized shrubs are too many to list in total.

ROSES

Roses and clematis are natural companions, each complementing the other. The best roses to associate with clematis are probably the old shrub roses, wall-trained climbers or ramblers and roses growing on posts, archways, pergolas or freestanding poles. On the whole it is best to use those clematis that belong to pruning group three because most roses growing in those locations need to be pruned at some point during the year, mostly of course in the late autumn or early spring. If you plant a clematis from pruning group one or two, the problem

of retaining its old growth (to achieve the spring and early summer flowers) will be difficult and very time consuming at pruning time, when the rose may require drastic pruning – although growing a host rose covered in early clematis flowers before it comes into bloom would certainly be something worth achieving.

Generally I recommend the late-flowering less vigorous species and their small-flowered cultivars, the large-flowered cultivars belonging to the C. 'Jackmanii' group of early summer-flowering clematis and the C. viticella group which are selected for those of us with little time and short tempers who dislike getting cold fingers at pruning time. C. viticella 'Polish Spirit' would be too vigorous for some wall-trained roses as it reaches at least 4.5 m (15 ft) in height and is rather dense in habit, but it would look outstanding grown over the climber Rosa 'Kiftsgate' or the rambler R. 'Bobbie James'. Of the clematis belonging to pruning group two, the easiest for this purpose are those that repeat flower or produce their flowers in the later part of early summer. These can be pruned hard in spring in the same way as group three. The early flowers are lost but the main crop is produced on the new growth, generally in midsummer. I do feel that some of these should be used as they add a wide range of colours to the C. 'Jackmanii' clan and also different-shaped flowers, thus giving added interest and form to the planting association. Some of this group are: C. ANNA LOUISE™ 'Evithree' Ⓝ (violet with red/purple bar), C. 'Elsa Späth' (mid blue), C. 'Gillian Blades' (white with wavy edges to the tepals), C. 'Kathleen Wheeler' (plummy purple with golden anthers), C. 'Lady Northcliffe' (Wedgwood blue), C. LIBERATION™ 'Evifive' Ⓝ (pink with cerise bar), C. 'Masquerade' (mauvish blue), C. 'Mrs Cholmondeley' (light lavender blue), C. 'Moonlight' (creamy yellow), C. 'Niobe' (deep red), C. 'Snow Queen' (white with red anthers), C. SUGAR CANDY™ 'Evione' Ⓝ (pinkish mauve with darker bar), C. 'The President' (rich purple), C. VINO™ 'Poulvo' Ⓝ (petunia red), C. 'Warsaw Nike' (rich purple) and C. 'Will Goodwin' (pale blue).

Other clematis that can be used in addition to the above and treated as pruning group three are C. 'Belle Nantaise' (lavender blue), C. 'General Sikorski' (deep blue), C. 'Henryi' (white), C. 'Marie Boisselot' (white), C. 'Ramona' (pale blue) and C. 'Violet Charm' (pale violet blue).

Of the small-flowered species and their cultivars, particularly recommendable are C. aethusifolia, which has foliage that would bring charm to any rose, C. 'Arabella' (a non-clinging rosy purple), C. 'Durandii' (a non-clinging clematis with large flowers of deep indigo-blue), C. 'Eriostemon' (a non-clinging semi-nodding purple blue), C. *flammula* (scented starry white flowers) and C. PETIT FAUCON™ 'Evisix' Ⓝ (non-clinging bronze foliage and intense deep blue semi-nodding flowers), which would be outstanding to cover the base of a rose up to 1 m (3¼ ft). Some of the C. *texensis* group would bring a variation of flower shape, for example the nodding-flowered cultivars C. *texensis* 'Etoile Rose' (deep pink) and C. *t.* 'Pagoda' (pink mauve), while C. × *triternata* 'Rubromarginata' with red-purple tips to its tepals and scented flowers would give charm and make a great combination with a large wall-trained rose.

Of the C. 'Jackmanii' group, which associate particularly well with the old shrub roses, good choices are: C. 'Ascotiensis' (bright blue), C. 'Comtesse de Bouchaud' (bright mauve pink), C. 'Gipsy Queen' (velvety violet

C. 'Mrs Cholmondeley' is ideal for growing over large tripods and through wall-trained shrubs or climbing roses.

purple), C. 'Hagley Hybrid' (mauve) for north walls, C. 'Jackmanii' (dark velvet purple), C. 'Jackmanii Superba' (rich velvet purple), C. 'John Huxtable' (the only white), C. 'Madame Edouard André' (dusky red), C. 'Madame Grangé' (dusky velvet purple), C. 'Perle d'Azur' (outstanding sky blue), C. 'Pink Fantasy' (pale pink), C. 'Prince Charles' (mauve blue), C. 'Rhapsody' (sapphire blue), C. 'Star of India' (purple blue with carmine bar), C. 'Victoria' (rosy purple) and C. 'Voluceau' (petunia red).

GROUNDCOVER & LOW-GROWING SHRUBS

Deciduous and evergreen groundcover plants are widely used to deter weeds and give both summer and winter interest. To use clematis successfully with groundcover plants it is best to give the latter a year, or perhaps two years, to become established before the clematis is planted. If you are starting from scratch, leave space for the clematis when you are planting the groundcover plants; where there are established areas of groundcover you may need to remove odd plants if no space is available. The distance between clematis

plants intended to grow over large areas should be 1.2–1.5 m (4–5 ft). The planting site will need to be prepared as described on page 38. A range of host plants can be used, including *Hedera* (ivy); *Pachysandra*; *Potentilla*; *Vinca*; *Euphorbia*; *Erica*; *Cotoneaster congestus*, *C. conspicuus*, *C. horizontalis*, *C. microphyllus*, and *C. prostratus*; *Ceanothus dentatus*, *C. diversiflorus*, *C. impressus* and *C. prostratus*; *Cistus* × *corbariensis*; *Cytisus albus*, *C.* × *kewensis* and *C. purpureus*; and *Juniperus horizontalis* 'Douglasii', *J.* × *pfitzeriana* 'Wilhelm Pfitzer', *J. sabina* 'Tamariscifolia' and *J. squamata*.

I believe the best clematis to be used are the mid- to late spring-flowering species and their cultivars and the midsummer- and early autumn-flowering species and their cultivars. The large-flowered cultivars can be used but their flowers will be damaged by slugs and splashed by rain. Their place is higher up in taller-growing plants and shrubs rather than in groundcover plants.

If a dense mat of growth is required and it does not matter if some of the groundcover plants are slightly spoiled by the spread of the clematis, the *C. alpina* and *C. macropetala* types can be used. In the wild, these clematis either cling on to a host or scramble around at ground level, where they will make a mat or mound about 30–45 cm (12–18 in) high and spread out over an area 1 × 1.5 m (3¼ × 5ft) after 3–4 years, depending upon the host. These very hardy scramblers or climbers will tolerate wind-exposed sites and still flower well each spring, producing outstanding seedheads and occasional summer flowers. They come in a range of colours, from light blue and dark blue to purple, pink and white. A mixed planting of these with variegated ivy or variegated large-leaved *Vinca major* 'Variegata' would be something worth trying out. A selection of all flower colours planted together would make a superb patchwork of colour.

The *C. texensis* group, especially the miniature tulip-shaped cultivars, are a must for ground-level clematis plantings as their delightfully shaped flowers can then be viewed from above, which is the best way to appreciate their full beauty. There are three well known and widely grown cultivars from the late 1800s and early 1900s: *C. texensis* 'Duchess of Albany' (pink), *C. t.* 'Gravetye Beauty' (stunning cherry red) and *C. t.* 'Sir Trevor Lawrence' (with bright bluish-crimson tepals and a darker bar). The light colour of *C. t.* 'Duchess of Albany' makes it versatile: I have grown it through *Caryopteris* × *clandonensis* and the mixture of the pale blue flowers of

the host and the pink tulip-like flowers of the clematis is a mouth-watering combination. Growing it over an established specimen of the prostrate blue-flowered *Ceanothus prostratus* would also be very successful.

The two darker-coloured cultivars need careful planning to achieve the best results. For *C. texensis* 'Gravetye Beauty' the tiny foliage of *Cotoneaster microphyllus*, although rather dark, is ideal to give contrast in foliage and between the small white flowers of the cotoneaster and the cherry red flowers of the clematis. The best planting combination I've achieved to date with *Clematis texensis* 'Sir Trevor Lawrence' is growing it in association with the summer flowering heather *Erica vagans* 'Lyonesse', the white flowers of the heather contrasting outstandingly with the colour of the clematis. The same effect could be achieved by planting this cultivar with any of the white potentillas such as *Potentilla fruticosa* 'Abbotswood' and *P. f.* 'Manchu'. Other suitable members of the *Clematis texensis* group, such as *C. t.* 'Ladybird Johnson' (purple red with a crimson central bar) and *C. t.* 'The Princess of Wales' (pink with deep pink central bar), are also becoming available.

Pachysandra, *Cotoneaster*, *Cistus*, *Cytisus*, and *Juniperus* as listed above all lend themselves splendidly to adornment by the Viticella group, while some of the best combinations are with summer- and winter-flowering heathers. The clematis can be treated slightly differently with regard to pruning so that a host plant that has winter beauty in shape, form or flower can be free of its clematis for the winter period; once mid-autumn is approaching, remove the top growth of the *C. viticella* to within about 30 cm (12 in) of ground level. If the winter is mild, some new growth may appear which can be pruned back in late winter or early spring.

The species *C. viticella*, which is generally mauve-purple, can be grown in any location but its flower colour lends itself nicely to an association with the blue-grey foliage of *Juniperus horizontalis* 'Turquoise Spreader' or *J. sabina* 'Tamariscifolia'. *Clematis viticella* 'Abundance', with wine-coloured semi-nodding flowers, also blends with glaucous-foliage hosts, and purple-leaved plants. *C. v.* 'Alba Luxurians', with green-tipped white flowers, is attractive with the winter-flowering heathers, as is *C. v.* 'Blue Belle' (a deep violet blue). In a heather bed with specimen shrubs or conifers, the latter two clematis look well if a few stems are allowed to grow up into these focal plants, giving a carpeting effect of colour throughout.

C. v. 'Betty Corning' has very elegant nodding scented pinkish-blue flowers which really need to be above eye level, so this clematis too can be allowed to scramble up into a neighbouring shrub. C. v. 'Etoile Violette' is a must for growing with golden-foliage heather, especially the summer-flowering *Calluna vulgaris* 'Robert Chapman', C. v. 'Golden Feather' and C. v. 'Gold Haze', its violet-purple flowers contrasting brilliantly, while *Clematis viticella* 'Little Nell's creamy bluish-white flowers and the stunning red flowers of C. v. 'Madame Julia Correvon' are perfect for growing with grey-foliage heathers such as *Erica tetralix* 'Pink Star' and *E. t.* 'Con Underwood'. *Clematis viticella* 'Margot Koster' (pink), C. v. 'Minuet' (white with mauve veins) and C.v.'Royal Velours' (deep purple), are also ideal for planting with heather and other groundcover plants of similar height.

There are some C. *viticella* cultivars that are not suitable with groundcover and low-growing plants. C. v. 'Polish Spirit' is too vigorous and its foliage is too dense. The very old double forms C. v. 'Purpurea Plena' (syn. C. v. 'Mary Rose') and C. v. 'Purpurea Plena Elegans' are best planted with large shrubs or small trees. However, C. v. 'Venosa Violacea', one of my favourite clematis, with 7.5 cm (3 in) white flowers with purple veins, can be grown very successfully through summer-flowering heathers and also looks perfect with grey-foliage spreading junipers, such as *Juniperus sabina* 'Tamariscifolia', giving a great combination of foliage and flower colour.

If the host plants are already established, the clematis may be planted as closely as possible, wherever the planting site can be prepared. The clematis stems can be carefully trained and tied in the first instance to the host to avoid them being blown off their intended course. In large areas of groundcover, such as heathers, *Vinca* or *Pachysandra*, the stems of the C. *viticella* types will need to be pinned in place using a long bent wire. This training is generally required only in the spring and early summer months when the new growth is being produced. Once the clematis leaf stalks have started attaching themselves you will only need to guide the stems so that an even coverage and effect is achieved.

PERENNIAL & MIXED BORDERS

The range of combinations here is so vast that it is practicable only to give some general guidelines about this type of mixed planting with clematis and low-growing shrubs and perennial plants. There are two ways to approach this: either make a detailed planting scheme before any planting takes place or let the border establish itself and then note down some combination ideas during the period when the border is flowering or is of some other particular interest. My planting of borders is never done to a precise plan: I have thought of the main feature or structure plants but I never get down to a detailed drawing, so my preference is for the second option.

At the back of a mixed border, there is often a wall or a line of shrubs or conifers to give shelter and a backdrop for the plants in front of it. Formal hedges, such as yew hedges, should be left uncluttered by clematis, but if the hedge is informal and will require autumn trimming C. *viticella* types can be used as an added splash of colour and interest for the mid- to late summer months.

Sometimes small trees, such as the golden-foliaged *Catalpa bignonioides* 'Aurea', are used as a foil to the colourful perennials that flower throughout the summer and these call for a colourful clematis, C. v. 'Royal Velours' perhaps, which will blend with other reds or blues planted in the border. In an informal border such as this, there may well be a range of deciduous and evergreen shrubs, together with summer-flowering perennials towards the front of the border, and perhaps the odd conifer to give height and structure during the winter months. The choice of clematis in these instances is obviously dictated by the prevailing colour theme of the border and by the habit of the clematis.

A clematis can be planted to enliven the border at all times of year. Evergreen clematis species and their cultivars, such as C. *cirrhosa* and C. c. 'Freckles', can be grown on a wall (generally a sheltered south or south-west-facing one), either alone or with other wall-trained climbers, to give foliage over the winter months and early flowers. C. *alpina* and C. *macropetala* types will provide early flowers, some summer flowers and interesting seedheads on a wall or fence, their density of growth giving protection to the perennials planted in front.

The early large-flowered cultivars, single, double and semi-double, could be grown with other deciduous or evergreen climbers or wall-trained shrubs to give early summer colour, some repeat blooming to give late summer colour also. These clematis are not suitable for fences or informal hedges but could be grown with structural evergreens such as free-standing *Ceanothus* or *Viburnum tinus*. However, they are placed best through wall-trained subjects which give protection to their large flowers.

C. 'Jackmanii' is well-suited to clambering through dahlias and summer bedding plants of similar size.

Most large-flowered clematis belonging to pruning group three can be used to grow at about 60 cm (2 ft) above ground level. C. 'Jackmanii', with its deep purple flowers, looks outstanding when grown through some of the red-flowered dahlias such as *Dahlia* 'Bishop of Llandaff' or *D*. 'Bednall Beauty'. The same clematis and C. 'Jackmanii Superba' make a pleasing contrast when grown with the variegated fuchsia, *Fuchsia magellanica* var. *gracilis* 'Variegata'. C. 'Madame Edouard André', with its dusky red flowers, also makes a good contrast when grown through other red or orange perennials, such as *Potentilla* 'Gibson's Scarlet'. The grey foliage of *Phlomis fruticosa* and its yellow flowers give the much-needed light background for the deep-purple clematis such as C. 'Madame Grangé'. The bright blue flowers of C. 'Ascotiensis' mix well with pink-flowering plants, and would be outstanding with any cluster roses or through the young foliage of *Rosa glauca* (formerly *R. rubrifolia*).

The C. *viticella* group lend themselves perfectly to scrambling, climbing or trailing through such a mixed border. Because of its vigour, C. *v*. 'Polish Spirit' is the only member of the group that I would not use in a border except at the back with other climbers on a wall or fence. C. *v*. 'Purpurea Plena Elegans' growing through an *Amelanchier* at the back of the border or with perhaps old cordon or wall-trained apples or pears is a very successful combination, bringing colour before they fruit. The same clematis looks marvellous growing through the apple

green foliage on *Hebe rakaiensis* at the front of the border.

Borders such as these are the natural home for the perennial clematis, such as the white heavily scented C. *recta* and its purple-foliage form C. *r*. var. *purpurea*, which may vary in height from 1.2 to1.8 m (4 to 6 ft) depending upon the form offered for sale. The shorter plants can clamber around and form colourful white mounds, while the taller forms will need the support of pea-sticks or perennial supports.

C. *integrifolia* (blue), C. *i*. 'Rosea' (pink) and C. *i*. 'Alba' (white) are splendid in mixed borders. They grow to about 60–75 cm (2–2½ ft) and can be supported by small twigs or pea-sticks or just allowed to form informal mounds. Their flowers are nodding open bell-shaped and C. *integrifolia* 'Alba' can be scented, though this is variable. The C. *heracleifolia* group, which are basically sub-shrubs, have enormous, usually pale green, leaves which give added dimension and form, and produce delightful pale blue hyacinth-shaped flowers which are generally scented, especially with C. *heracleifolia* var. *davidiana*, which also has scented leaves in the late autumn and grows to about 75 cm (2½ ft).

The non-clinging groups of clematis that originated from C. *integrifolia* many years ago are quite at home in a mixed border. The best is C. PETIT FAUCON™ 'Evisix' Ⓝ which is a new plant with deep blue flowers introduced from my Guernsey nursery. Its greatest attribute is its habit of flowering even in hot summers for at least three months. As it reaches only 1 m (3¼ ft), it can be used with many plants in a border. Of taller habit are C. 'Arabella' (rosy purple), C. 'Blue Boy' (pale blue), C. 'Durandii' (deep indigo blue) and C. 'Eriostemon' (purple-blue). A few other interesting clematis for this type of planting include the American species C. *addisonii* (purple to red pitcher-shaped flowers), C. × *aromatica* (highly scented purple flowers that look great with grey foliage plants), and C. × *jouiniana* 'Praecox' (bluish-white cluster flowers). The latter can be used to grow up a wall by itself or allowed to scramble at ground level, though as it is a bit invasive it will need to be kept within bounds. Other alternatives are C. *pitcheri*, whose purple pitcher-shaped flowers are charming but need a light background to be shown to the best effect, C. *songarica*, with starry white flowers and grey foliage, the C. *texensis* group and C. *viorna*, a North American species with pitcher-shaped flowers that vary from violet to bicoloured creamy and pinkish mauve.

CONTAINERS

For best effect choose the compact free-flowering early species such as C. *alpina*, C. *macropetala* and their cultivars, or the compact early large-flowered single, double and semi-double clematis. Most of the mid-season large-flowered types are too vigorous and do not produce enough flowers at one time, while the later flowering C. 'Jackmanii' types are generally too leggy, not producing enough flowers lower down the plant. The versatile C. *viticella* varieties for once are not ideal, as they too are vigorous and leggy. However, there are a few exceptions, these being: C. *v.* 'Betty Corning' (pinkish mauve), C. *v.* 'Madame Julia Correvon' (rich red), C. *v.* 'Royal Velours' (deep purple) and C. *v.* 'Venosa Violacea' (white with purple veins). Some of the later flowering species or cultivars can also be used, such as C. *florida* 'Sieboldii' and C. *f.* 'Plena' (both creamy white).

All the C. *alpina* and C. *macropetala* cultivars can be used successfully, either keeping to a single cultivar per container or perhaps a mixture of cultivars. A mix of pink, blue and white is charming, and combining several cultivars together does give a longer flowering period. A combination of C. *alpina* 'Pink Flamingo' (pink), which has probably the longest flowering period, with C. *a.* 'Frankie' (pale blue) and the white C. *macropetala* 'White Wings' is probably the best blend of colours that can be achieved. Plant them with any shallow-rooted small shrub such as heather, with perennials such as *Ajuga* or with summer or winter-flowering bedding plants, for example *Lobelia*.

CLEMATIS FOR CONTAINERS		
EARLY-FLOWERING SPECIES & THEIR CULTIVARS C. *alpina* cultivars C. *macropetala* cultivars **EARLY LARGE-FLOWERED CULTIVARS** ANNA LOUISE™ 'Evithree' Ⓝ 'Asao' 'Bees' Jubilee' 'Burma Star' 'Carnaby' 'Charissima' 'Dawn' 'Dr Ruppel' 'Edith' 'Edouard Desfossé' 'Elsa Späth' 'Etoile de Paris' 'Fireworks' 'Fujimusume' 'Gillian Blades' 'Guernsey Cream' 'Haku Ookan' 'Ken Donson' 'H. F. Young' 'King Edward VII' 'Lady Northcliffe'	'Lasurstern' 'Masquerade' 'Miss Bateman' 'Mrs N. Thompson' 'Nelly Moser' 'Niobe' 'Pink Champagne' 'Richard Pennell' ROYAL VELVET™ 'Evifour' Ⓝ 'Ruby Glow' 'Scartho Gem' 'Silver Moon' 'Snow Queen' SUGAR CANDY™ 'Evione' Ⓝ 'Sunset' 'The President' VINO™ 'Poulvo' Ⓝ 'Warsaw Nike' **DOUBLE & SEMI-DOUBLE LARGE-FLOWERED CULTIVARS** 'Arctic Queen' 'Daniel Deronda' 'Kiri Te Kanawa' 'Louise Rowe' 'Mrs George Jackman' 'Multi Blue' 'Royalty'	'Vyvyan Pennell' 'Walter Pennell' **MID-SEASON LARGE-FLOWERED CULTIVARS** 'General Sikorski' 'Henryi' 'Marie Boisselot' 'Ramona' 'Violet Charm' **VITICELLA TYPES & THEIR CULTIVARS** C. *viticella* 'Betty Corning' C. *v.* 'Madame Julia Correvon' C. *v.* 'Royal Velours' C. *v.* 'Venosa Violacea' **LATE-FLOWERING SPECIES & THEIR CULTIVARS** C. × *aromatica* 'Durandii' 'Eriostemon' C. *florida* PISTACHIO™ 'Evirida' Ⓝ C. *f.* 'Plena' C. *f.* 'Sieboldii' PETIT FAUCON™ 'Evisix' Ⓝ C. *viorna*

6

CONSERVATORY & CUT-FLOWER CLEMATIS

I n the garden many clematis, particularly the large-flowered cultivars, contribute an exotic presence with their showy flowers. Indoors, away from the competition of other garden vegetation, their appeal is accentuated and the scented species can be appreciated to the full.

CLEMATIS FOR THE CONSERVATORY

In large conservatories, some of the vigorous clematis, such as C. *armandii* with its huge pointed evergreen leaves, will give foliage interest year round, but this plant will need a space of about 4.5 × 3 m (15 × 10 ft) to be able to develop fully. Its scented early spring flowers are marvellous. C. *cirrhosa* and its forms, especially C. *c.* 'Freckles', would not require as much space: 2.4 × 1.5 m (8 × 5ft) would, with training, be enough for it to develop fully. C. *c.* 'Freckles' has delightful highly coloured bell-shaped flowers during mid- to late autumn under glass protection.

It is to the New Zealand species and their more recent cultivars that we should turn for added interest in early spring and for plants that are not quite so vigorous. C. *afoliata* has no true foliage other than rush-like stems with only the very occasional tiny leaf to be found. Its 2 cm (¾ in) long cream-coloured flowers are slightly scented. C. *australis* and C. *forsteri* both have creamy/green scented flowers, those of C. *forsteri* being the stronger scented, of lemon verbena. Both are early spring-flowering and have evergreen foliage, that of C. *forsteri* being very pale green while C. *australis* is some-what darker. C. *paniculata* has the largest flowers of all the New Zealand species and with selected forms, like

C. *paniculata* 'Bodnant', an evergreen that needs a sheltered, sunny place in a mild region (shown at twice normal size).

those of C. *p.* 'Bodnant', the flowers reach 5 cm (2 in) in diameter. They are pure white with pink stamens that contrast well with the dark green leaves. This plant is also early spring-flowering and can be kept within a similar space to that of C. *cirrhosa* 'Freckles'.

However, the clematis that is a must for colour and performance in early spring is C. × *cartmanii* 'Joe'. It will flower for a month, producing an abundance of 5 cm (2 in) wide white flowers that show up very well against its dark green, coarse, fern-like foliage. It is non-clinging and reaches about 1–2 m (3¼– 6½ ft) in height if allowed to grow freely, but can be contained down to 1 m (3¼ ft). For added interest, C. *gentianoides* from Tasmania can be used indoors. It is a distinctive and unusual clematis, growing to only 45–50 cm (18–20 in) with coarse narrow leaves and strongly scented white flowers.

The New Zealand evergreen clematis which are not entirely winter hardy in all locations and are, in fact, impossible to grow in areas below zones 7, 8 and 9, can be used to advantage under cover of glass conservatories or similar buildings. The C. *alpina* and C. *macropetala* types can be grown in a larger conservatory but their flowering period is too limited to use them widely.

The late spring and early summer large-flowered clematis, which include the single, semi-double and double large-flowered clematis listed for growing in containers on page 73, can be used most successfully in containers or grown in the soil in a conservatory. As they flower at slightly different times, you can choose cultivars to give you flowers over a long period of time. If the plant and the container in which it is growing are not too large, the plants can be grown outside and brought inside at the point of flowering, to be returned when they have finished.

One of the most rewarding of all clematis to grow in a conservatory is the C. *florida* group: C. *f.* 'Plena', C. *f.* 'Sieboldii' and the new cultivar C. *f.* PISTACHIO™ 'Evirida' Ⓝ. They are all very free-flowering and in my nursery in Guernsey we can flower them for 12 months with a little heat under glass. All of these clematis will grow well outside but they perform much better under glasshouse or conservatory conditions. They too can be grown in the soil or in containers. C. *f.* 'Plena' is a great favourite of mine, with its creamy-white double flowers that become greenish-white during the months with low light levels. C. *f.* 'Sieboldii' has a central boss of purple staminodes which give a dramatic contrast to the creamy-white tepals, which also become greener in the winter months. C. *f.* PISTACHIO™ 'Evirida' Ⓝ produces an outstanding crop of flowers with tepals the same colouring as C. *f.* 'Sieboldii' and a most unusual centre, with light pinkish-brown stamens and then a central green open tuft of aborted stigmas. These three forms of C. *florida* and C. × *cartmanii* 'Joe' would be my first choice for conservatory clematis, followed by a selection of the early large-flowered cultivars.

CLEMATIS AS CUT FLOWERS

Clematis have three attractions for flower arrangers: their foliage is extremely variable and most interesting; the flowers, also variable, lend themselves charmingly to mixed arrangements or to those composed purely from clematis flowers; and thirdly, the attractive seedheads produced by most clematis are a beautiful addition to fresh flower arrangements or to dried decorations. I have also used clematis flowers in bouquets and made a wedding bouquet for my daughter, Anna Louise, with flowers of C. ANNA LOUISE™ 'Evithree' Ⓝ, which was named after her, together with flowers of C. 'Edith', named after her grandmother. They lasted throughout the wedding day and looked charming with cream roses and cream freesias.

The evergreen species and their cultivars lend themselves naturally to arrangements in which long trails of foliage hang down from pedestals or similar large arrangements. The most interesting foliage can be cut from C. *armandii*, C. *australis*, C. × *cartmanii* 'Joe', C. *cirrhosa* (particularly C. *c.* var. *balearica*), C. *finetiana*, C. *forsteri*, C. *paniculata* and C. *uncinata*. The foliage of the large-flowered cultivars can be used as long as the base of the cut portion of the stem has become woody and the growing tip is

not too soft. Strands of the purple foliage of the pink-flowered C. *montana* cultivars can be arranged successfully as long as they too have become woody at their base. A wide selection of the later flowering small-flowered species and their cultivars may be used, again as long as the stems have a woody base. Some clematis with distinctly different foliage such as C. *aesthusifolia*, C. 'Blue Boy', C. 'Durandii', C. 'Eriostemon' and the outstandingly large leaves of the C. *heracleifolia* group would give extra interest, as would those of C. × *jouiniana* 'Praecox'.

I like to use a range of the small-flowered cultivars with seedheads in an informal 'cottage-style' arrangement. For large formal arrangements I combine the foliage of other plants, such as hostas, with single or double large-flowered clematis, sometimes again with their seedheads.

Clematis flowers can last up to 10 days in a cool room and even when I have used them as cut flowers in arrangements at the Chelsea Flower Show in the heat of the

C. × *cartmanii* 'Joe' is a useful evergreen clematis for the conservatory or a sheltered garden.

Great Marquee they have survived 5–6 days. For maximum longevity, it is important to condition them properly. First select a young flower whose tepals are just starting to open or are certainly no more than three-quarters of the way open – in other words, the tepals have opened enough for the stamens to be seen. At this point, they will still be held close to the style. The length of stem to be cut depends upon the natural habitat of the clematis and the group to which it belongs: with the evergreen and early to mid-spring flowering species and their cultivars only the flower stalk should be cut as it would be impossible to remove a length of stem successfully from the main plant, while in the case of the large-flowered cultivars, the cut stem could be 15–60 cm (6–24 in) depending upon the length of stem available and what is required. As soon as you have cut the flower from the plant, remove the leaves totally to reduce the amount of transpiration and put the cut stem immediately into a bucket of water while you cut the other flowers for your arrangement. When you have finished, recut the stems and place the bottom 2.5 cm (1 in) into boiling water for 15 seconds before placing them in a deep bucket of cold water. Leave the cut flowers in the water in a cool place overnight so that plenty of water is taken up by the stems. Next day, the conditioned cut flowers can be used in the arrangement and the stems recut to the required length.

SEEDHEADS

These may be used green or partially or fully dried and conditioned with glycerine for winter dried flower decorations. The early-flowering C. *alpina* and C. *macropetala* types produce numerous very attractive fluffy seedheads, while those of the early large-flowered cultivars, including the double-flowered clematis, are larger and the mid-season large-flowered clematis larger still. The later-flowering species produce interesting seedheads that are variable in size and form, some of the most noteworthy being C. *flammula* (small silvery seedheads); C. *fusca* var. *violacea* (outstanding large spiked seedheads); C. PETIT FAUCON™ 'Evisix'Ⓝ (neat round seedheads); C. *potaninii* var. *fargesii* (small silvery seedheads); C. *recta* and C. *r.* var. *purpurea* (abundant clusters of spiky seedheads); C. *serratifolia* (neat round seedheads); C. *tangutica* and its cultivars (masses of fluffy seedheads); C. *terniflora* (in hot climates producing masses of seedheads some of which have a purple colour); C. *tibetana* and its botanical variants and cultivars, similar to C. *tangutica*;

The attractive seedheads of C. 'Daniel Deronda' have an unusual top-knot effect.

and C. *vitalba* and its American cousins, C. *virginiana* and C. *ligusticifolia*, all with clusters of many small seedheads.

DRYING SEEDHEADS

The best clematis seedheads for drying are those that by late summer are at the silky stage but have not gone fluffy. Prepare a mixture of one-third glycerine and two-thirds boiling water, stir it well, and pour it into a jam jar or similar container to a depth of about 5 cm (2 in). Cut the stems and immediately put the bases into the mixture while it is still very hot. Do not pack them tightly. Place the container in a cool dry place out of bright light. The stalks and leaves will turn rich brown (you can remove the leaves if you prefer), while the seedheads become a slightly lighter colour and retain their silky texture. Check the level of the mixture in the container on a regular basis; it may require topping up with warm solution to keep the depth at about 5 cm (2 in). The correct time to remove the stems from the mixture is when the colour is even, which should take 2–3 weeks, though you should keep a check on them. If the leaves are left on the stems, they become slightly oily to the touch. The dried stems, leaves and seedheads should not be put into water or a damp atmosphere.

Long stems with trails of seedheads of the C. *vitalba* group or the Meclatis Section can be treated most successfully in this way. However, they must be cut and treated before they reach the fluffy stage.

7

CLEMATIS IN NORTH AMERICA

Until recently, there has been only a rather limited range of clematis species and cultivars available for most gardens in the USA and Canada. Many hobby gardeners or collectors of this fine genus have obtained the more unusual species or cultivars from overseas, from some forward-thinking mail-order companies or, of course, by swapping plants with other keen growers of clematis. The Steffen Clematis Nursery of Rochester, New York State, has been responsible for introducing many newer clematis from Europe, thus widening the range available to wholesale growers and retailers.

Many nurserymen and retailers have been under the false impression that it is possible to grow only the tried and tested old cultivars, such as C. 'Jackmanii', C. 'Nelly Moser', C. 'Henryi', C. 'Ville de Lyon' and C. 'Comtesse de Bouchaud', due to the fact that these were always readily available from sources in Holland and that they were known to be grown successfully in most areas of the USA and Canada. In fact the range of clematis that can be grown is by no means limited to these old cultivars, though much depends on location. The USDA zones given in the A–Z of Species & Cultivars are a guide as to which clematis can be grown where.

It is unfortunate that more has not been made of the USA and Canadian species in breeding and development programmes in the past, Dr Frank Skinner in the mid- to late 1940s really being the only successful breeder. J. E. Spingarn, writing a chapter in Ernest Markham's book Clematis, published in 1935, remarked that the USA and Canadian species had met with more interest and appreciation in Europe than at home, pointing out that C. texensis, a native of Texas, had been proved surprisingly winter-hardy in New York, New England and Ottawa; from what I have experienced myself when visiting gardens in North America I can only agree with his remarks. However, it has to be said that some of the North American species are more suitable for a woodland garden than for the typical modern small garden.

THE NORTH AMERICAN SPECIES

There are three basic groups of North American species and these are spring or mid to late summer flowering. The spring-flowering species are closely related to C. alpina from Central Europe belonging to the Atragene Section, flowering from the previous season's stems in mid to late spring and also producing occasional summer flowers. They are noted for their attractive silky seedheads. The most gardenworthy ones are C. occidentalis var. occidentalis, C. o. var. dissecta, C. o. var. grosseserrata and C. columbiana var. tenuiloba.

The mid to late summer-flowering species belong to two different sections: C. viorna (the American pitcher-shaped species) and those related to the European species C. vitalba. Both sections flower on current season's stems. The Viorna Section has very good gardenworthy clematis, the best and most readily available being C. addisonii, C. crispa, C. hirsutissima var. scottii (syn. C. douglasii var. scottii), C. hirsutissima var. scottii 'Rosea' (syn C. douglasii var. scottii 'Rosea'), C. pitcheri, C. texensis and C. viorna. All bear their pitcher-shaped flowers freely, usually until early autumn, and also have attractive seedheads.

C. 'Fireworks' has extremely large flowers that need a light background to be shown to best effect.

The species similar to C. *vitalba*, C. *ligusticifolia*, C. *pauciflora* and C. *virginiana* of Section Clematis, are less gardenworthy, being rather invasive if allowed to get out of hand. Their flowers, borne in late summer to early autumn, are small and lack interest, but their seedheads are most attractive, lasting well into winter in the garden. They can also be used for decoration in the house.

EVERGREEN SPECIES

Generally the evergreens are of little use in the northern states of the USA and Canada, except in the milder areas, the USDA zones giving the general guidelines. C. *armandii*, its clones and cultivars (Zones 7–9) and C. *cirrhosa* and its botanical variants and cultivars (Zones 6–9) are really the only types to be considered. C. *cirrhosa* 'Freckles' is the most winter hardy and worth trying out. Certainly C. *armandii* is grown successfully in the warmer southern areas of British Columbia and in Washington and Oregon, as well as further south in California and South Carolina. C. *cirrhosa* is also possible in these areas, C. c. 'Freckles' enjoying the Mediterranean climate of California. For the best results, both these clematis should be planted against south- or southwest-facing locations in full sun where their stems can be ripened to produce more winter-hardy stems for overwintering and to provide masses of spring flowers, except for C. c. 'Freckles', which flowers in the autumn.

The other clematis belonging to the evergreen group are suitable only for the particular zones specified or for growing under the protection of conservatories, garden rooms or glasshouses with some background heating to give frost protection. The following are the most worthy contenders for growing under protection: C. × cartmanii 'Joe', C. *forsteri* (for its outstanding scent), C. *gentianoides* (also for its scent), C. *marmoraria* for container culture in the alpine house, C. *paniculata* (male forms) and C. *uncinata*. For outdoor planting, try C. *armandii*, C. *armandii* 'Apple Blossom' and C. *cirrhosa* 'Freckles'.

EARLY-FLOWERING SPECIES & THEIR CULTIVARS

The C. *alpina* and C. *macropetala* species and cultivars are some of the most reliably winter-hardy clematis for all areas. They are ideal for cold exposed sites, and can be expected to perform well with a generous annual crop of flowers in any location in any state.

C. *macropetala* 'White Wings', one of the best white cultivars in the Atragene Section, has attractive silky seedheads.

The following cultivars of C. *alpina* and C. *macropetala* are some of the most free-flowering and are recommended for North American gardens:

C. *alpina* 'Blue Dancer' (blue, single)
C. *a.* 'Constance' (purple-pink, semi-double)
C. *a.* 'Frankie' (blue, pretty inner skirt, single)
C. *a.* 'Helsingborg' (blue-purple, single)
C. *a.* 'Pink Flamingo' (pink, semi-double)
C. *a.* 'White Columbine' (white, single)
C. *a.* 'Willy' (pink, single)

C. *macropetala* (blue, double)
C. *m.* 'Ballet Skirt' (pink, double)
C. *m.* 'Pauline' (blue, fully double)
C. *m.* 'Lagoon' (deep blue, double)
C. *m.* 'Markham's Pink' (pink, double)
C. *m.* 'White Wings' (white, double).

The C. *montana* group has not established itself in large numbers in North America, but in theory these plants should grow successfully within the zones recommended. They can be grown on large wall areas, up into trees, on fences, on low walls and in any positions recommended for growing these vigorous climbers in Europe. I have not seen large established plants in full flower in North America, as one can see in great abundance in central England during late spring every year, but I feel sure this group is worth growing. The following cultivars are recommended for North America:

C. *m.* 'Elizabeth' (pink)
C. *m.* 'Freda' (deep pink)
C. *m.* f. *grandiflora* (white)
C. *m.* 'Mayleen' (pink)
C. *m.* 'Pink Perfection' (pink)
C. *m.* 'Tetrarose' (deep pink)
C. *m.* 'Vera' (pink)

THE EARLY, DOUBLE & SEMI-DOUBLE & MID-SEASON LARGE-FLOWERED CLEMATIS

The early, double and semi-double and mid-season large-flowered cultivars can all flower from the ripened leaf axil buds from the previous season and are winter hardy to zones 4–9. The number of flowers produced from the ripened previous season's stems naturally depends upon the severity of the winter and whether the top growth has been killed to ground level or not. Gardeners in severe or very severe winter areas have little hope of retaining the previous season's stems other than in an exceptionally mild winter and they must be prepared to settle for flowers on the current season's stems in mid to late summer. These flowers will be smaller than those produced from the previous season's ripened stems, but they will be produced in profusion. Gardeners in somewhat less severe winter areas will have the chance from time to time of obtaining some early large flowers, even when the stems are not protected. However, some protection can be given by lowering the old stems to ground level and covering them with straw or similar material before snow falls. This will help with protection and with added snow cover there will be a good chance of some old stems coming through the winter. Care must obviously be taken not to break the stems when lowering them and when returning them to their support. This does take time and dedication but the end results are truly worthwhile.

If you do not have time for this, there are several other options open. One is to leave the plants totally untouched and take a chance on a mild winter and snow cover to protect at least the bottom part of the plant; some old stems may survive, especially at the base. The second is to take the same action (or lack of it) but give some protection to the plant by leaning strong bamboo or hazel poles or similar against the wall where the clematis is growing. Push them into the soil about 30–45 cm (12–18 in) apart and about 60 cm (2 ft) away from the base of the wall and secure them at the top by tying them to nails or other fixings. Tie chicken wire to them to make a half wigwam structure, then thread evergreen material such as yew or other small conifer branches through the wire to give protection from severe winds. For extra protection, a layer of horticultural fleece can be secured to the poles before the chicken wire is laid over them. I have used this method in England to protect Californian plants and it has been most successful. The wigwam can be removed as soon as the worst of the winter weather is over and before new growth appears from the clematis leaf axil buds.

A third option is to treat these large-flowered clematis as if they belonged to pruning group three rather than pruning group two and prune back their top growth from late winter to early spring before bud break. This will not harm the plant but it may delay the flowering period by 4–6 weeks, depending upon the flowering habit of the clematis. Many North American gardeners tell me that they do not wait until winter to do their pruning of the group three clematis – they prune back all top growth to 30 cm (12 in) or lower in the late autumn.

If clematis are to be grown in containers for the patio or deck garden in cold climates they will need to be taken into a shed, garage or glasshouse where they can receive some protection from frost and damaging cold winds. They must not be allowed to become over-dry in their containers, and occasional watering will be

PLATE VI
DOUBLE AND SEMI-DOUBLE LARGE-FLOWERED CULTIVARS
IN SECOND FLOWERING
All flowers are shown at approximately ½ size

C. 'Daniel Deronda'

C. 'Beauty of Worcester'

C. 'Multi Blue'

C. 'Kiri Te Kanawa'

C. 'Jackmanii Rubra'

C. ARCTIC QUEEN™
'Evitwo' Ⓝ

C. 'Proteus'

C. 'Mrs George Jackman'

required. Once the worst of the winter has passed and before full bud break, the containers should be returned to their summer flowering positions. It is important to remember that the containers should be placed on bricks or other supports to raise them off the flat surface area to help with drainage.

In milder areas where the temperature will not drop below −8°C (18°F), horticultural fleece can be placed around the support on which the clematis is growing to protect the old wood and the important leaf axil buds. In areas where there is little chance of a cold winter with prolonged spells of cold frozen weather, the clematis may be left in their summer flowering positions. Again, remember that good drainage is very important as clematis hate to have cold wet root systems over winter.

The list of best clematis for growing in North America from this section is vast, but I would suggest the following as being the first ones to try.

EARLY LARGE-FLOWERED CULTIVARS

C. ANNA LOUISE™ 'Evithree'   (violet tepals with a red-purple bar) *
C. 'Bees' Jubilee' (mauve pink with a deeper bar) *
C. 'Carnaby' (deep pink with a darker bar) *
C. 'Dawn' (pearly with a pink bar) *
C. 'Dr Ruppel' (deep rose pink with a deeper bar) *
C. 'Elsa Späth' (mid-blue) *
C. 'Fireworks' (blue-mauve with a deep petunia-red bar) *
C. 'Gillian Blades' (white) *
C. 'H. F. Young' (wedgwood blue) *
C. 'Ken Donson' (deep blue) *
C. 'Lasurstern' (deep lavender blue) *
C. LIBERATION™ 'Evifive'   (deep pink with a deep cerise bar)
C. 'Masquerade' (mauvish-blue with a mauve bar) *
C. 'Miss Bateman' (white) *
C. 'Mrs Cholmondeley' (light lavender blue) *
C. 'Nelly Moser' (pale mauve with a deeper lilac bar) *
C. 'Niobe' (deep red) *
C. 'Pink Champagne' (purple-pink, darker margins) *
C. ROYAL VELVET™ 'Evifour'   (rich velvet purple) *
C. 'Ruby Glow' (ruby rosy mauve) *
C. 'Scartho Gem' (bright pink with a darker bar) *

C. 'Snow Queen' (white, tinged with pale bluish-pink) *
C. SUGAR CANDY™ 'Evione'   (pinkish-mauve with a darker bar)
C. 'Sunset' (deep plummy red) *
C. 'The President' (rich purple) *
C. VINO™ 'Poulvo'   (petunia red)
C. 'Warsaw Nike' (rich velvety red-purple) *
C. 'Will Goodwin' (mid-blue)

DOUBLE & SEMI-DOUBLE LARGE-FLOWERED CULTIVARS

C. ARCTIC QUEEN™ 'Evitwo'   (double white) * ❑
C. 'Belle of Woking' (double silvery-mauve) ❑
C. 'Daniel Deronda' (semi-double and single, deep purple blue) *
C. 'Duchess of Edinburgh' (double white) ❑
C. 'Louise Rowe' (double, semi-double and single, pale mauve to whitish mauve) *
C. 'Mrs George Jackman' (semi-double and single, creamy white) *
C. 'Multi Blue' (semi-double, reddish-purple-blue) * ❑
C. 'Royalty' (semi-double and single, rich purple-mauve) *
C. 'Vyvyan Pennell' (double and single, rosy-lavender to lilac)
C. 'Walter Pennell' (semi-double and single, mauve pink with a darker bar)

MID-SEASON LARGE-FLOWERED CULTIVARS

C. 'General Sikorski' (mid-mauve to deep blue) *
C. 'Henryi' (white) *
C. 'Marie Boisselot' (white)
C. 'Peveril Pearl' (pale lavender)
C. 'Ramona' (pale blue) *
C. 'Violet Charm' (pale violet blue) *
C. 'W. E. Gladstone' (pale blue)

* the best for container culture.
❑ produces double flowers on new growth.

LATE LARGE-FLOWERED CULTIVARS

This group is very versatile and can be used in every state. Their culture is very easy; they require either late

C. 'Bees' Jubilee', a suitable plant for container cultivation, best grown out of direct sun to avoid the flowers fading.

winter or early spring hard pruning (group three) or, as preferred by some North American gardeners, they can be pruned back hard during late autumn before the onset of winter. They are ideal for growing through a whole range of small trees, shrubs (wall-trained or free-standing), climber roses of all types, and perennial plants almost at ground level. Some are also suitable for container culture. They are extremely winter hardy to zones 3–9.

The following can be considered some of the best for North American gardens, from an extensive list now becoming available.

C. 'Ascotiensis' (bright blue) *
C. 'Comtesse de Bouchaud' (bright mauve-pink)
C. 'Dorothy Walton' (mauve-pink tinged mauve-blue) *
C. 'Ernest Markham' (magenta)

C. 'Gipsy Queen' (deep velvety violet-purple)
C. 'Hagley Hybrid' (rosy-mauve to shell pink) *
C. 'Jackmanii' (dark velvet purple)
C. 'Jackmanii Superba' (rich deep purple)
C. 'John Huxtable' (white)
C. 'Jan Pawel II' (pale pinkish white)
C. 'Madame Edouard André' (dusky red) *
C. 'Madame Grangé' (dusky velvet purple)
C. 'Perle d'Azur' (light blue)
C. 'Perrin's Pride' (bronze-purple) *
C. 'Pink Fantasy' (pink with peachy-pink highlights) *
C. 'Prince Charles' (mauve-blue to greenish-blue) *
C. 'Rhapsody' (sapphire blue) *
C. 'Rouge Cardinal' (velvety crimson) *
C. 'Star of India' (deep purple-blue with a crimson bar)
C. 'Victoria' (deep rosy mauve)
C. 'Voluceau' (petunia red)

* The best for container culture.

PLATE VII

LATE LARGE-FLOWERED
CULTIVARS
All flowers are
shown at
approximately
¾ size

C. 'Rouge Cardinal'

C. 'Star of India'

C. 'Ville de Lyon'

C. 'Rhapsody'

C. 'Comtesse de
Bouchaud'

C. 'Perrin's Pride'

C. 'Perle d'Azur'

C. 'Pink Fantasy'

C. 'John Huxtable'

C. 'Voluceau'

THE *CLEMATIS VITICELLA* GROUP

This is an extremely valuable group of plants for North American gardens and their use is almost endless. They can be grown with groundcover plants to give summer colour, with all types of smaller trees and large shrubs and with wall-trained shrubs and climbers. Some are also suitable for container culture. They bring additional summer colour when the early large-flowered cultivars may be resting or have finished flowering and are easy clematis requiring hard pruning (group three) either in the late autumn or in the late winter/early spring when all growth can be removed to just above the base of the previous season's stems. Any viticella types growing over groundcover evergreen plants should be pruned back in the autumn to allow their hosts to look uncluttered during the winter months. They are winter hardy to zones 3–9.

They really are all worth listing, but some of the best are as follows.

C. *viticella* 'Abundance' (single, wine-rose)

C. *v.* 'Alba Luxurians' (single, white with green tips)

C. *v.* 'Betty Corning' (single, pale pinkish-blue) *

C. *v.* 'Blue Belle' (single, deep violet-purple)

C. *v.* 'Etoile Violette' (single, violet-purple)

C. *v.* 'Madame Julia Correvon' (single, vibrant rich red) *

C. *viticella* is a European species that has given rise to a range of larger-flowered cultivars.

C. *v.* 'Polish Spirit' (single, intense purple-blue)

C. *v.* 'Purpurea Plena Elegans' (double, dusky violet-purple)

C. *v.* 'Royal Velours' (single, deep velvety purple)

C. *v.* 'Venosa Violacea' (single, white with a network of purple veins *

* The best for container culture.

THE LATE-FLOWERING SPECIES & THEIR SMALL-FLOWERED CULTIVARS

The plants in this section are very diverse in their habit, leaf and flower forms, height of growth attained annually and their uses as garden plants. Below is a summary of some of the clematis from this section that are available in North America and worthy of consideration, but do not disregard plants not listed here as there are many others worthy of cultivation. This list should be considered bearing in mind the zones given in the A–Z of Species & Cultivars.

C. × *aromatica* (single, star-shaped, dark violet-purple) *

C. 'Blue Boy' (single, semi-nodding, blue)

C. *campaniflora* (single, nodding, white)

C. *crispa* (pitcher-shaped, nodding, lavender to purple)

C. 'Durandii' (single, semi-nodding, indigo blue) *

C. 'Eriostemon' (single, semi-nodding, purple-blue)

C. × *fargesioides* 'Summer Snow', syn. C. × *f.* 'Paul Farges' (single, creamy white)

C. *florida* 'Plena' (double, creamy white to greenish white) *

C. *f.* 'Sieboldii' (semi-double, creamy white tepals, purple centre) *

C. *heracleifolia* var. *davidiana* 'Wyevale' (small cluster, pale blue)

C. *integrifolia* 'Alba' (single, nodding, white)

C. *i.* 'Rosea' (single, nodding, pink)

C. × *jouiniana* 'Praecox' (cluster of single bluish-white to mauve)

C. PETIT FAUCON™ 'Evisix' Ⓝ (single, nodding, intense deep blue) *

C. *recta* (single, small white flowers in panicles)

C. *tangutica* 'Bill Mackenzie' (single, nodding, yellow)

C. *t.* 'Helios' (single, nodding, yellow)

C. *terniflora* (single small white flowers in panicles)

C. texensis 'Duchess of Albany' (single, upright tulip-like, pink)

C. t. 'Gravetye Beauty' (single, upright tulip-like, red)

C. t. 'Sir Trevor Lawrence' (single, upright tulip-like, dusky purple red)

C. × *triternata* 'Rubromarginata' (panicles of scented single tiny white flowers with red tips)

C. viorna (pitcher-shaped, purple to pinkish)

∗ The best for container culture.

CULTIVATION IN NORTH AMERICA

There is little to say concerning the culture of growing clematis in North America and similar climates other than the advice given in Chapter 3. However, North American gardeners may find the following list of quick tips a useful reference guide.

1 Always buy clematis plants from a good source. Short, stocky, well-rooted plants are as good as, or better than, poorly established plants in large containers.

2 Check the zone rating before purchase to avoid disappointment.

3 In cold climates, plant in the early spring so that the clematis becomes established before the following winter.

4 In mild, warm climates, plant in the autumn to obtain root establishment before the following year's hot summer.

5 Select the winter-hardy forms for extremely cold climates.

6 Select the New Zealand or Mediterranean species and their cultivars for hot climates, such as California, along with the more traditional species and cultivars.

7 Always plant the root crown an extra 5–7.5cm (2–3in) deeper than the soil level of its container to help root establishment and give extra protection to the root crown during the heat of summer and the winter cold.

8 Protect the plant's top growth in extremely cold climates (see page 81).

9 Protect container-grown clematis over winter so that the old wood can be retained to produce the large early flowers.

10 In cold areas do not expect the clematis to reach the heights given in the A–Z of Species & Cultivars, which apply to the British climate. These must be used as a guide only.

11 Plant deep-coloured or white-flowered clematis plants in hot sunny positions.

12 Plant the pale colours in shady positions to avoid the flowers fading prematurely.

13 Make sure the root crown is well protected by plant material or stone slabs in very hot climates to give the required cool root system.

14 Never underestimate the amount of water required for newly planted clematis, or for established plants in periods of dry weather.

C. texensis 'Sir Trevor Lawrence', a very attractive cultivar with miniature tulip-shaped flowers.

A–Z OF SPECIES
& CULTIVARS

EARLY-FLOWERING SPECIES
& THEIR CULTIVARS

The early-flowering clematis species and their cultivars encompass both evergreen and deciduous plants. The evergreen species and their cultivars are generally not fully winter hardy, some being suitable only for growing under glasshouse conditions. They are mostly natives of the southern hemisphere with the exception of C. *cirrhosa*, which comes from southern Europe. However, with the correct growing conditions and the right locality some may be grown in gardens in central and southern England, Ireland, southern Europe and the warm climates of the USA. The deciduous species and their cultivars are variable in winter hardiness (see zone ratings). Some, such as C. *alpina* and C. *macropetala*, are very winter hardy (zone 3) and are valuable plants for growing in extremely cold areas in northern Europe, the northern USA and Canada.

These species all flower from ripened stems produced the previous season, usually in early to mid-spring. They belong to pruning group one, requiring only light pruning after flowering, when dead or damaged stems may be removed (see page 46). Some clematis within this section are scented and this is stated in the relevant entries. The foliage is green unless otherwise stated.

C. *afoliata* A New Zealand evergreen species introduced to England in 1908 which is almost afoliate (produces no true leaves) with long stems that are somewhat rush-like in appearance. It has 2 cm (¾ in) long nodding pale yellow flowers which open gradually to display cream anthers. They have 4–6 tepals and are borne solitarily and 2–6 grouped in axillary cymes. This semi-climbing species of sprawling habit will grow successfully in central and southern England. *Flowering period:* early to mid-spring; *height:* 2.5 m (8¼ ft); *zones:* 8.

C. *alpina* var. *alpina* (Section Atragene) A deciduous climber native to the mountains of central Europe and northeast Asia. It was introduced into England from Europe in 1792, and was commonly known as the alpine virgin's bower. Its stems are somewhat ribbed and its leaves are biternate, the leaflets ovate-lanceolate, coarse serrate. The flowers are borne on short flower stalks, generally solitary directly from the leaf axil buds ripened the previous season, and are semi-nodding to nodding. The overall depth of the flowers is 5 cm (2 in). The colour varies slightly from blue to mauve. The tepals are normally four and are 2.5–5 cm (1–2 in) in length. These surround a large boss of cream petaloid staminodes, the outer ones being the longest and slightly spoon-shaped. The seedheads are large and most attractive in their shape and form.

The species has given rise to a range of different-coloured cultivars from white to pink, mauve, blue and purple, some becoming semi-double and similar to the double flowers of C. *macropetala*, a closely related species from China. These plants are very winter hardy to −35°C (−31°F) and extremely valuable as garden plants as they can be grown in very exposed locations. *Flowering period:* mid to late spring; *height:* 2–3 m (6½–10 ft); *zones:* 3–9.

C. *a.* 'Albiflora' Creamy white flowers, 5 cm (2 in) long. *Flowering period:* mid to late spring; *height:* 2.5–3 m (8½–10 ft); *zones:* 3–9.

C. *alpina* 'Cyanea', bred by Magnus Johnson to withstand the rigours of the Swedish winters (shown at twice normal size).

C. a. 'Blue Dancer' Most attractively shaped very pale blue flowers with long, narrow, twisted tepals 5–7.5 cm (2–3 in) long. *Flowering period:* mid to late spring; *height:* 3 m (10 ft); *zones:* 3–9.

C. a. 'Burford White' A cultivar with attractive light green foliage and creamy white tepals which produce a full flower 5 cm (2 in) deep. A chance seedling from C. *alpina* raised in North Wales and introduced by the author. *Flowering period:* mid to late spring; *height:* 2–3 m (6½–10 ft); *zones:* 3–9.

C. a. 'Columbine' Very pale blue tepals 5 cm (2 in) long with pointed tips and pale green foliage. A very pretty plant when in full flower. *Flowering period:* mid to late spring; *height:* 2–3 m (6½–10 ft); *zones:* 3–9.

C. a. 'Constance' Rich purple-pink semi-double flowers, 5 cm (2 in) deep. A seedling from C. a. 'Ruby', raised in England by Kathleen Goodman and introduced by the author. A free-flowering plant which is a great improvement on its parent. *Flowering period:* mid to late spring; *height:* 3 m (10 ft); *zones:* 3–9.

C. a. 'Cyanea' A very pretty deepish blue flower with tepals 5 cm (2 in) long and four blue inner tepals with pointed tips. It is free flowering and has pleasant green foliage. A new introduction to England but first catalogued by the raiser, Magnus Johnson of Sweden, in 1960. *Flowering period:* mid to late spring; *height:* 2–3 m (6½–10 ft); *zones:* 3–9.

C. a. 'Foxy' A very pale pink broad-tepalled flower, 5 cm (2 in) deep, with pointed tips to the tepals and a very pretty pink inner skirt. It has light green foliage. A sport of C. a. 'Frankie', raised and introduced by the author. *Flowering period:* mid to late spring; *height:* 3 m (10 ft); *zones:* 3–9.

C. a. 'Frankie' Mid-blue flowers with broad tepals 5 cm (2 in) long and a very pretty inner skirt, the outer petaloid stamens having a pale blue tip. One of the most free-flowering alpina cultivars, raised in Lincolnshire, England, by Frank Meecham and introduced by the author. *Flowering period:* mid to late spring; *height:* 3 m (10 ft); *zones:* 3–9.

C. a. 'Helsingborg' Deep blue/purple flowers 5 cm (2 in) deep with dark purple petaloid stamens. Very free-flowering. Raised in Sweden by Tage Lundell and introduced to England by the author. *Flowering period:* mid to late spring; *height:* 3 m (10 ft); *zones:* 3–9. ♛

C. a. 'Jacqueline du Pré' A cultivar with large, freely borne semi-nodding flowers and pale green foliage, raised in England by Barry Fretwell. The four tepals, 5 cm (2 in) in length and 2.5 cm (1 in) across, are pale pink with the reverse veined in pale maroon, especially the base of the tepals, the margins being pale pink. *Flowering period:* mid to late spring; *height:* 3 m (10 ft); *zones:* 3–9.

C. a. 'Pamela Jackman' A deep blue old cultivar with short 4 cm (1½ in) stubby flowers, but still attractive. *Flowering period:* mid to late spring; *height:* 2–3 m (6½–10 ft); *zones:* 3–9.

C. a. 'Pink Flamingo' Pale pink 4 cm (1½ in) semi-double flowers with delightful red veins. Raised by Elizabeth Jones in Brecon, Wales, as a seedling from C. *alpina* and introduced by the author. The best of the alpina types for length of flowering season. *Flowering period:* mid to late spring, and mid to late summer; *height:* 3 m (10 ft); *zones:* 3–9.

C. a. 'Ruby' Purple-pink flowers with tepals 4–5 cm (1½–2 in) long. This plant has a very strong growing habit. *Flowering period:* mid-spring and occasional autumn flowers; *height:* 3–4 m (10–13 ft); *zones:* 3–9.

C. a. 'Tage Lundell' Dark rose-purple flowers with 4–5 cm (1½–2 in) long tepals, a distinct strong colour. Raised by Tage Lundell in Sweden and introduced to England by the author. *Flowering period:* mid to late spring; *height:* 3 m (10 ft); *zones:* 3–9.

C. a. 'White Columbine' Clear white flowers with 4–5 cm (1½–2 in) long pointed tepals and attractive light green foliage. Raised as a seedling in England from C. a. 'Columbine' and introduced by the author. *Flowering period:* mid to late spring; *height:* 2–3 m (6½–10 ft); *zones:* 3–9.

C. a. 'Willy' Pale pink flowers, which are darker on the outside of the 4–5 cm (1½–2 in) long tepals. Vigorous habit. *Flowering period:* mid to late spring and some flowers in late summer; *height:* 2–3 m (6½–10 ft); *zones:* 3–9.

C. a. var. ochotensis A deciduous scrambling species native to eastern Siberia, Kamchatka, Korea and Japan, its foliage and flower shape being similar to C. *alpina*. The leaves are biternate, the leaflets ovate-lanceolate, cordate at base and coarse serrate. The flowers are nodding, borne on short flower stalks, generally solitary directly from the leaf axil buds ripened the previous season. The four tepals are 5 cm (2 in) in length and slate-blue in colour. They surround a large boss of petaloid staminodes. The plant grown by the author came from Kamchatka via Magnus Johnson, probably collected by Eric Hulten in 1922. A useful plant for future breeding work, due to its larger flower size than C. *alpina*. Magnus Johnson has already produced some interesting cultivars with large flowers. *Flowering period:* late spring to early summer; *height:* 2 m (6½ ft); *zones:* 3–9.

C. a. var. ochotensis 'Carmen Rose' A good garden plant raised by Magnus Johnson in 1950. It is a very free-flowering and showy clematis with purplish-pink flowers 6–7 cm (2¼–2¾ in) in length with broad outer tepals. *Flowering period:* late spring to early summer; *height:* 3 m (10 ft); *zones:* 3–9.

C. a. var. ochotensis 'Frances Rivis' (syn. C. *a.* 'Blue Giant') There is some question as to the true form of this cultivar. The plant that is generally grown and sold is the one described here. The flowers are large, with pale blue, very broad tepals which are slightly twisted and 5–6 cm (2–2¼ in) long. A very free-flowering plant. *Flowering period:* mid to late spring; *height:* 3 m (10 ft); *zones:* 3–9. ♀

C. a. var. sibirica (syn. C. *sibirica*) A plant that some classify as a form or botanical variant of C. *alpina*, native to northern Europe, northern Norway, Finland to eastern Siberia and the central Ural Mountains. It is a short-growing deciduous plant with attractive pale green foliage and pointed clear white four-tepalled flowers with petaloid staminodes of creamy white. They are open bell-shaped and 5 cm (2 in) deep. Magnus Johnson and Hans Reudi Horn-Gfeller from Switzerland have made a great

study of this plant, the latter undertaking many expeditions to find good forms. *Flowering period:* late spring; *height:* 2 m (6½ ft); *zones:* 3–9.

C. a. var. sibirica 'Flavia' (syn. C. *sibirica* var. *flavia*) A variety with light yellow flowers 5 cm (2 in) deep. *Flowering period:* late spring; *height:* 2 m (6 ½ ft); *zones:* 3–9.

C. aristata (Section Aspidantera) A rampant climber from Australia with evergreen pointed leaves, leaflets toothed or entire. Occasionally there is a silver vein down the centre of the leaves or leaflets. The star-shaped white, or occasionally pinkish-white, flowers are 2 cm (¾ in) across, produced in small panicles. A plant for indoor cultivation except in zone 9: southern Georgia, Florida, southern Texas, coastal areas of California and southern Europe. *Flowering period:* early to mid-spring; *height:* 3–4.5 m (10–15 ft); *zones:* 9.

C. armandii (Section Flammula) An evergreen species from China found over a very large geographical area, introduced to England in 1900 by Ernest Wilson. A very rampant climber with large, pointed, dark green leaves, generally trifoliate. They have a leathery texture when mature and an attractive bronze colour when young. The foliage is prone to damage by wind and late spring frosts may kill the new young growth, so except in the warmest areas it is best planted on a south- or southwest-facing aspect against a large wall. The creamy-white to pure white flat, open flowers are 4–5 cm (1½–2 in) in diameter, have off-white anthers and are produced on short flower stems in clusters from the leaf axil buds. They have a scent like that of hawthorn. Good forms are most attractive when in full flower, with a great abundance of blooms. *Flowering period:* early to mid-spring; *height:* 4.5–6 m (15–20 ft); *zones:* 6–9.

C. a. 'Apple Blossom' An old pink-flowered form which is similar in growth to the species, but with blunter and wider leaflets which are slightly more bronze. The 5 cm (2 in) wide flowers are whitish pink with the reverse of the tepal being pale pink. The flower buds and flower stem are also pink. The flowers are scented strongly of vanilla. *Flowering period:* early to mid-spring; *height:* 4.5–6 m (15–20 ft); *zones:* 6–9.

C. a. 'Jefferies' A white-flowered form of the species with long, narrow, more pointed leaflets. Discovered by the author in the old nursery of Jefferies of Cirencester growing over a shed and selected because it occasionally produces a crop of summer flowers. The 5 cm (2 in) flowers are white and more gappy than in the more rounded fuller-flowered forms of the species. *Flowering period:* early to mid-spring; *height:* 5–6 m (16½–20 ft); *zones:* 6–9.

C. a. 'Snowdrift' I am not sure if anyone has or knows of the true form of this name, though many plants are sold under it. The true plant should have white, 6 cm (2¼ in) fully rounded flowers and somewhat more blunt, more rounded leaflets, a great plant from the old descriptions. *Flowering period:* early to mid-spring; *height:* 5–6 m (16½–20 ft); *zones:* 6–9.

C. australis A New Zealand evergreen species which has trifoliate, generally dark green, leaves. The forms I know have panicles of semi-nodding, star-shaped pale yellow flowers which are 2 cm (¾ in) in diameter and scented. It is only partially hardy. *Flowering period:* early to mid-spring; *height:* 2 m (6½ ft); *zones:* 8–9.

C. AVALANCHE™ 'Blaaval' ⊘ A marvellous evergreen clematis raised by Robin White at Blackthorn Nurseries, England, introduced in 1998 and protected by Plant Breeder's Rights. A strong, vigorous plant, similar in growth to C. *paniculata* and in flower habit to C. × *cartmanii* 'Joe'. It is winter hardy to –8°C (18°F) in well-drained soil. The fleshy, leathery, dark green leaves are very dissected, their glossy surface making them most attractive. The open, flat flowers, 7–8 cm (2¾–3 in) in diameter, are borne in panicles in great profusion. They have 4–7 but mainly six pure white tepals, short dark yellow stamens and no styles. A useful plant for conservatory and container culture, it can be pruned to keep it compact, flowering only from the previous season's ripened stems. *Flowering period:* early to mid-spring; *height:* 3–4 m (10–13 ft); *zones:* 7–9.

C. × cartmanii 'Joe' Raised in the early 1980s in Scotland from seed sent by Joe Cartman from Christchurch, New Zealand, and the result of a cross between C. *marmoraria* and C. *paniculata*, both New Zealand evergreen species. An extremely valuable conservatory

or glasshouse plant, it is hardy to –5°C (23°F) at least and may be grown outside in well-drained soil under the shelter of a warm dry wall. It is non-clinging but will attain 2 m (6½ ft) if trained, otherwise it will form a mound of dense evergreen foliage. The semi-nodding, open cup-shaped 2.5 cm (1 in) wide white flowers are so profusely borne as to almost hide the foliage. *Flowering period:* early to mid-spring; *height:* to 2 m (6½ ft) with support; *zones:* 7–9.

C. chiisanensis (Section Atragene) A deciduous Korean species which is a climber or scrambler with trifoliate leaves, the leaflets cordate-ovate, coarse-dentate, often trilobed to ternate. The flowers are borne solitarily or in groups of threes from both the previous season's and current season's stems. The colour is variable, ranging from pale yellow to brownish orange yellow, having darker colouring at the base of the tepals which are ribbed and spurred. The flowers are 5 cm

C. chiisanensis, a Korean species with strange spurs at the base of the tepals, looking like an aquilegia.

(2 in) long and nodding. The form known to the author is pale yellow and has reddish to yellow colouring on the outside base of the tepals, which are ribbed and spurred. *Flowering period:* late spring to summer; *height:* 2–3 m (6½–10 ft); *zones:* 5–9.

C. chrysocoma (Section Montana) A Chinese species of deciduous climbing habit. The leaves are trifoliate, the leaflets broad ovate to narrow-obovate, coarsely and irregularly serrate and sometimes trilobed. The stems, leafstalks and leaflets appear downy, being covered by browny-yellow hairs. The flowers can be white or pink, and are borne generally on new growth with solitary flowers in each leaf axil, some forms flowering from ripened stems from the previous season. The 5 cm (2 in) diameter or sometimes smaller flowers are cup-shaped when they open, expanding to a flat flower with 4–6 tepals, sometimes more, and a large boss of short yellow stamens. In the wild it grows only to 60 cm (2 ft) but in cultivation may reach 2 m (6½ ft). In cultivation it needs free-draining soil and is only semi-hardy. *Flowering period:* early to late summer; *height:* to 2 m (6½ ft); *zones:* 8–9.

C. c. 'Continuity' A cultivar raised by Albert Voneshan, production foreman of Jackmans of Woking. It was bred and selected in the late 1950s/early 1960s for its long flower stalks, for use as a cut flower. The plant was given to the author by Roland Jackman many years ago to propagate and distribute. Like the species, it is not winter-hardy. The foliage is not as covered with hairs as that of the typical species. The leaf stalks (petioles) are very long, 12.5–15 cm (5–6 in), as are the flower stems (pedicels) at 20 cm (8 in). The 5 cm (2 in) wide flowers have generally four but sometimes five or six tepals of a mid-pale pink with a satiny texture to the surface, with blunt tips and darker pink reverse, long filaments and deep yellow anthers. This plant needs a well-drained soil and a sheltered aspect to grow well outside, but can be grown with safety under cover. Recommended as a cut flower. *Flowering period:* early to late summer; *height:* 2 m (6½ ft); *zones:* 8–9.

C. c. hybrid This plant was thought to be the type plant until Roy Lancaster reintroduced the species from Yunnan in China in the early 1980s and it was realized this must be of hybrid origin, possibly as a result of crossing

C. chrysocoma with a pink form of *C. montana*. It too has most attractive bronze downy foliage, especially when young. The somewhat fleshy leaves are a bronze green becoming greener with age but turning bronze when they fully mature. The attractive cup-shaped flowers are usually 5 cm (2 in) in diameter with four tepals and stubby yellow anthers. A vigorous free-flowering plant when fully established, it is not as winter hardy as *C. montana* but is hardier than the species. *Flowering period:* late spring; *height:* 5 m (16½ ft); *zones:* 7–9.

C. cirrhosa var. cirrhosa (Section Cheiropsis) An evergreen species from the Mediterranean area of southern Europe, widespread in the Balearic Islands, southern Spain and Italy to Cyprus, Israel and parts of North Africa, introduced to England in the 1590s. It is a very variable species with clear light greenish-yellow flowers to those lighter in base colour but covered in brown-purple blotches. The flowers are 4 cm (1½ in) deep. It prefers a sheltered situation in full or partial sun (to ripen the flowering stems) and well-drained soil, similar to the dry soils of its native habitat, where it goes into a summer dormancy. Its foliage is most attractive, usually dark green and glossy, its leaves varying between simple, dentate or trilobed, or ternate to biternate with dentate to lobed leaflets. Its leaf stalks (petioles) cling very tightly to its support. The flowers are broad campanulate and are solitary or in axillary fascicles, with two calyx-like bracts. *Flowering period:* mid to late winter; *height:* 3–4 m (10–13 ft); *zones:* 7–9.

C. c. var. balearica A fine form of the species introduced from the Balearic Islands to England in 1783. It has delightful cut-leaf foliage which turns bronze during winter when it is grown outside. It is not as vigorous as *C. cirrhosa*, nor so dense in its habit. Its 5 cm (2 in) deep flowers are narrower and longer, the four tepals being slightly twisted, with reddish-brown blotches that show through on the reverse, giving the flower a slightly creamy-pink appearance when aged. *Flowering period:* mid to late winter; *height:* 3 m (10 ft); *zones:* 7–9. ♀

C. c. 'Freckles' A cultivar raised by the author in 1987 from seed collected in the Balearic Islands and introduced in 1989. It has larger leaves than the species, either simple or trifoliate. Occasionally this cultivar goes into a slight summer dormancy before producing new growth in mid to late autumn, when it bears its large flowers. It has exceptionally long 6–7 cm (2¼–2¾ in) slender flower stalks and four-tepalled flowers 7.5 cm (3 in) in length. The base colour is creamy pink, with the inside of the flower highly coloured with red-maroon blotches. This has become a most useful garden plant as it produces its main crop of flowers before the onset of winter, thus avoiding the damage usually caused by frost to the other forms in mid to late winter. In Worcestershire in England it has been found to be hardy to –12°C (10°F). It flowers well in California and obviously in the warmer climate of southern Europe. *Flowering period:* mid to late autumn; *height:* 3–4 m (10–13 ft); *zones:* 7–9. ♀

C. c. 'Ourika Valley' A vigorous evergreen climber, raised by Captain Peter Erskine from seed collected in the Ourika Valley, High Atlas Mountains, Morocco in December 1986. The leaves are rich green and are divided into three coarsely toothed leaflets. The unspotted pale yellow flowers have four tepals which are non-overlapping and cream anthers; they are nodding bell-shaped, 4–5 cm (1½–2 in) long. This cultivar has proved to be more winter hardy than C. c. var. *balearica*, more resistant to cold winds and more free-flowering. *Flowering period:* late winter to early spring; *height:* 3–4 m (10–13 ft); *zones:* 7–9.

C. c. 'Wisley Cream' A cultivar introduced by the author in the 1970s, raised by the late Ken Aslet at the RHS Garden at Wisley from seed collected in southern Europe. The leaves are generally simple and lighter green; the four-tepalled 4 cm (1½ in) deep flowers are greenish-cream without blotches or markings of any kind. *Flowering period:* mid to late winter; *height:* 3–4 m (10–13 ft); *zones:* 7–9.

C. columbiana var. columbiana (Section Atragene) A semi-woody deciduous scrambler, having ternately twice-compound leaves, with nine leaflets with prominently toothed margins, sometimes lobed or further divided. The solitary nodding blue-purple flowers are 4 cm (1½ in) deep and are borne on the previous season's ripened stems. A native of British Columbia to Colorado and Oregon. *Flowering period:* late spring; *height:* 1 m (3¼ ft); *zones:* 3–9.

C. c. var. tenuiloba (syn. C. *tenuiloba*) A procumbent deciduous vine native to western USA, South Dakota to Arizona. The leaves are biternate, leaflets usually pinnatisect with the segments ovate to lanceolate. The open bell-shaped blue to purple flowers are 3–4 cm (1¼–1½ in) deep. *Flowering period:* late spring; *height:* 15 cm (6 in); *zones:* 3–9.

C. fasciculiflora (Section Flammula) A slightly untidy scrambling evergreen plant from southwestern China with trifoliate leaves, leaflets oval-oblong, with a purple tint and sometimes a central silver bar to each leaflet. The nodding, 3–4 cm (1¼–1½ in) bell-shaped flowers are a muddy creamy white and are borne in axillary clusters. A collector's plant of little horticultural value. *Flowering period:* early to mid-spring; *height:* up to 4.5 m (15 ft); *zones:* 8–9.

C. finetiana (Section Flammula) A climbing evergreen species from central and western China with trifoliate foliage, bright green similar to C. *armandii* but somewhat smaller and finer in texture. The leaves are trifoliate, the leaflets somewhat coriaceous, narrow-ovate, acute, rounded somewhat cordate at base, entire, bright green, glabrous, three-veined. The star-shaped 4 cm (1½ in) wide white flowers are borne in threes or sometimes seven on short pedicels from the leaf axil. It needs a well-protected site to grow well and flower. Its flowers are strongly scented. *Flowering period:* late spring to early summer; *height:* 3–4 m (10–13 ft); *zones:* 8–9.

C. forsteri A dioecious New Zealand evergreen climbing species. The form I grow is a male selection. It has delightful apple-green leaves, trifoliate and lanceolate to broad-ovate, entire. Its semi-nodding, open, star-shaped creamy lime green flowers are 2–3 cm (¾–1¼ in) wide and strongly scented, resembling lemon verbena. They are borne in large clusters, producing a massed effect. *Flowering period:* mid-spring; *height:* 2 m (6½ ft); *zones:* 8–9.

C. gentianoides (Section Aspidantera) A creeping non-clinging evergreen species from Tasmania with simple or trifoliate leaves, leaflets lanceolate to lanceolate-ovate. The somewhat star-shaped flowers, 2.5–4 cm (1–1½ in) wide, have four white tepals and are solitary or occasionally in clusters. It needs a good sunny situation to do well, when it will flower for three months non-stop, producing hawthorn-scented blooms. *Flowering period:* early to mid-spring; *height:* 45–60 cm (1½–2 ft); *zones:* 8–9.

C. gracilifolia var. gracilifolia (Section Montana) A deciduous species from western China. I know of two forms which are very similar, one collected by Professor Harry Smith in 1935 and the other collected by myself in 1981 in western Sichuan. My form has rather more gappy flowers. It is a deciduous climber to 4 m (13 ft) in the wild. The leaves are ternate or pinnate with 3–5–7 leaflets, somewhat hairy. The leaflets are ovate, acute, coarse-serrated or trilobed. The white four-tepalled open flowers are 5 cm (2 in) in diameter and are grouped like those of C. *montana* from the previous season's ripened leaf axil buds. It is rather a pretty plant with attractive foliage, flowering earlier than C. *montana* but after C. *alpina*. *Flowering period:* mid to late spring; *height:* 5 m (16½ ft); *zones:* 6–9.

C. glycinoides (Section Aspidantera) An Australian species, similar to C. *aristata*, but with thin-textured evergreen leaves made up of three leaflets which are broad and sparsely toothed. Occasionally there is a silver-coloured vein down the centre of each leaflet. The star-shaped, white, four-tepalled flowers are 2 cm (¼ in) across and are produced in small panicles. *Flowering period:* early to mid-spring; *height:* 3–4.5 m (10–15 ft); *zones:* 9.

C. japonica (Section Bebaeanthera) A climbing species native to Japan, with trifoliate leaves, the leaflets with serrated margins and a pleasant pale green colour, especially in the paler flowered clones. It is deciduous, flowering from the old wood in spring. Some forms have almost too much foliage, nearly hiding the bell-like nodding flowers, which measure 3 cm (1¼ in) and are normally borne singly, or in small clusters, on short pedicels direct from the leaf axil buds ripened the previous season. The pedicels have a pair of small bracts and the four fleshy tepals are unusually wax-like, recurving at the tips. It is a variable species with purple-red to maroon to pale yellow flowers. It looks charming in its wild habit in Japan, clambering about in small trees or shrubs. A useful collector's plant

for a sunny aspect, not difficult to grow but hard to find. *Flowering period:* early summer; *height:* 2 m (6½ ft); *zones:* 6–9.

C. koreana var. koreana (Section Atragene) A Korean species which is a deciduous climber or scrambler with trifoliate leaves, leaflets cordate-ovate coarse-dentate often trilobed to ternate. Solitary open bell-shaped flowers are produced from the previous season's ripened stems, while on current season's growth they are borne in clusters. They have generally four tepals in a reddish-purple, 7.5 cm (3 in) long with pointed tips, being elliptic to lanceolate in form. The petaloid staminodes are generally creamy yellow. *Flowering period:* late spring to

A good, dark-coloured form of C. *japonica*, photographed growing in the wild in Japan.

early summer; *height:* 2–3 m (6½–10 ft); *zones:* 5–9.

C. k. var. *fragrans* This form was collected in Korea in 1976 by the Nordisk Arboretum. It has fragrant flowers with pointed tepals 9 cm (3½ in) long. *Flowering period:* late spring to early summer; *height:* 2–3m (6½–10 ft); *zones:* 5–9.

C. k. var. *lutea* A form with most attractive yellow flowers of an unusual shade. *Flowering period:* late spring to early summer; *height:* 2–3 m (6½–10 ft); *zones:* 5–9.

C. *macropetala* (Section Atragene) A species native to northern China and eastern Mongolia and known to be growing northeast of Beijing. It was introduced to the British Isles in 1910. A deciduous climber, it has leaves up to 10 cm (4 in) long, biternate, leaflets ovate to lanceolate, irregularly coarsely serrate and deeply lobed. The open bell-shaped flowers are pendulous, borne solitarily from the leaf axil buds ripened the previous season. The tepals are normally four, 4–5 cm (1½–2 in) long, blue to violet blue; the staminodes are numerous, giving the appearance of a double flower, the outer staminodes bluish in colour, the inner ones generally bluish-white to white. The species produces an abundance of fluffy seed-heads from midsummer to late autumn which can be used for summer floral arrangements or dried for winter decorations. It can be grown in a wide variation of locations and must be utilized for its extreme winter hardiness in exposed locations. It has given rise to a range of beautiful cultivars with larger flowers in a range of colours from blue, purple, pink and mauve through to white. *Flowering period:* mid to late spring; *height:* 2 m (6½ ft); *zones:* 3–9.

C. m. 'Alborosea' Pinkish-mauve flowers with outer tepals 5 cm (2 in) long and pretty petaloid staminodes which are lighter in colour. Raised by Magnus Johnson in Sweden in 1974 and introduced to the British Isles by the author. *Flowering period:* mid to late spring; *height:* 3 m (10 ft); *zones:* 3–9.

C. m. 'Anders' A good lavender-blue cultivar with 4–5 cm (1½–2 in) long flowers, raised by Magnus Johnson in Sweden in 1980 and introduced to England by the author. *Flowering period:* mid to late spring; *height:* 2–3 m (6½–10 ft); *zones:* 3–9.

C. m. 'Ballet Skirt' A very attractive large flower, with fully double deep pinkish tepals and petaloid staminodes. Raised in Canada in 1981 by Stanley J. Zubrowski and introduced to England from Sweden by the author. Not so vigorous as other cultivars but worth growing for its 6 cm (2¼ in) deep flowers. *Flowering period:* mid to late spring; *height:* 2 m (6½ ft); *zones:* 3–9.

C. m. 'Blue Bird' Mauve-blue outer tepals which are very slim and twisted, rather a gappy flower 6 cm (2¼ in) in diameter, petaloid staminodes paler in colour, becoming creamy white in the centre. A vigorous plant raised in 1962 by Dr Frank Skinner in Canada. *Flowering period:* mid to late spring with some summer flowers; *height:* 3 m (10 ft); *zones:* 3–9.

C. m. 'Floralia' Pale blue, stubby 4 cm (1½ in) flowers but very attractive, borne on purple-red flower stalks. Raised by Magnus Johnson in Sweden and introduced by the author to the British Isles in the 1980s. *Flowering period:* mid to late spring; *height:* 2 m (6½ ft); *zones:* 3–9.

C. m. 'Harry Smith' A pretty flower with pale lavender-blue colouring, only 4 cm (1½ in) long but freely produced. Introduced to Sweden by Professor Harry Smith from China (Chili province) in 1922 and introduced into the British Isles from Magnus Johnson by the author. *Flowering period:* mid to late spring; *height:* 2–3 m (6½–10 ft); *zones:* 3–9.

C. m. 'Jan Lindmark' Raised in Sweden by Jan Lindmark, named by Magnus Johnson and introduced to the British Isles in 1983 by the author. It has mauve-purple flowers only 4 cm (1½ in) long, slightly twisted outer tepals, a good colour and the first of all the alpina and macropetala types to flower each year. The foliage can become untidy, but it is worth growing for the early flowers. *Flowering period:* mid to late spring; *height:* 2.5 m (8¼ ft); *zones:* 3–9.

C. m. 'Lagoon' The darkest of all the blue cultivars with large spiky flowers, 6 cm (2¼ in) deep, in a very deep blue. It needs a light background to show off the flowers to their best advantage. It is later flowering than most macropetala types. *Flowering period:* mid to late spring; *height:* 2–3 m (6½–10 ft); *zones:* 3–9.

C. m. **'Lincolnshire Lady'** Raised by Frank Meecham and introduced by the Valley Clematis Nursery in the 1990s. It has fully double nodding flowers with four outer tepals in two obvious pairs and up to 14 long and thin inner tepals. The flowers are 4–7 cm (1½–2¾ in) long, the outer tepals dusky blue, the inner tepals paler. It produces plenty of silky seedheads. *Flowering period:* mid to late spring with occasional summer flowers; *height:* 3 m (10 ft); *zones:* 4–9.

C. m. **'Maidwell Hall'** There are many cultivars about under this name, but the true plant has pale blue to lavender fully double flowers, 5 cm (2 in) deep, somewhat stunted in appearance and held more out-facing than other cultivars. Raised about 1956 by Oliver Wyatt at Maidwell Hall, Northants, England. *Flowering period:* mid to late spring; *height:* 2 m (6½ ft); *zones:* 3–9. ♚

C. m. **'Markham's Pink'** Raised by Ernest Markham and introduced in 1935. A free-flowering plant with deep pink fully double flowers 5 cm (2 in) long and attractive pale green foliage. *Flowering period:* mid to late spring; *height:* 3 m (10 ft) ; *zones:* 3–9. ♚

C. m. **'Pauline'** A very useful newish macropetala raised in England by Washfield Nursery in 1966, with extra-large flowers 5–7 cm (2–2¾ in) long. It has long pointed outer tepals in a good mid to dark blue with a very attractive inner skirt of petaloid staminodes, these being longer than in other clones and of the same colour as the outer tepals. It is a very good plant, strong-growing and of free-flowering habit. *Flowering period:* mid to late spring; *height:* 3 m (10 ft); *zones:* 3–9.

C. m. **'Rosy O'Grady'** Raised by Dr Frank Skinner in Canada in 1964, this is a strong-growing plant with pinky-mauve spiky flowers, very open in form, with the inner skirt lighter in colour. The outer tepals are 5–7 cm (2–2¾ in) in length. *Flowering period:* mid to late spring; *height:* 3 m (10 ft); *zones:* 3–9.

C. m. **'White Moth'** (syn. *C. alpina* ssp. *sibirica* 'White Moth') Stubby, creamy white flowers, 3–4 cm (1¼–1½ in) long, the outer tepals spreading when mature, and attractive pale green foliage. The latest of the alpina and macropetala to flower each year and not very vigorous, but useful for a small garden. *Flowering period:* late spring; *height:* 2 m (6½ ft); *zones:* 3–9.

C. m. **'White Swan'** Creamy-white fully double semi-nodding flowers 5–6 cm (2–2¼ in) in length, good pale green foliage, but a slow plant to establish. Raised in 1961 by Dr Frank Skinner in Canada. *Flowering period:* late spring; *height:* 2 m (6½ ft); *zones:* 3–9.

C. m. **'White Wings'** A cultivar with creamy white fully double flowers 5–6 cm (2– 2¼ in) in length and attractive pale green foliage. It is very free-flowering and the best of the white macropetala types. Raised in Sweden by Magnus Johnson in 1970 and introduced to the British Isles by the author. *Flowering period:* late spring; *height:* 2–3 m (6½–10 ft); *zones:* 3–9.

C. marmoraria A dwarf evergreen New Zealand species reaching only 10–12.5 cm (4–5 in) in height, this plant has been described as resembling a rigid clump of parsley. The deep glossy green leaves are trifoliate, the leaflets deeply and closely divided. It has a suckering habit. The creamy white flowers start off greenish, are only 2 cm (¾ in) wide and are borne close to the foliage. A marvellous plant for an alpine house, growing in a container. *Flowering period:* early spring; *height:* 10–12.5 cm (4–5 in); *zones:* 8–9.

C. meyeniana (Section Flammula) A vigorous ever-green climber from southwestern China which the author has found in the Hong Kong region. A close relation to *C. armandii* with trifoliate leaves, the leaflets broad-ovate to lanceolate and of a thick texture. The flowers are 2.5cm (1in) in diameter, borne in racemes. The four tepals are narrow oblong, white or pink. A plant for only the most sheltered garden. *Flowering period:* early to mid-spring; *height:* 4.5–5 m (15–16½ ft); *zones:* 9.

C. microphylla (Section Aspidantera) An evergreen Australian climber of a thin structure with very narrow foliage, the leaves biternate or triternate. The flowers, borne in short panicles, are 2.5 cm (1 in) wide with very thin narrow tepals which become twisted with age, followed by silky seedheads. A collector's plant, it needs a dry, sunny, sheltered location. *Flowering period:* early spring; *height:* 2 m (6½ ft); *zones:* 9.

C. montana var. *montana* (Section Cheiropsis Subsection Montanae) A rampant variable deciduous species, native of central and western China and the Himalayas, introduced to the British Isles in 1831 from the Himalayas by Lady Amherst. This vigorous clematis grows to 8 m (26 ft). The leaves are trifoliate, the leaflets ovate-lanceolate, quite deeply trilobed with tapered points, rounded at the base, coarse-serrate, rarely entire. The flat, open, white flowers are 5 cm (2 in) in diameter, normally with four tepals, generally a gappy flower. They are grouped in pairs or in fives and are borne from the ripened leaf axil buds from the previous season, with occasionally some summer flowers. The species and its botanical variant *C. montana* var. *rubens* have given rise to a range of most useful garden plants, valuable for covering large wall areas or for growing up into large evergreen trees. They are not fully winter hardy in very cold locations such as Scandinavia or North America and they have never become large fully-established plants even in the warmer areas of North America. *Flowering period:* late spring to early summer; *height:* 8 m (26 ft); *zones:* 7–9.

C. m. 'Alexander' A plant introduced from India by Colonel R. D. Alexander. It has much larger leaves than the species, the foliage being of a good green colour. The flowers too are larger at 6 cm (2¼ in) in diameter. The flower shape is fully round, and the white tepals are offset by creamy anthers. This form needs a position in full sun to flower well as the previous season's stems need to be ripened fully to achieve a good crop of flowers. *Flowering period:* late spring to early summer; *height:* 8 m (26 ft); *zones:* 7–9.

C. m. 'Broughton Star' An unusual plant with interesting trifoliate leaves which are deeply serrated, bronze when young becoming dark green when mature. The very attractive semi-double to fully double flowers, 4–7 cm (1½–2¾ in) in diameter, are most unusual for this group of clematis; they have four outer tepals with many inner tepals, forming a cup-shaped flower. They are deep dusky pink with slightly darker veins. A useful cut flower for small flower arrangements. The plant does best in a sunny position. Raised and introduced by Vince and Sylvia Denny in Preston in England in 1988. *Flowering period:* late spring to early summer; *height:* 4–5 m (13–16½ ft); *zones:* 7–9.

C. m. 'Elizabeth' A most attractive pale pink cultivar with a satiny sheen, raised by Jackmans in 1958. The 6 cm (2¼ in) wide flowers are slightly gappy with long filaments and spiky anthers and have a beautiful vanilla scent. The attractive bronze foliage turns to green as it matures. *Flowering period:* late spring to early summer; *height:* 8–10 m (26–33 ft); *zones:* 7–9. ♔

C. m. 'Freda' A deep pink cultivar with 5 cm (2 in) flowers with dark pink/red margins and contrasting yellow anthers, set off by attractive very deep bronze foliage. The deepest-coloured of all the montanas currently available, raised in Suffolk and introduced by Jim Fisk in 1985. A more compact plant and useful for smaller gardens. *Flowering period:* late spring to early summer; *height:* 6–8 m (20–26 ft); *zones:* 7–9 .

C. m. 'Gothenburg' A form given to the author by Magnus Johnson in the early 1980s, raised at the Gothenburg Botanical Gardens in Sweden. An interesting cultivar with attractive foliage, the bronze leaflets having a central silver band. Long flower stalks (pedicels) support the creamy pink rounded flowers which are 4–6 cm (1½–2¼ in) across. *Flowering period:* late spring to early summer; *height:* 5 m (16½ ft); *zones:* 7–9.

C. m. grandiflora The true plant is not fully established in cultivation, having only recently been reintroduced by Brickell & Leslie from China. In the wild I'm told the flowers are as large as a person's hand. *Flowering period:* late spring to early summer; *height:* 5 m (16½ ft); *zones:* 8–9.

C. m. f. grandiflora The plants sold under this name originate from a plant I obtained from Percy Picton under the incorrect name of *C. chrysocoma* 'Sericea'. This very strong-growing and vigorous clematis is ideal for covering large areas. It has dark green foliage and clear white flowers 7.5 cm (3 in) in diameter which are freely produced. It is the hardiest of all the *C. montana* plants known to me. *Flowering period:* late spring to early summer; *height:* 10–11 m (33–36 ft); *zones:* 6–9. ♔

C. m. 'Margaret Jones' Semi-double star-like flowers 5 cm (2 in) in diameter with four long thin pointed outer tepals and an inner ring of smaller, shorter, petaloid stamens, both in a creamy-green white (stamens being absent) with a green style. The trifoliate leaves have long pointed leaflets. It is not free-flowering, therefore best planted in a sunny south- or southwest-facing position. Raised by Anne Smyth, Norfolk, England, named after her mother and introduced by Thorncroft Clematis Nursery in 1991. *Flowering period:* late spring to early summer; *height:* 4.5m (15 ft); *zones:* 7–9.

C. m. 'Marjorie' Raised by Mrs Marjorie Free in Suffolk and introduced in 1980 by Jim Fisk, the first of all the semi-double *C. montana* cultivars to be introduced. During cold springs the 6 cm (2¼ in) flowers open a greenish pink but when exposed to sunlight age to a creamy pink. It does best in full sun. *Flowering period:* late spring to early summer; *height:* 8 m (26 ft); *zones:* 7–9.

C. m. 'Mayleen' Introduced by Jim Fisk in 1984, the best scented montana currently available, with a strong vanilla scent. Bronze foliage offsets the satiny pink fully rounded flowers, 6 cm (2¼ in) in diameter, with contrasting yellow anthers. *Flowering period:* late spring to early summer; *height:* 8–10 m (26–33 ft); *zones:* 7–9.

C. m. 'Pink Perfection' A good vanilla-scented cultivar with rounded pink almost cup-shaped flowers on opening, yellow anthers and bronze foliage. The flowers are 6 cm (2¼ in) in diameter. A strong-growing plant. *Flowering period:* late spring to early summer; *height:* 8–10 m (26–33 ft); *zones:* 7–9.

C. m. var. *rubens* A pink form of the species introduced by Ernest Wilson from China in the early 1900s. Sadly the original form appears to be lost to cultivation, and there are many variable clematis on sale under this name, with flowers of about 5 cm (2 in). It is therefore best to obtain a named pink-flowered cultivar. The pink form of the true species reportedly has bronze foliage and rosy-red flowers. *Flowering period:* late spring to early summer; *height:* 8–10 m (26–33 ft); *zones:* 7–9.

C. montana 'Vera', a strong-growing plant with vanilla-scented flowers and larger leaves than most montanas.

C. m. var. rubens 'Picton's Variety' A compact form with deep mauve pink flowers 5 cm (2 in) wide and bronze foliage. The spring/early summer flowers have four tepals, while the occasional midsummer flowers have six. Raised by Percy Picton during the 1950s. *Flowering period:* late spring to early summer, occasional midsummer flowers; *height:* 4.5m (15 ft); *zones:* 7–9.

C. m. 'Tetrarose' A tetraploid form of *C. m.* var. *rubens* raised at the Boskoop Research Station in Holland in 1960. It has large trifoliate leaves, bronze green in colour maturing to deep bronze purple. The leaflets have deeply serrated edges. This attractive foliage off-sets the large 7.5 cm (3 in) wide cup-shaped flowers with a large cluster of deep yellow stamens. The four deep rosy-mauve tepals are rather thick and have a satin sheen. *Flowering period:* late spring to early summer; *height:* 8 m (26 ft); *zones:* 7–9.

C. m. 'Vera' A cultivar raised in Cornwall, England, in the mid-1900s which produces large bronze green leaves and deep pink 5–7 cm (2–2¾ in) wide flowers, pleasantly scented of vanilla. A very strong-growing plant. *Flowering period:* late spring to early summer; *height:* 10 m (33 ft); *zones:* 7–9.

C. m. var. wilsonii A form collected by Ernest Wilson from central China in the early 1900s and thought to have been lost to cultivation until about 1983, when Lawrence Banks of Hergest Croft, Herefordshire, England, told the author of a plant he had of *C. montana* that flowered in midsummer. His plant exactly matched the details of the plant described by Veitch and in the *Curtis's Botanical Magazine* (t8365), the plant being acquired by his grandfather before the 1914–18 war. However, this form does not have the scent of choco-late as described by some authors. The author has prop-agated and distributed this plant. The leaves are somewhat more fleshy than those of typical *C. montana*. It has the same vigour and its 5 cm (2 in) flowers are borne on long flower stems (pedicels); the four tepals are creamy white and there is a large boss of sta-mens. It is more difficult to propagate than other *C. montana* forms and cultivars. *Flowering period:* mid to late summer; *height:* 10 m (33 ft); *zones:* 6–9.

C. napaulensis (Section Cheiropsis) A deciduous climbing species native to north India and southwest-ern China. Although it has winter foliage it does go into a summer dormancy. In Europe it loses its foliage by late summer and resumes growth by late autumn. The new leaves are bright green and are either three- or five-foli-olate, the leaflets slender oval-lanceolate. The flowers are nodding, grouped together in axillary clusters. The four tepals are creamy white and only 2.5 cm (1 in) long. It has very prominent stamens longer than the tepals, with purple-red anthers. The seedheads are large and fluffy. *Flowering period:* early winter; *height:* 3–4 m (10–13 ft); *zones:* 8–9.

C. occidentalis var. occidentalis (Section Atragene) A native of the eastern parts of Canada and the USA which can be found on the Niagara Escarpment on Mount Nemo and in the Blue Ridge Mountains of North Carolina and Virginia. It makes a climbing or trailing shrub. The young stems are grooved, the deciduous leaves trifoliate, leaflets lanceolate to ovate, margins entire to 2–3-lobed, often serrate and downy beneath when young. The solitary, nodding flowers, produced from the previous season's ripened stems, are blue to blue-purple, sometimes rosy mauve, and are 4 cm (1½ in) deep. *Flowering period:* late spring to early summer; *height:* 2 m (6½ ft); *zones:* 3–9.

C. o. var. dissecta Native to the Cascade Mountains, Washington State. A variety with finely cut leaves and rosy-mauve to indigo flowers 4 cm (1½ in) long, seldom attaining 1 m (3¼ft) in height. *Flowering period:* late spring to early summer; *height:* 1 m (3¼ ft); *zones:* 3–9.

C. o. var. grosseserrata A native of the western part of the USA, Yukon, Colorado in the northwest USA and Saskatchewan in Canada, with leaflets usually entire, rarely 2–3-lobed, with 6 cm (2¼ in) long flowers, indigo occasionally white. *Flowering period:* late spring; *height:* 3 m (10 ft); *zones:* 3–9.

C. paniculata A variable New Zealand evergreen species which is dioecious, the male forms having stun-ning pink anthers while the female forms only produce a style and have generally smaller flowers, though they can have attractive leaves with a brown central bar to the leaflets. The dark shining green leaves are trifoliate, the leaflets ovate, obtuse, rounded or somewhat cordate at the base, entire or sometimes lobed. The white flowers are semi-nodding, saucer-shaped and 5 cm (2 in) across, borne in axillary clusters. A very good plant for a sunny, probably south-facing, wall with good drainage. *Flowering period:* early to mid-spring; *height:* 3–5 m (10–16½ ft) or possibly more; *zones:* 7–9.

C. p. 'Lobata' This plant has deeply lobed leaves and white flowers which are rather sparser and only 4 cm (1½ in) across. *Flowering period:* early to mid-spring; *height:* 2–3 m (6½–10 ft); *zones:* 7–9.

C. p. 'Bodnant' A very free-flowering plant which is hardy in North Wales, where it was raised at Bodnant Gardens by Lord Aberconway. This clone has slightly larger foliage in a bright green and larger flowers, 6 cm (2¼ in) in diameter. The tepals are white with a large central boss of pink stamens. *Flowering period:* early to mid-spring; *height:* 3–4 m (10–13 ft); *zones:* 7–9.

C. patens A variable species from China which has blue to white 10–12.5 cm (4–5 in) wide flowers with 6–8 tepals and red or yellow anthers. It is a deciduous climber, the leaves pinnately 3–5-foliolate, the leaflets ovate to oval-lanceolate, acute, entire. It has a compact habit, useful in a container. Only good forms should be used for garden cultivation. *Flowering period:* late spring to early summer; *height:* 2 m (6½ ft); *zones:* 4–9.

C. sibirica See *C. alpina* var. *sibirica*.

C. s. var. flavia See *C. alpina* var. *sibirica* 'Flavia'.

C. tenuiloba See *C. columbiana* var. *tenuiloba*.

C. × vedrariensis 'Highdown' (Section Montana) A deciduous, vigorous climbing cultivar raised from *C. chrysocoma* × *C. montana* var. *rubens*, and has the somewhat downy foliage of *C. chrysocoma*. The pink slightly cup-shaped flowers resemble the flowers of *C. chrysocoma* and are 5 cm (2 in) in diameter, with yellow anthers. *Flowering period:* late spring to early summer; *height:* 6 m (20 ft); *zones:* 7–9.

C. williamsii (Section Cheiropsis) A deciduous Japanese species with attractive foliage and a vigorous habit when established. The leaves are trifoliate, the leaflets

C. patens, a Chinese species photographed growing in the wild in Japan, where it has naturalized.

deeply serrated. Those borne from the previous season's stems in early spring are greyish-green and have a silver central band down the leaflet; the new leaves produced after flowering are a bright green. The nodding flowers, borne on the ripened previous season's stems, are 4 cm (1½ in) across and have four tepals, which are pointed, reflexing when old, cream in colour with pronounced cream stamens. As this plant is new to my collection its exact winter hardiness is unknown at present. It is best grown in a well-drained site on a south-facing or warm, sheltered wall, or under glass. *Flowering period:* early to mid-spring; *height:* 3 m (10 ft); *zones:* 7–9.

EARLY LARGE-FLOWERED CULTIVARS

The early large-flowered cultivars have been largely derived from *C. patens*, a species native to China and naturalized in Japan. They are generally compact in habit, growing to 2–3 m (6–10 ft). This group is decidu-

ous and the leaves are simple to trifoliate. The foliage is normally light to mid-green. They flower in late spring or early summer from the previous season's ripened stems and produce attractive seedheads. Many produce further flowers in the late part of the summer or early autumn and some are almost continuously flowering. Some bear a good second or even third crop of flowers on new growth. The length of new growth produced before the single terminal flower appears will vary from cultivar to cultivar, some producing growth of only 10–15 cm (4–6 in) before flowering, others some 60 cm (2 ft). Their main use as a garden plant is growing naturally through other wall-trained shrubs. However, because of their compact free-flowering habit, many of them are ideal for growing in containers with supports in small gardens or patios where clematis cannot be planted in the garden soil. Several of this group are scented, and this is stated in the individual entries.

These clematis belong to pruning group two and are winter hardy to zones 4–9 as a garden plant. Plants grown in severe climates will be killed down to ground

C. ALABAST™ 'Poulala' Ⓝ, an unusual greenish-cream clematis raised in Denmark and belonging to the early large-flowered section. For the best effect this cultivar should be grown out of direct sun.

level some winters, thus delaying the flowering season by 4–6 weeks, when flowers will be borne on new growth. In this case all old growth will need to be removed down to ground level. Clematis grown in containers in severe climates will require frost protection.

C. ALABAST™ 'Poulala' Ⓝ This Evison/Poulsen cultivar raised in Denmark in the late 1980s has 12–15 cm (4¾–6 in) wide greenish-cream well-formed round flowers with 6–8 tepals and creamy-yellow anthers in late spring. The mid and late summer flowers are smaller at 9 cm (3½ in). It has attractive slightly glaucous foliage. *Flowering period:* late spring to early summer, and late summer; *height:* 3 m (10 ft); *zones:* 4–9.

C. 'Andrew' This cultivar was raised from C. 'Prins

Hendrik' by Magnus Johnson in Sweden in about 1952. It is a compact plant with flowers 15–20 cm (6–8 in) across comprising eight overlapping tepals with wavy margins and purple to purplish-violet anthers and white filaments. The tepals are bluish-violet with shades of purple at the base of the middle bar. It has neat trifoliate leaves. *Flowering period:* early summer to late summer; *height:* 2 m (6½ ft), *zones:* 4–9.

C. 'Anna' A compact and free-flowering cultivar raised in Sweden in 1974 by Magnus Johnson, this clematis has 15 cm (6 in) wide rosy-pink fully rounded flowers with 6–8 tepals and red anthers. The early spring flowers are sometimes not the true colour, being rather greenish-pink. It does best in a sunny location. *Flowering period:* late spring to early summer, and late summer; *height:* 2.5 m (8¼ ft); *zones:* 4–9 .

C. ANNA LOUISE™ 'Evithree' An Evison/Poulsen cultivar with a very strong-coloured flower introduced by the author in 1993. It has 15 cm (6 in) wide violet flowers with 6–8 tepals with a contrasting reddish-purple central bar and striking reddish-brown anthers. Its compact free-flowering habit and long flowering make it ideal for container cultivation. *Flowering period:* late spring to early autumn; *height:* 2.5 m (8¼ ft); *zones:* 4–9.

C. 'Asao' A Japanese cultivar introduced by the author from Japan in the early 1980s, this plant has deep pink 15 cm (6 in) wide flowers which have the deepest colour at the edges of the 6–8 tepals and yellow anthers. It has attractive bronze foliage in the late spring. It has a very compact habit and is ideal for growing in a container. *Flowering period:* late spring to early summer, and late summer; *height:* 2.5 m (8¼ ft); *zones:* 4–9 .

C. 'Barbara Dibley' An old Jackman cultivar, raised in 1949, with 18 cm (7 in) deep petunia red flowers with 6–8 pointed tepals in the spring, the later flowers being much paler in colour and thinner in texture. The anthers are red. It is best on a west- or east-facing location. It has medium-sized attractive seedheads which have curly seed tails. *Flowering period:* late spring to early summer, and late summer ; *height:* 2.5–3 m (8¼–10 ft); *zones:* 4–9.

C. 'Barbara Jackman' A Jackman cultivar raised in 1952, with 6–8 mauve tepals which have a petunia-coloured central bar and contrasting yellow anthers. The 12–15 cm (4¾–6 in) wide flowers fade in strong sunlight so it is best on west- or east-facing locations. *Flowering period:* late spring to early summer, and late summer; *height:* 2.5–3 m (8¼–10 ft); *zones:* 4–9.

C. 'Bees' Jubilee' Raised in 1958 by Bees of Chester and named to commemorate their 25th anniversary. Its 15 cm (6 in) wide flowers have 6–8 mauve-pink tepals with a much deeper central bar and light brownish anthers. It is a very compact free-flowering plant, ideal for growing in a container and also suitable as a cut flower. It has medium-sized, attractive, spherical seedheads. *Flowering period:* spring to late summer; *height:* 2.5–3 m (8¼–10 ft); *zones:* 4–9. ♉

C. BLUE MOON™ 'Evirin' , an ideal plant for container cultivation and for the smaller garden.

C. BLUE MOON™ 'Evirin' ⊘ An Evison/Poulsen cultivar raised by the author and introduced in 1997, this is a compact free-flowering plant suitable for any position in the garden, the flowers retaining their colour best in a shady situation. The flowers measure 15–18 cm (6–7 in) across and have a base colour of white, which is suffused with pale lilac becoming darker at the edges of the eight tepals, shown to great effect by the contrasting dark red anthers. The tepals have most attractive wavy edges, a stunning feature of the flower. The slightly smaller summer flowers, 10 cm (4 in) across, are generally darker in colour. It is an ideal plant for container culture, for the patio or small garden and is a very good cut flower. *Flowering period*: late spring to early summer, and late summer to early autumn; *height*: 2.5–3 m (8¼–10 ft); *zones*: 4–9.

C. 'Bracebridge Star' A cultivar raised by Pennells of Lincoln in 1956 with 15 cm (6 in) wide star-shaped flowers which have 6–8 lavender-blue tepals with a carmine central bar and brownish-red anthers. *Flowering period*: late spring to early summer, and early autumn; *height*: 2.5–3 m (8¼–10 ft); *zones*: 4–9.

C. 'Burma Star' A very compact free-flowering cultivar with fully formed 11.5–12.5 cm (4½–5 in) flowers, raised by Barry Fretwell in the late 1980s/early 1990s. It has 6–8 very deep rich purple-blue tepals with red highlights and red anthers. It is an ideal plant for a container. *Flowering period*: late spring to early summer; *height*: 2.5 m (8¼ ft); *zones*: 4–9.

C. 'Carnaby' This compact free-flowering plant ideal for container culture was introduced by the author from the USA in the early 1980s. It has 6–8 deep pink tepals with a darker bar and red anthers in spring and paler flowers in the late summer. The flowers are 11.5–12.5 cm (4½–5 in) across. *Flowering period*: late spring to early summer, and late summer to early autumn; *height*: 2.5 m (8¼ ft); *zones*: 4–9.

C. 'Caroline' A cultivar from Barry Fretwell, raised in the 1990s, with a compact, neat habit and terminal flowers. The neat flowers are 9–11.5 cm (3½–4½ in) across and have 6–8 closely overlapping tepals with occasional thin inner tepals. They are a lovely pale dusky pink with a darker central bar at the base of the tepals, which also

C. 'Dawn', a compact plant well-suited to the small garden or container culture.

have a thin darker edge. The flower is a delightful pale pink on the reverse and has yellow anthers and prominent styles. The leaves are small, somewhat coarse, with 3–5 leaflets with crinkled edges. It is a useful compact plant, ideal for the small garden, but best grown out of direct sunlight to avoid the flower fading further. *Flowering period*: early summer to midsummer, and late summer; *height*: 2 m (6½ ft); *zones*: 4–9.

C. 'Charissima' This cultivar raised by Pennells of Lincoln and named in 1974 has a large flower 15–18 cm (6–7 in) across with 6–8 cerise pointed tepals, a deeper bar and deeper coloured veins throughout the flower. The anthers are dark maroon. It is a very attractive clematis with a free-flowering habit. *Flowering period*:

late spring to early summer; *height:* 2.5–3 m (8¼–10 ft); *zones:* 4–9.

C. **'Corona'** A compact plant raised in Sweden by Tage Lundell and introduced to the British Isles by the author in 1972. The profusely borne spring flowers are 10–15 cm (4–6 in) wide, with 6–8 light purple-pink tepals and red anthers. The late summer flowers are lighter in colour and fewer in number. It has medium-sized, attractive, spherical seedheads. *Flowering period:* late spring to early summer, and late summer; *height:* 2 m (6½ ft); *zones:* 4–9.

C. **'Dawn'** A very compact free-flowering plant ideal for a container, this cultivar was raised in Sweden by Tage Lundell and introduced to the British Isles by the author in 1969. It has bronze foliage in the spring and 12 cm (4¾ in) wide fully formed flowers with 6–8 pearly white tepals, suffused with pink, and deep red anthers, fading in strong sunlight. This plant is slightly more winter-hardy than most old-wood flowering clematis. It is suitable as a cut flower and has medium-sized, attractive, spherical seedheads. *Flowering period:* late spring to early summer, and late summer; *height:* 2 m (6½ ft); *zones:* 4–9.

C. **'Dorothy Tolver'** A cross between C. 'Vyvyan Pennell' and C. 'Niobe', raised by Jonathon Gooch and introduced by Thorncroft Nursery in 1993. The following is Ruth Gooch's description, as I am only just starting to grow this new cultivar. Flowers 15 cm (6 in) across, six overlapping tepals with textured, satiny surface and rounded, lightly crimpled edges, tapering to a point. The satiny tepals are mauve at the base, heavily overlaid with deep mauve-pink, and have bright buttercup-yellow anthers. *Flowering period:* late spring to early summer, and early to mid-autumn; *height:* 2.5–4 m (8–13 ft); *zones:* 4–9.

C. **'Dr Ruppel'** Raised in the Argentine and introduced by Jim Fisk in 1975, this is a very good compact, very free-flowering clematis, one of the best for container culture. It has 15 cm (6 in) wide flowers with 6–8 deep rose-pink tepals and a much deeper central bar. The anthers are light brown. It is suitable as a cut flower and has large, attractive, spherical seedheads with curly seed tails. *Flowering period:* late spring to early summer,

C. 'Edith', raised by the author and named after Edith Evison, his mother.

and late summer to early autumn; *height:* 2.5–3 m (8¼–10 ft); *zones:* 4–9. ♛

C. **'Edith'** The first cultivar raised by the author, this is a chance seedling from C. 'Mrs Cholmondeley' introduced in 1974. The 12 cm (4¾ in) wide flowers have 6–8 white tepals which have a central green bar in late spring and dark red anthers. It is very compact in habit, ideal for container culture. It is also suitable as a cut flower and has medium-sized, attractive, spherical

PLATE VIII

**EARLY LARGE-
FLOWERED CULTIVARS
FOR SMALL GARDENS
& CONTAINERS**

All flowers
are shown at
approximately
½ size

C. 'John Warren'

C. 'Burma Star'

C. 'Niobe'

C. 'Masquerade'

C. 'Lady Northcliffe'

C. 'Carnaby'

C. 'Gillian Blades'

C. 'Mrs
Cholmondeley'

seedheads. *Flowering period:* late spring to early summer, and late summer ; *height:* 2 m (6½ ft); *zones:* 4–9. ♔

C. 'Edouard Desfossé' This very compact clematis was raised in France by Desfossé and introduced in 1880. It is a very free-flowering plant in the spring, ideal for container culture. It has eight-tepalled, pale blue, 12 cm (4¾ in) wide flowers with a slightly darker bar and red anthers. The attractive seedheads are small and rounded. *Flowering period:* late spring to early summer; *height:* 2 m (6½ ft); *zones:* 4–9.

C. 'Elgar' A recent introduction with a good compact free-flowering habit, this cultivar has single to almost semi-double flowers 15–20 cm (6–8 in) across with 6–8 tepals when single and 11–12 tepals when double. The tepals are blue-mauve, reddish when young, and have pointed tips that reflex on themselves, being of slightly floppy habit. It has contrasting yellow anthers with pale mauve filaments, prominent styles and a delightful reverse to the tepals, revealing a whitish central band with purple ribs and a pretty mauvish-blue edge. The leaflets are large and have three pointed tips. It is a useful plant for container culture. *Flowering period:* late spring to early summer, and late summer; *height:* 2–3 m (6½–10 ft); *zones:* 4–9.

C. 'Elsa Späth' Raised in Berlin in 1891 by Späth, this is a very rewarding free-flowering, strong-growing plant which blooms over a long period. It has 15–18 cm (6–7 in) wide rounded flowers with mid-blue tepals, darker when first open, and deep red anthers. It is suitable as a cut flower. *Flowering period:* late spring to early autumn; *height:* 2.5–3 m (8¼–10 ft); *zones:* 4–9. ♔

C. 'Etoile de Paris' A very compact plant, ideal for growing in a container, raised in France by M. Christen of Versailles in 1885. It is free-flowering in late spring, bearing 12.5 cm (5 in) flowers with 6–8 mauve-blue very pointed tepals and red anthers. The seedheads are large and attractive, the seed tails forming a neat sphere shape. *Flowering period:* late spring to early summer; *height:* 2 m (6½ ft); *zones:* 4–9.

C. EVENING STAR™ 'Evista' Ⓢ A 1997 Evison/Poulsen cultivar raised by the author, this very large-flowered clematis has 20 cm (8 in) blooms with 6–8 broad tepals

C. EVENING STAR™ 'Evista' Ⓢ produces very large early summer flowers and a good crop of late flowers.

that overlap when young, become twisted with age and have wavy edges. The base colour is a plummy mauve which fades quickly to mauve, each tepal having a deep cerise bar and on the reverse three purple-red veins running down the central midrib. The centre of the flower has a very large boss of golden-yellow anthers and prominent styles in pinkish-yellow. The leaves are large, trifoliate with long petioles. This is a strong-growing plant suitable for a container but not in an exposed position because of the size of the flowers. It is very useful as a cut flower for large flower arrangements. *Flowering period:* early summer to late summer; *height:* 3 m (10 ft); *zones:* 4–9.

C. 'Fair Rosamond' A compact plant ideal for growing in a container, raised by Jackmans in 1871. It is free-flowering in the late spring. It has a scent like that of violets. The flowers are 12.5–15 cm (5–6 in) wide, with 6–8 white tepals with a pale pink central bar which fades gently. They have dark red anthers and medium-sized, well-shaped, rounded seedheads. *Flowering period:* late spring to early summer; *height:* 2 m (6½ ft); *zones:* 4–9.

C. 'Fireworks' This cultivar raised by John Treasure of Burford House Gardens in the early 1980s is a vigorous plant when established. It has large 18–20 cm (7–8 in) wide flowers in the late spring and early summer, with 6–8 blue-mauve tepals with a very deep petunia-red bar and dark red anthers. The late summer flowers are 12.5–15 cm (5–6 in) across. It is a dramatic flower, suitable for cut-flower arrangements. *Flowering period:* late spring to early summer, and late summer to early autumn; *height:* 3 m (10 ft); *zones:* 4–9. ♛

C. 'Fujimusume' A marvellous Japanese cultivar with delightful powdery blue flowers and yellow anthers, raised by Sejurn Arai in 1952. The 10–12.5 cm (4–5 in) wide flowers with 6–8 tepals are freely produced on this compact plant, ideal for a container. *Flowering period:* late spring to early summer, and late summer to early autumn; *height:* 2.5 m (8¼ ft); *zones:* 4–9.

C. 'Gillian Blades' A seedling from C. 'Lasurstern', introduced by Jim Fisk in 1975, this is a very free-flowering compact plant with beautifully shaped 12.5–15 cm (5–6 in) wide white flowers which have 6–8 pointed tepals with wavy edges. The anthers are creamy white. It is an ideal clematis for a container and is suitable as a cut flower. The flowers are followed by attractive spherical seedheads of medium size. *Flowering period:* early summer to late summer; *height:* 2.5 m (8¼ft); *zones:* 4–9. ♛

C. 'Guernsey Cream' This cultivar raised by the author and introduced in 1989 is a compact plant, free-flowering in the late spring. It has well-formed full 12.5 cm (5 in) wide flowers with 6–8 creamy-yellow overlapping tepals and yellow anthers. The late summer flowers are paler and only 7.5 cm (3 in) across. It is ideal for a container. *Flowering period:* late spring to early summer, and late summer; *height:* 2.5 m (8¼ ft); *zones:* 4–9.

C. 'Hainton Ruby' This is a strong-growing, repeat-flowering plant, introduced by Keith and Carol Fair in Lincolnshire in 1993. It has 15 cm (6 in) wide flowers which generally have six tepals. These are ruby red with purple highlights, giving the colour good depth, and the anthers are red. The flower has a gappy look because of the space between the base of the tepals, which just about overlap before the tips recurve. The leaves are trifoliate with broad leaflets. *Flowering period:* late spring to early summer, and late summer to early autumn; *height:* 3 m (10 ft); *zones:* 4–9.

C. 'Haku Ookan' A cultivar introduced by Jim Fisk in 1971 from Japan, the name translating as The White Royal Crown. It is a very free-flowering compact plant ideal for a container, with violet-blue 15 cm (6 in) wide flowers, eight overlapping tepals with pointed tips and contrasting yellow-white anthers. It is suitable as a cut flower and has small, well-formed, spherical seedheads. *Flowering period:* late spring to early summer, and late summer; *height:* 2.5 m (8¼ ft); *zones:* 4–9.

C. 'Helen Cropper' This cultivar raised by Vince and Sylvia Denny of Preston, England, in the early 1990s has 15–18 cm (6–7 in) wide flowers of eight overlapping tepals with wavy edges. The tepals are dusky pinky-mauve, with a darker central band when young and the colour deeper towards the edges of the tepals. The overall appearance of the colouring gives a mottled look to the flower. The filaments are creamy white and the anthers red. The reverse of the flowers is as pretty as the top side, with three central reddish ribs bounded by a band of white returning to a pinkish-mauve at the edges of the tepals. It has neat trifoliate leaves with pointed tips. *Flowering period:* late spring to early summer, and late summer; *height:* 2–3 m (6½–10 ft); *zones:* 4–9.

C. 'H. F. Young' Raised by Pennells of Lincoln and named in 1962, this is probably the most compact free-flowering plant, ideal for container culture. It has 12.5–15 cm (5–6 in) wide flowers with 6–8 wedgwood blue tepals and pale yellow anthers and well-formed, attractive, spherical seedheads with the seed tails arranged in swirls. *Flowering period:* late spring to early summer, and late summer; *height:* 2 m (6½ ft); *zones:* 4–9. ♛

C. 'Horn of Plenty', a free-flowering plant both in early spring and late summer.

C. 'Horn of Plenty' A compact plant, raised in Holland around 1962, which is very free-flowering in both early and late summer. In late spring and early summer, 18 cm (7 in) wide flowers are produced with 6–8 dark rosy-mauve overlapping tepals with a deeper central bar and crinkled edges. The anthers are red. The late summer flowers are produced more freely but are only 10–12.5 cm (4–5 in) wide and paler in colour. It is suitable as a cut flower and has attractive seedheads. It is ideal for a container. *Flowering period:* late spring to early summer, and late summer; *height:* 2–3 m (6½–10 ft); *zones:* 4–9. ♇

C. 'Ivan Olssen' Raised by Magnus Johnson in Sweden from C. 'The President' in 1955, this cultivar generally produces 10–12.5 cm (4–5 in) wide single flowers with 6–8 tepals, but occasionally semi-doubles. It is a com-

pact free-flowering plant with most unusual colouring. The pale blue to very pale mauve tepals have a creamy white broad central bar, the whole flower fading to ice blue. Contrasting neat red anthers are held on pinky-cream filaments. There is very pretty colouring to the reverse of the tepal, with a greenish-cream central band and three ribs with white to pale blue edges, darkest at the edges. The leaves are neat trifoliate, the leaflets lanceolate and apiculate. This plant has a repeat-flowering habit. *Flowering period:* late spring to early summer, and early autumn; *height:* 2 m (6½ ft); *zones:* 4–9.

C. 'James Mason' A cultivar raised by Barry Fretwell in 1984. The well-formed flowers, 10–12.5 cm (4–5 in) across, have 6–8 clear white tepals and contrasting dark red anthers. *Flowering period:* late spring to early summer, and late summer; *height:* 2.5–3 m (8¼–10 ft); *zones:* 4–9.

C. 'Joan Picton' Raised by Percy Picton and introduced by Jim Fisk in 1974, this is a compact plant, free-flowering in the spring. It has 12.5–15 cm (5–6 in) wide fully rounded lilac flowers, each of the 6–8 tepals having a lighter central bar, and red anthers. They are followed by small, neatly formed, spherical seedheads. This clematis is ideal for a container. *Flowering period:* late spring to early summer, and early autumn; *height:* 2 m (6½ ft); *zones:* 4–9.

C. 'John Warren' This cultivar raised by Pennells of Lincoln and named in 1968 has a very distinctive large flower up to 23 cm (9 in) in diameter with 6–8 very pointed overlapping tepals. The tepal colour is French grey, with three carmine bars and deep carmine edges, and the anthers are red. Because of the very large flowers it is best grown out of strong winds. *Flowering period:* late spring to early summer, and late summer to early autumn; *height:* 2.5–3 m (8¼–10 ft); *zones:* 4–9.

C. 'Kacper' A strong-looking plant with large, healthy, dark green, pointed leaflets, raised by Brother Stefan Franczak in Poland about 1970. It has a very large, imposing, full flower, 23 cm (9 in) in diameter, with 6–8 wavy-edged tepals which are deep mauve/ blue/purple with a deeper central band, fading gradually. The reverse of the tepals shows a broad central band of white with mauve margins. The anthers are red and the filaments clear white, and the seedheads are large. It is compact in habit, ideal for a container, but not in a windy position. *Flowering period:* late spring to early summer, and late summer to early autumn; *height:* 2.5 m (8¼ ft); *zones:* 4–9.

C. 'Kakio' See C. 'Pink Champagne'.

C. 'Kathleen Wheeler' Raised by Pennells of Lincoln and named in 1967, this cultivar is identical in habit to C. 'John Warren'. It has very large late spring and early summer flowers up to 23 cm (9 in) in diameter, with a good crop of late flowers. The flowers, with 6–8 plummy-purple tepals and delightful contrasting golden-yellow anthers, fade gently and are followed by attractive seed-heads. They are suitable as a cut flower. This clematis is best grown out of strong wind. *Flowering period:* late spring to early summer, and late summer to early autumn; *height:* 2.5–3 m (8¼–10 ft); *zones:* 4–9.

C. 'Ken Donson' Raised by Pennells of Lincoln and named in 1976, this cultivar has handsome large foliage and well-formed flowers 18 cm (7 in) across with 6–8 deep blue overlapping tepals and golden-yellow anthers. This clematis produces the most delightful, almost perfectly formed, spherical seedheads, where the seed tails are arranged very neatly – the best seedheads seen by the author. It is suitable as a cut flower and is ideal for a container. *Flowering period:* late spring to early summer, and late summer; *height:* 2.5–3 m (8¼–10 ft); *zones:* 4–9. ♈

C. 'King Edward VII' A compact free-flowering plant in the late spring and early summer which is ideal for container culture. It was raised by Jackmans in 1902. The lilac-mauve flowers are 15 cm (6 in) across with a pink central bar, sometimes with white tips, and light brown anthers. The 6–8 tepals may be greenish in colour in late spring. The later flowers are of a thinner texture. It is suitable as a cut flower. *Flowering period:* late spring to early summer, and late summer; *height:* 2.5 m (8¼ ft); *zones:* 4–9.

C. 'King George V' Raised by Jackmans before 1935, this is generally a shy-flowering cultivar with 6–8 mottled pale pink tepals which have a much darker central bar and pointed tips. The 15 cm (6 in) wide flowers have contrasting chocolate-coloured anthers. Occa-

sional semi-double flowers are produced. *Flowering period:* early summer and midsummer; *height:* 2.5 m (8¼ ft); *zones:* 4–9.

C. 'Königskind' A very compact, very free-flowering plant raised by F. M. Westphal in Germany in 1989, ideal for container culture for the patio or small garden. The mauve-blue flowers have a broad lighter-coloured central band with attractive veining. The 8–9 tepals are overlapping and the flower is cup-shaped and only 9–11 cm (3½–4¼ in) across, giving the impression of a small, almost semi-double, flower. The anthers are red, and the prominent styles are white. The flowers fade to give it a fairly ordinary clematis flower colour, but it is worth growing for its marvellously compact habit. *Flowering period:* late spring to early autumn; *height:* 2 m (6½ ft); *zones:* 4–9.

C. 'Lady Londesborough' Raised by Noble about 1868, this very compact plant ideal for a container is free-flowering in the spring, producing fully rounded flowers 12.5–15 cm (5–6 in) wide with 6–8 pale pinkish-mauve blue tepals and contrasting red anthers. They have a slight scent of violets and are followed by attractive seedheads. *Flowering period:* late spring to early summer, and late summer; *height:* 2 m (6½ ft); *zones:* 4–9.

C. 'Lady Northcliffe' A very good plant, free-flowering over a long period, which was raised by Jackmans in the early 1900s. It has a compact habit which makes it ideal for a container or small area. The 12 cm (4¼ in) diameter flowers have 6–8 wedgwood blue tepals and contrasting greenish-yellow anthers which often have black tips. *Flowering period:* early summer to late summer, and early autumn; *height:* 2 m (6½ ft); *zones:* 4–9.

C. 'Lasurstern' A fine, handsome clematis with well-formed flowers of overlapping wavy-edged tepals, introduced in Germany about 1905. The 18 cm (7 in) flowers have 6–8 deep lavender-blue flowers and contrasting yellow anthers. It has a compact but vigorous habit, ideal for a container. It is suitable as a cut flower and its seedheads are among the most outstanding, being large, attractive, neatly formed spheres. *Flowering period:* late spring to early summer, and late summer to early autumn; *height:* 2.5–3 m (8¼–10 ft); *zones:* 4–9. ♈

C. 'Lemon Chiffon' A cultivar raised by Dennis Bradshaw from Busheyfield Nursery, England, in the early 1990s which is a most useful addition to the pale yellow large-flowered clematis. It has attractive, small, rounded leaflets and neat open flowers with eight rounded, overlapping tepals. The flowers are 10–14 cm (4–5½ in) across and are pale yellow-cream with a hint of pale purple-pink on some. The anthers are yellow and the seedheads large. It has a compact habit, ideal for a container, and is a useful plant for a shady spot, but not too shady as this may cause the early flowers to open green. *Flowering period:* late spring to early summer, and early autumn; *height:* 2–3 m (6½–10 ft); *zones:* 4–9.

C. LIBERATION™ 'Evifive' ℕ, named in 1995 to commemorate the 50th Anniversary of the Liberation of the Channel Islands.

C. LIBERATION™ 'Evifive' ℕ A strong-growing Evison/Poulsen cultivar, raised by the author and introduced in 1995. The late spring flowers are huge, 23 cm (9 in) across, the later summer flowers much smaller and more gappy. The 6–8 pointed tepals are deep pink with a very deep cerise central band. These are offset by contrasting golden-yellow anthers which have pinkish-grey filaments. *Flowering period:* late spring to early summer, and late summer to early autumn; *height:* 3 m (10 ft); *zones:* 4–9.

C. 'Lincoln Star' Raised by Pennells of Lincoln and named in 1954, this cultivar has refreshing raspberry-pink tepals with a much deeper bar and contrasting red anthers. The flowers measure 15 cm (6 in) across and the 6–8 tepals are pointed. The late summer flowers are much paler in colour. It is suitable as a cut flower and does best out of full sun. *Flowering period:* late spring to early summer, and late summer to early autumn; *height:* 2.5–3 m (8¼–10 ft); *zones:* 4–9.

C. 'Lord Nevill' This cultivar raised by Cripps & Sons in about 1873 has very attractive 15 cm (6 in) wide flowers with pretty wavy edges to the 6–8 overlapping deep blue tepals which contrast with the deep red anthers. The flowers fade gently and are followed by smallish, open, spherical seedheads. It is suitable as a cut flower. *Flowering period:* late spring to early summer, and late summer; *height:* 2.5–3 m (8¼–10 ft); *zones:* 4–9. ♔

C. 'Marcel Moser' This attractive clematis raised by Moser of France in 1896 has been overshadowed by C. 'Nelly Moser', its flowers not being so dramatic. They are star-shaped, 15–18 cm (6–7 in) across, with 6–8 mauve tepals with a darker central bar and contrasting red anthers. It is suitable as a cut flower and has smallish, neatly sphere-shaped seedheads. *Flowering period:* early summer and mid-autumn; *height:* 2.5–3 m (8¼–10 ft); *zones:* 4–9.

C. 'Masquerade' This plant is of unknown origin and was named and introduced by the author in 1993. It has good large early summer flowers and a plentiful crop of lighter-coloured late summer flowers. The flowers, 18 cm (7 in) in diameter, have 6–8 mauvish-blue pointed tepals with a mauve central band and dark red anthers. Its free-flowering and compact habit make it ideal for a container. *Flowering period:* late spring to early summer, and late summer to early autumn; *height:* 3 m (10 ft); *zones:* 4–9.

C. 'Minister' This cultivar was raised in Estonia by Uno Rivistik in 1982 with C. 'Hagley Hybrid' as one of its parents, giving it its short, compact, free-flowering habit. The fully rounded 13–15 cm (5¼–6 in) wide flowers have 6–8 overlapping tepals which are red-purple fading to mauve, delightful contrasting yellow anthers on red filaments and prominent styles. The greenish central mid-rib to the reverse of the tepals is also most unusual. It has smooth trifoliate leaves. A useful plant for a small garden and for container culture, only just becoming available in western Europe. *Flowering period:* early summer, and late summer to early autumn; *height:* 2 m (6½ ft); *zones:* 4–9.

C. 'Miss Bateman' This old cultivar raised by Charles Noble in the mid-1860s has a compact free-flowering habit in the early summer. The fully rounded 12.5–15 cm (5–6 in) wide flowers have 6–8 clear white tepals and contrasting red anthers and are scented slightly of violets. Some further flowers appear in late summer to early autumn. It is suitable as a cut flower and has medium-sized, well-formed, spherical seedheads. This is an ideal clematis for a small garden or for container culture. *Flowering period:* late spring to early summer, and late summer to early autumn; *height:* 2 m (6½ ft); *zones:* 4–9. ♈

C. 'Moonlight' (syn. C. 'Yellow Queen') A distinctive variant of C. *patens*, possibly of wild origin, obtained by the author from Tage Lundell in Sweden in the 1970s. The attractive leaves are cordate to trifoliate, as with most large-flowered clematis, but though the margins are entire they are undulating. The delightful creamy-yellow flowers with yellow anthers have 6–8 tepals which overlap and become slightly twisted with age. The early summer flowers are 18 cm (7 in) in diameter and produce very attractive small to medium, very elegantly sphere-shaped seedheads. This clematis has a slight scent of violets. It is sometimes a shy grower but can be vigorous once established. *Flowering period:* late spring to early summer, and late summer; *height:* 2.5 m (8¼ ft); *zones:* 4–9.

C. 'Mrs Cholmondeley' A classic clematis raised by Charles Noble in 1873, with very large, somewhat gappy early summer flowers and a good crop of later flowers. The 18 cm (7 in) wide light lavender-blue flowers have 6–8 tepals and light chocolate-coloured anthers. It is free-flowering over a long period and is suitable as a cut flower. Medium-sized, rather spiky seedheads follow the flowers. *Flowering period:* late spring to early autumn; *height:* 2.5–3 m (8¼–10 ft); *zones:* 4–9. ♈

C. 'Mrs N. Thompson' A very compact clematis raised by Pennells of Lincoln and named in 1961, free-flowering in late spring to early summer and ideal for a small garden or for container culture. The 12.5–15 cm (5–6 in) wide, bluish-purple flowers are impressive, with a dark petunia central band to each of the 6–8 tepals and red anthers. *Flowering period:* late spring to early summer, and late summer; *height:* 2.5 m (8¼ ft); *zones:* 4–9.

C. 'Mrs P. B. Truax' This very early flowering cultivar thought to have been raised by Jackmans before 1939 has extremely pretty periwinkle blue 12.5 cm (5 in) wide flowers with 6–8 tepals and attractive pale yellow anthers. The flowers are followed by smallish, well-formed, spherical seedheads. It is compact, ideal for a small garden or container culture. *Flowering period:* late spring to early summer, and late summer; *height:* 2 m (6 ½ ft); *zones:* 4–9.

C. 'Myojo' A colourful Japanese cultivar, raised by Seidjuro Arai in the early 1980s, with violet-purple 12.5–15 cm (5–6 in) wide flowers with a dominant central boss of golden anthers. Each of the 6–8 tepals has a colourful darker bar. Its compact habit makes it ideal for a small garden or container culture. *Flowering period:* late spring to early summer, and late summer; *height:* 2.5 m (8¼ ft); *zones:* 4–9.

C. 'Natascha' This compact and free-flowering cultivar raised in Germany by F. M. Westphal in 1989 has rich mauve-blue flowers, the six tepals having pointed tips which recurve as they mature. The flowers are 12–14 cm (4¾–5½ in) in diameter and have prominent red anthers on pinkish-red filaments. The reverse of the tepals is also attractive, possessing a white central band and mauve margins. The flower colour fades pleasantly. This clematis has three narrow pointed leaflets. It is a useful plant for the smaller garden and for container culture.

PLATE IX

EARLY LARGE-FLOWERED CULTIVARS SUITABLE FOR WALL-TRAINED SHRUBS

All flowers are shown at approximately ½ size

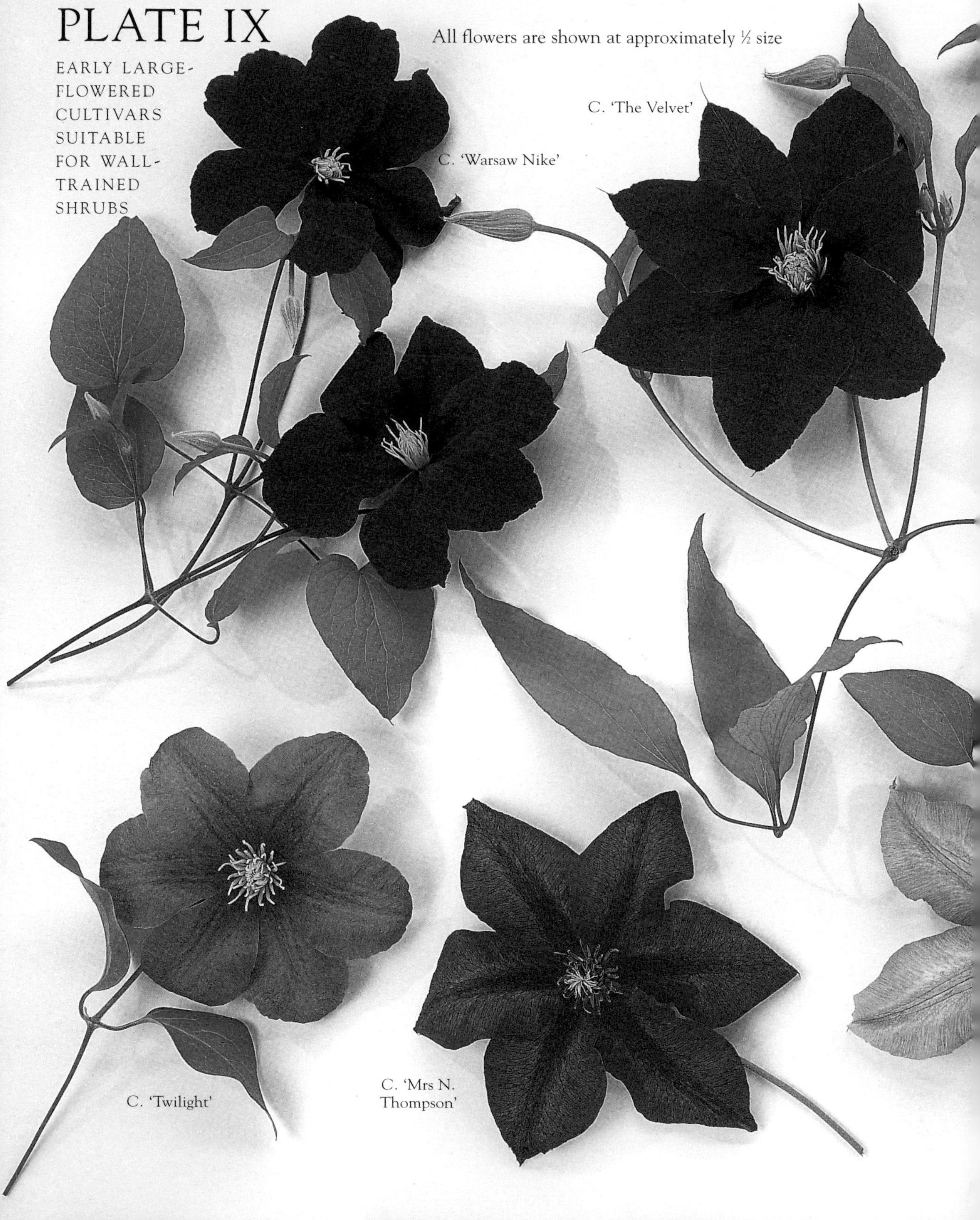

C. 'Warsaw Nike'
C. 'The Velvet'
C. 'Twilight'
C. 'Mrs N. Thompson'

C. 'Kacper'

C. 'Sealand Gem'

C. 'Ivan Olssen'

C. 'Helen Cropper'

Flowering period: late spring to early summer, and late summer; *height:* 2.5 m (8¼ ft); *zones:* 4–9.

C. 'Nelly Moser' Raised by Moser in France in 1897, this is probably the second most famous clematis name after C. 'Jackmanii' and is a plant that has proved its worth, always performing well. Its biggest disadvantage is that it fades badly in strong sunlight, but it does very well in full shade. The cartwheel-like 15–18 cm (6–7 in) wide flowers have 6–8 pointed pale mauve tepals with a deeper lilac central bar and dark red anthers. They are followed by very attractive, large, well-formed, spherical seedheads. It is ideal for container culture, and is suitable as a cut flower. *Flowering period:* late spring to early summer, and late summer to early autumn; *height:* 2.5–3 m (8¼–10 ft); *zones:* 4–9. ♀

C. 'Niobe' Raised in Poland by Wladyslaw Noll and introduced by Jim Fisk in 1975, this clematis has become a bestseller throughout the world. It is free-

C. 'Pink Champagne' (syn. C. 'Kakio'), an ideal plant for container cultivation.

flowering over a long period, making it ideal for container culture. The deep red 15 cm (6 in) wide flowers with 6–8 tepals become very dark in hot climates and have contrasting yellow anthers. It is suitable as a cut flower. *Flowering period:* late spring to early autumn; *height:* 2.5–3 m (8¼–10 ft); *zones:* 4–9. ♀

C. 'Pink Champagne' (syn. C. 'Kakio') A Japanese cultivar introduced by the author to Europe in the early 1980s, this is a good free-flowering plant of a compact nature, ideal for container culture. The 15 cm (6 in) wide flowers have 6–8 purplish-pink tepals which are darker at the margins. The tepals overlap, making a full flower. It has contrasting compact yellow anthers with a prominent style and medium-sized, attractive, spherical seedheads. *Flowering period:* late spring to early summer, and late summer to early autumn; *height:* 2.5 m (8¼ ft); *zones:* 4–9.

C. 'Prince Philip' A plant reintroduced by the author from the USA in the 1980s, with 15 cm (6 in) flowers. The 7–8 blue-mauve tepals have a plum-coloured central bar and crimpled edges. As they mature the tepals become twisted but to begin with they overlap at the base. The anthers are a light brown. It is pleasant flower when young but fades badly, though the plant has a useful free-flowering habit. The leaves are trifoliate, the leaflets being long and pointed with long petiolules. *Flowering period*: late spring to late summer; *height*: 3 m (10 ft); *zones*: 4–9.

C. 'Richard Pennell' A very handsome clematis raised by Pennells of Lincoln in 1974 with 15–18 cm (6–7 in) wide flowers. The 6–8 tepals are a rich purple-blue which fades gently, and overlap to make a full flower. The anthers are golden-yellow and have unusual red filaments. *Flowering period*: early summer to late summer, and early autumn; *height*: 2.5–3 m (8¼–10 ft); *zones*: 4–9.

C. ROYAL VELVET™ 'Evifour' Ⓢ This extremely free-flowering clematis of compact habit is an Evison/Poulsen cultivar raised by the author and introduced in 1993. It is ideal for a small garden or container culture. It has slightly bronze-coloured foliage in the spring and the 15 cm (6 in) wide flowers have 6–8 rich velvet purple tepals and dark red anthers. *Flowering period*: late spring to early autumn; *height*: 2 m (6½ ft); *zones*: 4–9.

C. 'Ruby Glow' Introduced by Jim Fisk in 1975, this compact plant is very free-flowering in the spring and also produces a good crop of late summer flowers. It is ideal for a small garden or container culture. The 15–18 cm (6–7 in) wide flowers have 6–8 rosy mauve tepals with a ruby glow and red anthers. *Flowering period*: late spring to early autumn; *height*: 2.5 m (8¼ ft); *zones*: 4–9.

C. 'Scartho Gem' This plant was raised by Pennells of Lincoln and named in 1973. The 15–18 cm (6–7 in) wide flowers are very pretty, the 6–8 bright pink tepals having a much deeper-coloured central band. The tepals are overlapping and have slightly wavy edges and the anthers are light pinkish-brown. The later season's flowers are paler in colour and smaller, at 15 cm (6 in). *Flowering period*: late spring to early summer, and late summer; *height*: 2.5 m (8¼ ft); *zones*: 4–9.

C. 'Sealand Gem' Raised by Bees of Chester in 1957 from the same batch of seedlings as C. 'Bees' Jubilee', this is not the most free-flowering plant but it has interesting 12.5 cm (5 in) wide lavender flowers, each of the 6–8 tepals having a dark pink central bar. The anthers are light brown. *Flowering period*: early to late summer; *height*: 3 m (10 ft); *zones*: 4–9.

C. 'Sho Un' A strong-growing clematis raised in Japan by Mr Sakurai before 1977. The six overlapping tepals are blue with purple highlights and make a fully rounded flower 18 cm (7 in) across. The anthers are a contrasting yellow. *Flowering period*: early summer to early autumn; *height*: 2.5–3 m (8¼–10 ft); *zones*: 4–9.

C. 'Silver Moon' This very compact clematis was raised by Percy Picton and introduced by Jim Fisk in 1971. It has a most unusual-coloured flower in silvery mauve, profusely borne in the late spring and early summer. The flowers are 15 cm (6 in) across, with creamy-white anthers, and the 6–8 tepals overlap, making a very full flower. Occasional late summer flowers are produced. It is ideal for a small garden or container culture. *Flowering period*: late spring to early summer, and late summer; *height*: 2 m (6½ ft); *zones*: 4–9. ♛

C. 'Sir Garnet Wolseley' This compact clematis raised by Jackmans in about 1874 is generally the first large-flowered clematis to flower. It is free-flowering in the late spring and early summer, with occasional late summer flowers. The fully rounded 12.5–15 cm (5–6 in) flowers have 6–8 mauve-blue tepals which fade gently and red anthers. They are slightly violet-scented. It is ideal for the small garden or container culture. *Flowering period*: late spring to early summer, and late summer; *height*: 2.5 m (8¼ ft); *zones*: 4–9.

C. 'Snow Queen' Raised by Alister Keay in New Zealand and introduced by Jim Fisk in 1983, this very good plant has large well-formed early summer flowers 15–18 cm (6–7 in) across and plenty of late summer flowers measuring 10 cm (4 in). The 6–8 tepals are white tinged with pale pink and sometimes very pale blue, and the anthers are red. It is of compact habit, ideal for container culture, and is suitable as a cut flower. *Flowering period*: late spring to early summer, and late summer to early autumn; *height*: 2.5 m (8¼ ft); *zones*: 4–9.

C. 'Souvenir du Capitaine Thuilleaux' This old French cultivar of compact habit, raised by J. Thuilleaux of St Cloud in 1918, is ideal for the small garden or for container culture. It has lightly violet-scented, fully rounded 15 cm (6 in) wide flowers with 6–8 creamy-pink tepals which have deeper pink bands and crinkled edges to the tepals. The anthers are dark red. It is very free-flowering in the late spring and early summer. *Flowering period:* late spring to early summer, and late summer ; *height:* 2 m (6½ ft); *zones:* 4–9.

C. 'Special Occasion' This is a seedling from 'Mrs Cholmondeley', raised by amateur breeder Ken Pyne and introduced by Pennells Nurseries in the mid 1990s. The 10–12.5 cm (4–5 in) wide flowers have 6–8 rounded tepals which are pale bluish-pink, lighter in the centre of the tepal, and contrasting light brown anthers. It is a compact plant, suitable for growing in a container. *Flowering period:* early summer to midsummer; *height:* 2 m (6½ ft); *zones:* 4–9.

C. SUGAR CANDY™ 'Evione'Ⓢ An strong-growing Evison/Poulsen cultivar introduced in 1994 which is free-flowering both in early summer and late summer. It has 15–18 cm (6–7 in) wide flowers with 6–8 pointed tepals of a pinkish-mauve colour with a darker central bar and contrasting yellow anthers with grey filaments. For the best colour, grow it out of strong sunlight. *Flowering period:* late spring to early autumn; *height:* 3 m (10 ft); *zones:* 4–9.

C. 'Sunset' A very good free-flowering plant, raised in the USA by Steffens Clematis Nursery in the 1980s and introduced to Europe by the author. It has 15 cm (6 in) early summer flowers and masses of late summer flowers. The 6–8 tepals are deep plummy red with purple highlights and the anthers are a good yellow. *Flowering period:* late spring to early autumn; *height:* 2.5 m (8¼ ft); *zones:* 4–9.

C. 'The President' Raised by Charles Noble in 1876, this is a classic clematis with a long flowering period. It has 15 cm (6 in) wide rich purple flowers with dark red anthers. The 6–8 tepals overlap, making a very full flower, the tips being somewhat pointed. Its compact habit makes it ideal for a small garden and for container culture. It is suitable as a cut flower and has attractive rather open,

spiky seedheads. *Flowering period:* late spring to early autumn; *height:* 3 m (10 ft); *zones:* 4–9. ♕

C. 'The Velvet' This cultivar raised in Japan by Hirashi Hayakawa in the 1990s has 6–8 pointed tepals which give it a star-like appearance. The 18 cm (7 in) wide flowers have overlapping blue tepals which have a purple central bar and contrasting yellow anthers. The reverse of the flower is attractive, with three red veins on a central white band and pale blue edges. It has a good repeat flowering habit. *Flowering period:* late spring to early summer, and late summer to early autumn; *height:* 2–3 m (6½–10 ft); *zones:* 4–9.

C. 'Twilight' This cultivar raised by Percy Picton in the 1970s has a well-rounded flower, 13–15 cm (5¼–6 in) across. The 6–8 tepals open deep mauve-pink, with pink shading at the base, fading slowly to light mauve-pink; the anthers are yellow. It has a compact, free-flowering habit, ideal for the small garden or container culture. *Flowering period:* late spring to late summer; *height:* 2.5 m (8¼ ft); *zones:* 4–9.

C. 'Ulrique' This cultivar was raised by Magnus Johnson in Sweden in 1952 but was not sold until 1970. It is a plant of vigorous habit with flowers 12.5–18 cm (5–7 in) across, the six tepals having somewhat wavy margins and pointed tips. They are lavender violet with a broad central bar of amethyst, and the anthers are wine-purple – an interesting flower but not distinct in comparison to others of similar colouring. *Flowering period:* early summer to midsummer, and late summer; *height:* 2.5 m (8¼ ft); *zones:* 4–9.

C. VINO™ 'Poulvo'Ⓢ This is an Evison/Poulsen cultivar raised in Denmark in the early 1990s, bearing stunning petunia-red flowers 15–18 cm (6–7 in) across with 6–8 tepals and contrasting yellowy-cream anthers. The late summer flowers are much paler in colour and 10–12.5 cm (4–5 in) across. It has attractive foliage and is suitable as a cut flower. It is ideal for container culture. *Flowering period:* late spring to late summer ; *height:* 3 m (10 ft); *zones:* 4–9.

C. 'Wada's Primrose' This plant was introduced by the author from Kiyoshi Wada of Hakoneya Nurseries in Japan in the 1970s. It is very close to C. *patens* and may well be a form of it. It is sometimes slow-growing but thrives and flowers very well in hot climates, such as that of California. The flowers are 15 cm (6 in) in diameter with yellow anthers and 8–10 attractive creamy-yellow tepals that fade to creamy-white; they have a slight primrose scent. It has medium-sized, rather attractive, spherical seedheads. *Flowering period:* late spring to early summer; *height:* 2.5 m (8¼ ft); *zones:* 4–9.

C. 'Warsaw Nike' (syn. C. 'Warszawska Nike') Raised by Brother Stefan Franczak in Poland and introduced by Jim Fisk in 1986, this clematis has a very dramatic coloured flower, 15 cm (6 in) in diameter, with 6–8 rich velvety red-purple tepals and contrasting pale yellow anthers. It needs a light background to show the flowers off to best effect. It is a very free-flowering plant, generally flowering on the new growth but with some old-wood flowers. *Flowering period:* early to late summer, and early autumn; *height:* 2.5–3 m (8¼–10 ft); *zones:* 4–9.

C. 'Warszawska Nike' See C. 'Warsaw Nike'.

C. 'Will Goodwin' This clematis raised by Pennells of Lincoln and named in 1961 has an attractive clear mid-blue flower 15 cm (6 in) across with 6–8 overlapping tepals which have pointed tips and wavy margins. The anthers are bright yellow. It flowers very well in late summer and is suitable as a cut flower. *Flowering period:* early summer to late summer, and early autumn; *height:* 3 m (10 ft); *zones:* 4–9. ♈

C. 'William Kennett' A reliable old cultivar raised by Mr H. Cobbet in Surrey, England, in 1875. The six pale lilac-blue tepals form a fully rounded flower 12.5–15 cm (5–6 in) across. They are pointed and overlapping, and when young have wavy edges. The anthers are dark red. *Flowering period:* early summer to late summer; *height:* 2.5 m (8¼ ft); *zones:* 4–9.

C. 'Yellow Queen' See C. 'Moonlight'.

DOUBLE & SEMI-DOUBLE LARGE-FLOWERED CULTIVARS

The double and semi-double cultivars have mostly been derived from the old Japanese double or semi-double cultivars introduced in the 19th century, or by seedlings as clones of C. *patens*, or as sports (mutations) from single large-flowered types. The main crop of double or semi-double flowers is produced from the previous season's ripened stems in the very late spring or early summer. Some cultivars produce single flowers on the current season's stems later in the summer or in early autumn though some are always double or semi-double, the later flowers generally not being so fully double as the early summer flowers. Some may produce both double and single flowers at the same time. Only one is scented – C. 'Veronica's Choice'. The length of flowering stem, as with the early-flowering large-flowered cultivars, varies from cultivar to cultivar. These clematis are deciduous and the leaves are simple to trifoliate.

Their main use as garden plants is to take advantage of their large attractive flowers and grow them through other wall-trained shrubs to give added colour. The foliage and framework of these other shrubs gives the large double flowers much-needed protection from rain and wind. This group may also be used as container-grown plants for the patio, though the very large-flowered types should not be placed in a windy position.

C. ARCTIC QUEEN™ 'Evitwo' Ⓝ is the best double white clematis available.

The double and semi-double cultivars belong to pruning group two and are winter hardy to zones 4–9 as a garden plant. Those grown in extremely cold climates will be killed to ground level in some winters and therefore no early flowers will be produced, only the mid-summer blooms, so cultivars which flower double on old and current season's growth should be chosen. Clematis grown in containers in severe climates will require frost protection to retain the previous season's ripened stems.

This group of clematis is best planted in a position facing south, west or east. If planted on a shady north-facing position, the first crop of flowers may open slightly green or misshapen due to poor light levels.

C. Arctic Queen™ 'Evitwo' ⊘ An outstanding double clematis that is an Evison/Poulsen cultivar, raised by the author and introduced in 1994. This plant far out-performs any other double clematis currently available for the amount of flowers produced, and they are double on both old and new growth. They are 10–18 cm (4–7 in) in diameter, with clear creamy-white tepals and yellow anthers. This plant is ideal for a small garden or container culture, has good foliage and is suitable for cut flowers. *Flowering period:* early summer to early autumn, always double; *height:* 3 m (10 ft); *zones:* 4–9.

C. 'Beauty of Worcester' Raised by Richard Smith & Co. of Worcester and introduced in 1886, this is a marvellously coloured clematis but a shy grower. The 12.5–15 cm (5–6 in) fully double flowers in early summer are deep blue with a hint of red, while the late summer single flowers reveal contrasting yellowy-cream anthers. It is suitable as a cut flower. *Flowering period:* early summer (double), late summer (single); *height:* 2.5 m (8¼ ft); *zones:* 4–9.

C. 'Belle of Woking' Raised by Jackmans in 1875, this is somewhat weak in constitution but a pleasing plant when established. The flowers, 10 cm (4 in) in diameter and always double, open silvery-mauve and fade gradually to silvery-grey. They have creamy-white anthers. The tepals are small but it is a very fully double flower in early summer. It is suitable as a cut flower and as a container plant. *Flowering period:* early summer to late summer, always double; *height:* 2.5 m (8¼ ft); *zones:* 4–9.

C. 'Countess of Lovelace' A cultivar raised by Jackmans before 1876 which has very attractive 12.5 cm (5 in) wide semi-double to double flowers with pale lavender tepals which are narrow and very pointed at the tips in early summer. The anthers are yellow. It produces slightly gappy single flowers in mid to late summer, being floppy in habit also. It is suitable for container culture. *Flowering period:* early summer (double), late summer (single); *height:* 2.5 m (8¼ ft); *zones:* 4–9.

C. 'Daniel Deronda' A strong-growing plant raised by Charles Noble in 1882 with very large 18–20 cm (7–8 in) wide semi-double or single flowers in early summer and smaller single flowers mid to late summer, produced in good numbers. The flowers have tepals which fade gradually from the deep purple-blue with plummy highlights at opening to a purple-blue, with creamy-yellow anthers – a pleasing flower. This plant is ideal for container culture and produces the most unusual and attractive seedheads of any clematis, with seed tails that form a sphere and then have a further twist, or topknot, at the top. *Flowering period:* early summer (semi-double), midsummer to early autumn (single); *height:* 2.5 m (8¼ ft); *zones:* 4–9. ♀

C. 'Duchess of Edinburgh' An old classic clematis, raised by Jackmans before 1876 and the best double white until the introduction of C. Arctic Queen™ 'Evitwo' ⊘. By comparison, it is shy flowering. It was described by Moore & Jackman as having a scent to fill a room, though in fact its scent seems slight. It retains its foliage much later than most large-flowered clematis. The fully double flowers (on old and new growth) have several rows of green outer tepals and occasionally the flower can be fully green in the early summer. It has creamy-white anthers. The early flowers are 12.5 cm (5 in) in diameter, the later flowers smaller. It is suitable as a cut flower. *Flowering period:* early summer to early autumn, always double; *height:* 2.5–3m (8¼–10 ft); *zones:* 4–9.

C. 'Glynderek' A plant with attractive deep blue double flowers in early summer and single flowers in midsummer, introduced by Jim Fisk in 1985. The early flowers are 12.5 cm (5 in) in diameter and the single flowers reveal purple-violet anthers. *Flowering period:* early summer (double), mid to late summer (single); *height:* 2.5 m (8¼ ft); *zones:* 4–9.

C. 'Jackmanii Alba' This plant raised by Charles Noble before 1877 by crossing C. 'Jackmanii' with C. 'Fortunei' has the vigour of the former and the flower form of the latter. It produces 15 cm (6 in) diameter pointed flowers, semi-double in early summer, with outer tepals which are bluish-mauve, often splashed with green and with green tips, the inner tepals being a bluish-white. The midsummer single flowers are creamy bluish-white and show light choco-late-coloured anthers. *Flowering period:* early summer (semi-double), midsummer to early autumn (single); *height:* 3 m (10 ft); *zones:* 4–9.

C. 'Jackmanii Rubra' This is an old cultivar with very attractive semi-double and single flowers, introduced before 1877 by Charles Noble, Sunningdale Nurseries, Berkshire, England. The semi-double flowers are 12.5 cm (5 in) in diameter with crimson, slightly purple tepals, while the single flowers have a clear crimson colour. The anthers are a contrasting yellow. It is strong-growing and free-flowering when established, with a good crop of single flowers. *Flowering period:*

C. JOSEPHINE™ 'Evijohill' Ⓢ is an outstanding cultivar which always produces double flowers.

early summer (semi-double), midsummer to early autumn (single); *height:* 2.5 m (8¼ ft); *zones:* 4–9.

C. JOSEPHINE™ 'Evijohill' Ⓢ A fascinating new double cultivar found by Josephine Hill in England and introduced by the author as an Evison/Poulsen cultivar in 1998. This is probably a sport from another large-flowered early-flowering clematis but its history is not available. During the early summer, the flowers when first opening generally have 6–8 base tepals which are almost bronze in colour, tinged with green, with a darker bar. The colour becomes more lilac with a pink bar in mid summer. As with most doubles, the inner tepals are slower to open, giving an almost three-layered appear-ance. The inner tepals are also tinged with green, and have a narrow central bar. As the flower ages, the base or outer tepals fall, creating a pompom effect. There are no anthers. It is marvellous for flower arranging and a great plant for container culture or for the small garden. It is best to plant it in partial to full sun otherwise the full beauty of its flower colour will not be achieved, though if green flowers are required for unusual floral arrangements it can be planted in a shady northeast or northwest position. The most flowers will be produced in a full sun position. It has neat trifoliate leaves. *Flowering period:* early summer to early autumn (always double); *height:* 2.5 m (8¼ ft); *zones:* 4–9.

C. 'Kathleen Dunford' A cultivar introduced by Jim Fisk in 1962 with semi-double or single flowers. The semi-double flowers are 18 cm (7 in) across with only 2–3 layers of tepals which are narrow and pointed at the tips. They are purplish-pink in colour, becoming mottled and mauve-blue at the margins. The anthers are deep red. Occasionally, the single flowers have extra inner tepals. *Flowering period:* early summer (semi-double), late summer to early autumn (single); *height:* 2.5 m (8¼ ft); *zones:* 4–9.

C. 'Kiri Te Kanawa' A stunning very free-flowering fully double clematis on both old and new growth, raised by Barry Fretwell in 1986. The early flowers are 15 cm (6 in) in diameter, becoming smaller towards late summer. The tepals are deep blue and reveal a centre of cream anthers. It is suitable for container culture and as a cut flower. *Flowering period:* early summer to early autumn always double; *height:* 3 m (10 ft); *zones:* 4–9.

C. 'Lady Caroline Nevill' A fine old cultivar, raised by Cripps & Sons before 1866, which has been used as a commercial cut flower clematis in the past. It is strong-growing but not very free-flowering. The early semi-double flowers are at least 15 cm (6 in) across and the tepals are of a soft white, with a mauve bar and light chocolate-coloured anthers. The single flowers produced in summer are paler in colour and have overlapping tepals with tapered points. It is suitable as a cut flower. *Flowering period:* early summer (semi-double), mid to late summer (single); *height:* 3 m (10 ft); *zones:* 4–9.

C. 'Louise Rowe' Introduced by Jim Fisk in 1984, this cultivar occasionally produces very attractive double, semi-double and single flowers all at the same time. The early flowers can be 12.5–15 cm (5–6 in) across. The colour varies with light levels and ages from pale mauve to nearly white, with cream anthers. The single summer flowers are paler in colour, but still pretty. It is ideal for container culture and suitable as a cut flower. *Flowering period:* early summer (double), mid to late summer (single); *height:* 2–2.5 m (6½–8¼ ft); *zones:* 4–9.

C. 'Miss Crawshay' A cultivar raised by Jackmans before 1877 which has charming semi-double flowers in early summer, single later. They are 12.5 cm (5 in) wide, pink shaded with lilac, a soft colouring with a slight bronze-coloured bar. The inner tepals are rather short and narrow. The pretty single flowers have pale brown anthers. It is not very free-flowering but has dark green, very full foliage, retaining the colour well into late summer. *Flowering period:* early summer (semi-double), mid to late summer (single); *height:* 2.5 m (8¼ ft); *zones:* 4–9.

C. 'Mrs George Jackman' A delightful clematis raised by Jackmans before 1877 with clear fresh foliage, very clean creamy-white tepals and light brown anthers. The semi-double flowers have a marvellous form and seem almost perfect. The early flowers are 15 cm (6 in) across and are fully rounded, with overlapping tepals tapering to pointed tips. The single flowers are produced in profusion. It is ideal for container culture and suitable as a cut flower. *Flowering period:* early summer (semi-double), mid to late summer (single); *height:* 2.5 m (8¼ ft); *zones:* 4–9. ♔

C. 'Mrs George Jackman', a charming white semi-double or single-flowered plant.

C. 'Mrs Spencer Castle' This cultivar raised by Jackmans in about 1913 has semi-double and single flowers, the former resembling a pink water-lily. The 15 cm (6 in) early flowers have long pointed outer tepals and rather shorter inner tepals which protrude from the centre of the flower. The colour is a sugary soft pink with occasional hints of red, set off by creamy yellow anthers. The single flowers are also attractive. It is not very free-flowering. *Flowering period:* early summer (semi-double), mid to late summer (single); *height:* 3 m (10 ft); *zones:* 4–9.

C. 'Multi Blue' A sport from 'The President' developed in Boskoop, Holland. Discovered in 1983 and not yet fully stabilized. The author has selected four clones, one reverting back to 'The President' but stronger and more vigorous in habit. The general description of this unusual flower is as follows; 6–8 outer tepals of a deep navy blue forming a well-rounded flower. The inner tepals are either blue or reddish-purple-blue in colour, very narrow in form, producing a central tuft of many tepals which remain when the outer tepals have fallen away. They have white tips to the points of the tepals, giving a spiky appearance. The anthers are absent. The early flowers are up to 15 cm (6 in) across and are generally more fully double than the later flowers. It flowers over a long period and is always double or semi-double when stable. It is suitable as a cut flower and is ideal for the small garden or for container culture. *Flowering period:* early summer (fully double), midsummer until early autumn (fully to semi-double); *height:* 2.5 m (8¼ ft); *zones:* 4–9.

C. 'Proteus' A cultivar raised by Charles Noble of Sunningdale 1876 which produces large double, semi-double and single flowers. The double flowers often have a mixture of green or purple-pink outer tepals, making the flower look ragged, but the centre is pretty with many soft pinkish-purple inner tepals. The semi-double flowers are more attractive, lacking the green outer tepals. The early flowers are 15–20 cm (6–8 in) across. The single flowers produced on new growth later in the summer are a soft mauve-pink with pale yellow anthers and are smaller, being 10–15 cm (4–6 in) across. It is a vigorous plant when fully established, with large leaves. It is best planted out of full sun but not north-facing. *Flowering period:* early summer (double and semi-double), midsummer to late summer (single); *height:* 3 m (10 ft); *zones:* 4–9.

C. 'Royalty' Raised by John Treasure at Burford House Gardens about 1985, this very compact plant is ideal for container culture. It has many semi-double flowers in early summer and a very good crop of single flowers in late summer. The double flowers, which are 10–12.5 cm (4–5 in) across, are rich purple-mauve with slightly more blue inner tepals. The single flowers are smaller at 7.5 cm (3 in) across and also a little lighter in colour, revealing a centre boss of yellow anthers on purple filaments. It is ideal for a small garden and does best in some sun, so is not for a north-facing position. *Flowering period:* early summer (semi-double), midsummer to late summer (single); *height:* 2 m (6½ ft); *zones:* 4–9.

C. 'Sylvia Denny' Raised by Vince and Sylvia Denny about 1980 and introduced by the author, this cultivar has compact smallish semi-double flowers about 10 cm (4 in) across, looking a little like a camellia. The tepals are pure white and well-formed on the semi-double flowers. The single flowers reveal pale yellow anthers. The young foliage is often bronze in colour. *Flowering period:* early summer (semi-double), late summer (single); *height:* 2.5 m (8¼ ft); *zones:* 4–9.

C. 'Veronica's Choice' This cultivar was raised by Pennells of Lincoln and named in 1973. It has double and single flowers, the former 15–18 cm (6–7 in) across and the latter 10–12.5 cm (4–5 in), with blunt tips to the outer overlapping tepals, the edges crimpled and giving a frilly appearance to the flower. They have a scent resembling that of primroses. The flower colour is a pretty pale mauve-lavender with hints of rose-pink and yellow anthers. It is suitable as a cut flower. *Flowering period:* early summer (double), midsummer to late summer (single); *height:* 2.5 m (8¼ ft); *zones:* 4–9.

C. 'Vyvyan Pennell' One of the most striking of the double clematis with large leaves and strong flower stems, this cultivar was raised by Pennells of Lincoln and named in 1958. Sadly, it does succumb to clematis wilt rather easily as a young plant. The large fully double early flowers are up to 15–20 cm (6–8 in) across. The large outer tepals are purple-mauve, occasionally with a greenish tinge, the inner tepals being rosy-lavender to lilac, fading to a deep lilac-mauve, there being quite a difference between the young and old flower colour. The later single flowers are also paler, a pleasing lilac mauve, with cream to light brown anthers. It is suitable as a cut flower and also for container culture. Do not plant in a north-facing aspect. *Flowering period:* early summer (double and semi-double), late summer (single); *height:* 2.5–3 m (8¼–10 ft); *zones:* 4–9. ⚥

C. 'Walter Pennell' A good free-flowering plant raised by Pennells of Lincoln and named in 1974, with semi-double and single flowers. The deep mauve-pink tepals have a slightly darker central bar contrasting with the cream anthers. The semi-double flowers are 15 cm (6 in) in diameter and the single are 10–12.5 cm (4–5 in). *Flowering period:* early summer (semi-double), late summer (single); *height:* 2.5m (8¼ ft); *zones:* 4–9.

MID-SEASON LARGE-FLOWERED CULTIVARS

The mid-season large-flowered cultivars have generally been derived from *C. lanuginosa* since its introduction from China in the mid-1880s. Most flower from the old stems or the previous season's ripened stems as well as from the current season's growth, the latter producing the most flowers. None of them are scented. The early flowers are sometimes enormous, reaching 25 cm (10 in) across. The length of stems produced before the solitary flowers are borne may vary but is generally 30–60 cm (1–2 ft), coming direct from the previous season's ripened stems. The length of new growth that is subsequently produced varies also but many, such as C. 'Marie Boisselot', will continue to grow and flower as late as early winter during mild weather, putting on several metres (yards) of growth annually, the later flowers being produced along the stem rather than solitarily.

This group is deciduous and the large leaves are simple or trifoliate. Their main use as garden plants is growing with large wall-trained shrubs or other climbers, or on uprights to archways or pergolas where they can grow up and then over the horizontal structure, falling back down to give a very attractive effect at flowering time. They are most pleasing when grown through other large freestanding shrubs or small trees such as magnolia and rhododendrons.

These clematis can be treated as pruning group two or three but if the large early summer flowers are required they must be treated as group two, leaving in some old ripened stems from the previous season. In severe climates such as northern Europe or North America, the top growth will be killed to ground level and the plants will always flower on the current season's stems, usually in midsummer. If later rather than earlier flowers are required hard pruning (group three) can be used. Some of the compact types which are extremely free-flowering may also be used in containers to give a later-flowering plant than the early large-flowered and double/semi-double types (see individual entries).

C. 'Beauty of Richmond' This cultivar raised by Russells of Sunningdale in 1935 has 18–20 cm (7–8 in) diameter well-rounded pale lavender-blue flowers with a large central boss of light chocolate-coloured anthers. The tepals recurve as the flower ages. It is not very free-flowering but is dramatic when in full flower. It is suitable for cut-flower arrangements. *Flowering period:* midsummer to early autumn; *height:* 3 m (10 ft); *zones:* 4–9.

C. 'Belle Nantaise' Though the flower shape, colour and stamens are very different this plant raised by Boisselot in France in 1887 is sometimes sold as *C. lanuginosa*, of which the true plant is believed to be lost to cultivation. This cultivar has large lavender-blue flowers, some 18–20 cm (7–8 in) in diameter. The tepals are pointed and have crimpled edges, giving a rounded but star-like appearance. The filaments and anthers are longer than normal and very prominent, the anthers being yellow. The second crop of flowers, during late summer and early autumn, are very freely produced. It is suitable as a cut flower. *Flowering period:* midsummer to early autumn; *height:* 3 m (10 ft); *zones:* 4–9.

C. 'Blue Ravine' Raised in British Columbia, Canada, by Conrad Eriandson about 1978 and possibly a cross between C. 'Nelly Moser' and C. 'Ramona'. This very strong-growing plant flowers well in the early summer and the autumn. It has large simple to trifoliate leaves and 18–20 cm (7–8 in) wide well-formed flowers with overlapping tepals on the early summer crop. The lilac-blue colour is suffused with pinkish-mauve. The late-summer flowers have more pointed tepals, being smaller and more star-like in appearance, and contrasting red anthers. It is a useful garden plant well-suited to North America, being similar in habit to C. 'Ramona', which is well known there and enjoys the hot summers, flowering very well. *Flowering period*: early summer to midsummer, and early autumn; *height*: 3 m (10 ft); *zones*: 4–9.

C. 'Boskoop Beauty' Raised in Holland about 1960 although not widely grown, this clematis has rounded leaflets and very large flowers which are 21.5 cm (8½ in) across, with 6–7 tepals. The young flowers have a very dramatic, very deep lilac purple bar which is set against a pale lilac-blue base colour, a stunning combination contrasting with dark red anthers and prominent white styles. The tepals are gappy at the base, and have attractive wavy edges. It is a strong-growing clematis but not very free-flowering. *Flowering period*: early summer to late summer; *height*: 3 m (10 ft); *zones*: 4–9.

C. 'Crimson King' (C. 'Crimson Star' of North America) A somewhat shy-flowering plant raised by Jackmans of Woking about 1915 and often sold under the wrong name. The true plant usually has single flowers, though they may occasionally be semi-double. It has a good crimson-red flower which can be 15–18 cm (6–7 in) across, with contrasting light brown anthers. When the flowers open they resemble a water-lily in the way they hold themselves, especially those that are semi-double. *Flowering period*: midsummer to late summer; *height*: 3 m (10 ft), *zones*: 4–9.

C. 'Crimson Star' See C. 'Crimson King'.

C. 'Duchess of Sutherland' This clematis raised by Jackmans of Woking about 1934 has flowers 12.5 cm (5 in) across of a good carmine red with contrasting deep yellow anthers. The flower tepal texture is rather thin, giving the flower a speckled appearance. The early flowers can sometimes be semi-double. It is not very free-flowering. *Flowering period*: midsummer to late summer; *height*: 3 m (10 ft); *zones*: 4–9.

C. 'Edomurasaki' A Japanese cultivar raised by Seijozo Arai in 1952 which has deep purple-blue flowers with red anthers. This plant can have some growth problems in the spring when it produces a lot of pale green foliage. It is not of the strongest constitution as a young plant.

The early flowers are 15–18 cm (6–7 in) across, the later flowers being smaller at 10–12.5 cm (4–5 in). *Flowering period*: midsummer to late summer; *height*: 3 m (10 ft); *zones*: 4–9.

C. 'Empress of India' This plant was raised by Jackmans then found in the USA by the author and reintroduced to England in the 1980s. The early flowers are 15–18 cm (6–7 in) across, fully rounded and a creamy rose red colour with the anthers being prominent in a pale creamy yellow. It is not a very free-flowering plant but is suitable as a cut flower. *Flowering period*: midsummer to late summer; *height*: 3 m (10 ft); *zones*: 4–9.

C. 'Etoile de Malicorne' This is a cultivar of French origin before 1968 with 15–18 cm (6–7 in) diameter flowers of a rich purplish-blue with slightly cupped tepals that fade on ageing. It has a narrow central bar of reddish-purple and contrasting dark red anthers. It is a free-flowering plant which is suitable as a cut flower. *Flowering period*: midsummer to early autumn; *height*: 3 m (10 ft); *zones*: 4–9.

C. 'Fairy Queen' A very large-flowered cultivar, raised by Cripps & Sons in 1875, with flowers that can measure 23–25 cm (9–10 in) across. The tepals are light pink with a rosy pink bar, fading quickly, and the anthers are light brown. It is not very free-flowering but has a strong habit when established. It is suitable as a cut flower. *Flowering period*: early summer to late summer; *height*: 3 m (10 ft); *zones*: 4–9.

C. 'General Sikorski' Raised in Poland by Wladyslaw Noll and introduced to the British Isles in 1980 by Jim Fisk, this is a very good strong-growing, free-flowering clematis. Early in the season the flowers are 15 cm (6 in) across, being smaller but more freely produced in late summer and early autumn. Generally, it has six broadly overlapping mid-mauve to deep blue tepals with a hint of rose-pink at their base, a well-rounded flower with yellow anthers. This is a good plant with climbing roses and is suitable as a cut flower. *Flowering period*: midsummer to early autumn; *height*: 3 m (10 ft); *zones*: 4–9. ♇

C. 'Henryi' Raised by Anderson-Henry of Edinburgh in 1870, this splendid clematis has proved its garden-worthiness over more than a century. It is a great favourite of North American gardeners. The white 15–20 cm (6–8 in) wide flowers are well formed and have contrasting chocolate-brown anthers. It flowers over a long season and is suitable as a cut flower. *Flowering period*: midsummer to mid-autumn; *height*: 3 m (10 ft); *zones*: 4–9. ♈

C. 'Imperial' This cultivar was raised by Magnus Johnson in Sweden in 1955, from C. 'Lasurstern'. The flowers are 15–20 cm (6–8 in) across and have eight overlapping, rounded tepals, making a well-rounded flower. Some flowers are almost semi-double with one row of shorter, inner tepals. The tepals are pale creamy pink with a deeper central band, which fades gradually. The anthers are light chocolate. It has a good strong-growing habit with large trifoliate leaves and smooth rounded leaflets. *Flowering period*: early summer to late summer; *height*: 3 m (10 ft); *zones*: 4–9.

C. 'Henryi' – one of the most popular white large-flowered clematis ever raised.

C. *lanuginosa* 'Candida' This is an old cultivar raised by Victor Lemoine, France, in 1862 which is grown widely in North America. The foliage and flowers closely resemble C. 'Marie Boisselot' though the plants may be more compact in habit. The trifoliate leaves have broad rounded leaflets on long petiolules. The flowers are 12.5–18 cm (5–7 in) across, with eight rounded overlapping tepals which are pure white, each one having two main central ribs. There is a large boss of yellow stamens, creamy when young. The tepals recurve as the flower ages. It is a strong-growing plant, good as a cut flower. *Flowering period*: late spring to early summer, and late summer to early autumn; *height*: 3 m (10 ft); *zones*: 4–9.

C. 'Lawsoniana' An old cultivar raised by Anderson-Henry in 1870 which has good flowers but not freely produced. They are lavender-blue with rosy-pink tones, 15–20 cm (6–8 in) wide, and with long pointed tepals giving a star-like flower. The anthers are light chocolate in colour and contrast well with the tepals. It is suitable as a cut flower. *Flowering period*: early summer to late summer; *height*: 3 m (10 ft); *zones*: 4–9.

C. 'Madame Le Coultre' See C. 'Marie Boisselot'.

C. 'Marie Boisselot' (syn. C. 'Madame Le Coultre') Raised by Boisselot in France in 1885, this is a great old classic clematis with well-formed slightly creamy white flowers and golden-yellow anthers. The overlapping tepals produce a well-rounded flower 15 cm (6 in) across, the flower colour maturing to pure white. The foliage is always of a good colour and strong in constitution, remaining green well into the autumn. In mild locations, the flowers can be produced as late as early winter. It is suitable as a cut flower. *Flowering period*: early summer to late autumn; *height*: 3.5m (12 ft); *zones*: 4–9. ♈

C. 'Maureen' This cultivar raised in Worth Park Nursery, Surrey, England, about 1955 has an outstanding flower colour when first open – an intense rich purple, fading slightly with age. It is a well-formed flower, 12.5–15 cm (5–6 in) across, with light chocolate-coloured anthers. The distinctive foliage has rounded leaflets. *Flowering period*: early to late summer; *height*: 3 m (10 ft); *zones*: 4–9.

C. 'Midnight' Raised by Keith and Carol Fair in Lincolnshire in the 1980s. The rounded 15 cm (6 in) flowers of this repeat-flowering cultivar have eight rounded tepals in a distinctive deep blue with a slightly paler central band and contrasting red anthers. The reverse of the flower is most attractive, having a cream central mid-rib which is green when the flower first opens. The leaves are large and simple to trifoliate. *Flowering period:* early summer to late summer; *height:* 3 m (10 ft); *zones:* 4–9.

C. 'Mrs Bush' This cultivar raised before 1935 has distinctive lavender-blue flowers 15–20 cm (6–8 in) across with narrow slightly pointed tepals that are ridged. The anthers are light chocolate-coloured and prominent. It is not free-flowering but has strong, healthy foliage. *Flowering period:* midsummer to early autumn; *height:* 3.5 m (12 ft); *zones:* 4–9.

C. 'Mrs Hope' This old cultivar raised by Jackmans of Woking in about 1875 is not free-flowering unless it is planted in a sunny location where the stems can ripen. It has profuse foliage, very often with simple leaves. The 15 cm (6 in) wide pale blue flowers have overlapping tepals with a slightly darker central band. The anthers are dark red, contrasting well with the tepals. *Flowering period:* midsummer to early autumn; *height:* 3.5 m (12 ft); *zones:* 4–9.

C. 'Percy Picton' Raised by Percy Picton and introduced by Jim Fisk in 1956, this clematis has a large mauve flower with rosy highlights. They are 15–18 cm (6–7 in) in diameter and well formed, with brownish-red anthers. This plant is not free-flowering but the blooms are a pleasing colour. They are suitable as cut flowers. *Flowering period:* early summer to late summer; *height:* 3 m (10 ft); *zones:* 4–9.

C. 'Peveril Pearl' This cultivar raised by Barry Fretwell in England in 1979 has lovely very pale lavender flowers that are 15–18 cm (6–7 in) in diameter with light pinkish-brown anthers. The broad tepals with rosy highlights become narrower on the later crops of flowers. It needs a dark background to show off the flowers to best effect. They make good cut flowers. *Flowering period:* early summer to early autumn; *height:* 3 m (10ft); *zones:* 4–9.

C. 'Prins Hendrik' A cultivar raised in Boskoop, Holland, in about 1900 which has very attractive, 15–18 cm (6–7 in) wide flowers with mid to pale blue tepals crimpled at the edges and dark red anthers. The well-rounded flower is somewhat star-shaped. The clematis was used as a cut flower for many years and sold in the Dutch flower markets. *Flowering period:* early summer to late summer; *height:* 3 m (10 ft); *zones:* 4–9.

C. 'Ramona' An old cultivar possibly raised in Holland or the USA and most widely grown in the USA and Canada, this clematis was first distributed in 1888 by the Jackson & Perkins Co., USA. It flowers best in a sunny location where the wood can ripen. It has large 15–18 cm (6–7 in) wide flowers which are pale blue and well formed, with contrasting dark red anthers. The foliage is strong and healthy, the leaves very often simple in format. *Flowering period:* early summer to early autumn; *height:* 3 m (10 ft); *zones:* 4–9.

C. 'Serenata' This cultivar was raised by Tage Lundell, Sweden, in 1960 and introduced to the British Isles by the author. The flowers are 12.5 cm (5 in) across and have dusky dark purple tepals with a reddish bar and contrasting golden-yellow anthers. They can be rather gappy, especially in the late summer and early autumn. It is free-flowering and suitable as a cut flower, but needs a light background to show the flowers to their best advantage. *Flowering period:* early summer to early autumn; *height:* 3 m (10 ft); *zones:* 4–9.

C. 'Titania' Raised by Magnus Johnson in Sweden in 1952 as a seedling from C. 'Nelly Moser', this is a plant of vigorous habit. It has large trifoliate leaves and very large flowers, sometimes up to 25 cm (10 in) across. They are white with a hint of violet and a broad pinkish-violet central bar which fades gradually. The eight tepals are overlapping, making a very well-rounded flower. The maroon anthers are on white filaments, which are well-proportioned to the size of the flower. It is sadly not a free-flowering plant, but if large clematis flowers are required for a short period in early summer it is a stunning sight. *Flowering period:* early summer to midsummer; *height:* 3 m (10 ft); *zones:* 4–9.

C. 'Torleif' This clematis was a seedling from C. 'Prins Hendrik', raised by Magnus Johnson in Sweden in 1955.

It is a large, vigorous plant with 18 cm (7 in) wide flowers composed of 6–8 tepals which are blue-mauve with a pronounced double central rib, reddish on some flowers. As the flowers age, the tepals become twisted. It has a contrasting large boss of red anthers on white filaments, and prominent white styles. The large leaves are trifoliate with pointed tips. *Flowering period:* early summer to late summer; *height:* 3 m (10 ft); *zones:* 4–9.

C. 'Violet Charm' A very free-flowering clematis, especially in late summer, making a good container plant. It was raised at Solihull Nurseries, Birmingham, England, in 1966. The well-formed, attractive, pale violet-blue flowers are 15–18 cm (6–7 in) in diameter with contrasting red anthers and slightly crimpled edges to the tepals. It has outstanding, healthy-looking foliage, better than most other cultivars in this group. It is suitable as a cut flower. *Flowering period:* early summer to early autumn; *height:* 3 m (10 ft); *zones:* 4–9.

C. 'W. E. Gladstone' A classic clematis with very large flowers some 18–20 cm (7–8 in) across, raised by Charles Noble in England in about 1881. It has pale blue tepals and red anthers, and though it is not free-flowering it will bloom over a long season. It has a strong habit once established and is suitable as a cut flower. *Flowering period:* early summer to early autumn; *height:* 3.5 m (12 ft); *zones:* 4–9.

LATE LARGE-FLOWERED CULTIVARS

The late-flowering large-flowered clematis have generally been developed from some of the early large-flowered cultivars of the mid-19th century, when cultivars of *C. viticella* were used in crosses with *C. lanuginosa* cultivars. This group of clematis flowers on the current season's growth towards the end of the growing stems, producing single flowers from midsummer onwards until early to mid-autumn depending upon locality and climate. None are scented. The length of stem varies between cultivars but is generally about 2–3 m (6½–10 ft), sometimes to 4 m (13 ft). The foliage is deciduous and the leaves generally have trifoliate leaflets.

These are most useful flowers, coming at a time when all early-flowering clematis have finished their first main blooming period. As their growth needs to be removed each spring they are particularly ideal for growing with climbing or rambling species or old roses,

giving additional colour when the rose has finished flowering or, with careful selection, while it is still in bloom. They can also be used to clamber around at ground level through perennial plants or summer-flowering bedding plants, or to grow into freestanding shrubs or small trees.

This group belongs to pruning group three so all stems should be removed down to ground level in early spring. They are winter hardy to zones 3–9.

C. 'Allanah' This is a compact plant, raised by Alister Keay in New Zealand and introduced to the British Isles by Jim Fisk in the early 1980s. The flower colour of this clematis is most unusual – a deep bright red, the anthers being almost black. The flowers are 10–12.5 cm (4–5 in) and have 6–7 tepals which are blunt-tipped. It does not flower along the stem but produces terminal flowers. *Flowering period:* early summer to early autumn; *height:* 2.5 m (8¼ ft); *zones:* 3–9.

C. 'Ascotiensis' This old cultivar raised by John Standish in 1874 is very free-flowering and vigorous once established. The bright mid-blue flowers are 12.5 cm (5 in) across and have darker veins to the broad tepals, which number 4–6. The anthers are greenish-chocolate in colour. It flowers well along the stem and can be used as a container plant to give late summer colour. It is ideal with red roses. *Flowering period:* midsummer to early autumn; *height:* 3 m (10 ft); *zones:* 3–9. ♔

C. 'Bagatelle' See *C.* 'Dorothy Walton'.

C. 'Cardinal Wyszynski' Raised by Brother Stefan Franczak in Poland and introduced by Jim Fisk in 1989, this is a very showy plant with 6–8 crimson tepals and anthers of the same shade. The flowers are 10–12.5 cm (4–5 in) in diameter and the plant should be grown against a light background to show them off to best effect. *Flowering period:* midsummer to early autumn; *height:* 2.5 m (8¼ ft); *zones:* 3–9.

C. 'Comtesse de Bouchaud' This classic clematis raised by Morel in France in about 1900 is still one of the best of this group, producing bright mauve-pink, 12.5 cm (5 in) wide, rounded flowers with cream anthers. They have 6–8 deeply textured tepals with a satin sheen, crimpled edges and blunt tips. It is extremely free-flowering and is ideal with roses. *Flowering period:* midsummer to early autumn; *height:* 3 m (10 ft); *zones:* 4–9. ♔

C. 'Dorothy Walton' (syn C. 'Bagatelle') This is an extremely free-flowering plant with star-like 12.5 cm (5 in) flowers, raised in France before 1930. The 6–8 very pointed, mauve-pink tepals have a hint of blue-mauve, the strongest colours being along the edge of the tepal and on the central bar. The anthers are coffee-coloured and it is a striking plant when in full flower. It is ideal to use as a container plant, giving late summer colour to a patio. *Flowering period:* early summer to early autumn; *height:* 2.5 m (8¼ ft); *zones:* 3–9.

C. 'Ernest Markham' A classic clematis, raised in a batch of seedlings at Gravetye Manor, Sussex and introduced and named by Rowland Jackman after Ernest Markham's death in 1937. It has magenta 10–12.5 cm (4–5 in) wide roundish flowers, the 6–8 broad tepals overlapping, tapering to a point with crimpled margins. The anthers are light brown. It flowers best when grown in full sun where the stems can be

C. 'Jackmanii Superba' has a stunning colour that fades as the flower matures.

ripened. *Flowering period:* midsummer to mid-autumn; *height:* 3–4 m (10–13 ft); *zones:* 3–9. ♔

C. 'Gipsy Queen' A classic clematis raised by Cripps & Sons in England in 1877 which will produce flowers from ripened stems from the previous year as well as the crop from the current season. The early flowers are 15 cm (6 in) across and are borne on very strong stems. The later flowers, only 10–12.5 cm (4–5 in) in diameter, are produced along the flowering growth in great profusion. The 4–6 tepals are a deep velvety violet-purple with dark red anthers. *Flowering period:* early summer to early autumn; *height:* 3 m (10 ft); *zones:* 3–9.

C. 'Hagley Hybrid' This clematis raised by Percy Picton at Hagley Hall and introduced by Jim Fisk in 1956 has already become a classic clematis on account of its profuse flowers and compact habit. The rosy-mauve to shell pink 10 cm (4 in) wide flowers have 4–6 tepals which have pointed tips and dark red anthers. The flowers fade quickly if planted in full sun, so a shady location is required for this plant. *Flowering period:* early summer to late summer; *height:* 2.5 m (8¼ ft); *zones:* 3–9.

C. 'Honora' A new cultivar which is similar in habit and in flower colour to C. 'Gipsy Queen', obtained from Holland in 1995. The 18 cm (7 in) wide flowers have six tepals and are rather gappy, especially as the flowers mature and the tepals become twisted and recurve at the tips. These are a rich purple, with a deep purple central bar, and have crimpled edges. The anthers are a stunning deep purple-red with light purple filaments. It is very free-flowering and and is an excellent plant to grow with roses, especially ramblers or climbers. The foliage is also interesting, with five leaflets and extra-long petiolules. *Flowering period:* early summer to early autumn; *height:* 3–4 m (10–13 ft); *zones:* 3–9.

C. 'Jackmanii' The most famous clematis of all, raised in 1858 by Jackmans of Woking and still the most widely grown clematis both in Europe and North America. It seems totally winter hardy, even in the coldest locations, flowering freely every year. The 10 cm (4 in) wide semi-nodding flowers, produced in profusion along the stem to the growing tip, are deep dark velvet purple, fading with age to a good bluish-purple. The tepals number 4–6 and the anthers are creamy green. The leaves are occasionally simple but generally trifoliate. It is a great plant for associating with roses and any type of perennial plant. *Flowering period*: midsummer to early autumn; *height*: 3 m (10 ft); *zones*: 3–9. ♀

C. 'Jackmanii Superba' This clematis was raised by Jackmans of Woking in 1878 and many other plants are sold under its name, including C. 'Jackmanii' and C. 'Gipsy Queen', though the true plant is quite distinct. In propagation, it is not so easy to produce as the latter two cultivars. The flowers measure 12.5 cm (5 in) across and have greenish-cream anthers. The four tepals are broader than in C. 'Jackmanii', almost square in appearance and a deeper rich purple at the point of opening, fading with age. Otherwise its habit is the same, except the leaves are generally simple, rather than trifoliate as in C. 'Jackmanii'. *Flowering period*: midsummer to early autumn; *height*: 3 m (10 ft); *zones*: 3–9.

C. 'Jan Pawel II' (syn. C. 'John Paul II') Raised by Brother Stefan Franczak in Poland and introduced by Jim Fisk in 1980, this clematis has pale whitish-pink flowers which have six overlapping tepals, each tapering to a point. The early flowers, which are 12 cm (4¾ in) across, have a satin sheen and a pearly white colour, as do the late flowers, though these are smaller at 7.5–10 cm (3–4 in). The anthers are dark red. For best flowering plant in sun, though the flower colour will fade quickly to white. *Flowering period*: midsummer to early autumn; *height*: 3.5 m (12 ft); *zones*: 3–9.

C. 'John Huxtable' This clematis was raised by John Huxtable in Devon, England, and given to the author by Rowland Jackman for introduction in 1967. It was a chance seedling from C. 'Comtesse de Bouchaud' which has retained most of its parent's characteristics, except that the flower colour is creamy-white – rare in this group. The flowers are 10 cm (4 in) in diameter, the 4–6 white tepals offset by yellow-white anthers. It is free-flowering. *Flowering period*: midsummer to late summer; *height*: 2.5–3 m (8¼–10 ft); *zones*: 3–9.

C. 'John Paul II' See C. 'Jan Pawel II'.

C. 'Lady Betty Balfour' A strong-growing clematis raised by Jackmans of Woking in 1910 which needs to be planted in full sun to obtain early flowers, otherwise the top growth and flowerbuds may be killed by early autumn frost before the flowers open. This clematis also seems prone to clematis wilt. The large 15 cm (6 in) wide purple-blue flowers have a dramatic colour which fades with age. The 6–8 tepals are broad and overlapping and the anthers are yellow, giving a good contrast to the flower. *Flowering period*: early autumn to mid-autumn; *height*: 3.5 m (12 ft); *zones*: 3–9.

C. 'Lilacina Floribunda' A very strong-growing but somewhat untidy clematis raised by Cripps & Sons in England in 1880 which flowers from both the old and the current season's stems. The old-wood flowers appear in early summer and are 12.5 cm (5 in) in diameter, larger than the later flowers. They are of a deep, rich purple with 6–8 pointed and somewhat gappy tepals and deep red anthers; the later summer flowers are of similar colour, fading with age. *Flowering period*: early summer to early autumn; *height*: 3 m (10 ft); *zones*: 3–9.

C. 'Madame Baron Veillard' Because of its late flowering habit, this old cultivar introduced by Baron Veillard in 1885 must be grown in a sunny location to obtain a good crop of flowers. It is very vigorous, ideal for covering large areas. The lilac-rose flowers are 10–12.5 cm (4–5 in) in diameter and have 6–8 overlapping tepals and greenish anthers. *Flowering period*: early autumn to mid-autumn; *height*: 3–4 m (10–13 ft); *zones*: 3–9.

C. 'Madame Edouard André' A very useful mid to late summer flowering plant, raised by Baron Veillard in 1892. The profusely borne 10 cm (4 in) wide flowers are slightly cup-shaped, the 4–6 tepals having a roundish shape, tapering to a point. They are a clear to dusky red, fading to a mauve-red as the flower ages, contrasting with the creamy-yellow anthers. This clematis has a compact habit and is therefore useful for growing in a container to give summer colour to a patio. *Flowering period*: midsummer to late summer; *height*: 2.5 m (8¼ ft); *zones*: 3–9. ♀

C. 'Madame Grangé' A late-flowering clematis with attractive boat-shaped tepals, raised by Grangé in France in 1875. The flowers, which are 10–12.5 cm (4–5 in) wide and freely produced along the stem to its tip, are made up of 4–6 tepals which are of a dusky velvet purple, with a red-purple central bar. As the tepals never open fully they reveal a dusky silver reverse. The anthers are light brownish-green. This plant must be grown against a light background to show the flowers off to the best advantage. *Flowering period:* midsummer to late summer; *height:* 3 m (10 ft); *zones:* 3–9.

C. 'Margaret Hunt' This vigorous cultivar was raised by Margaret Hunt and introduced by Jim Fisk in 1969. It has a gappy, dusky mauve-pink flower with 6–8 tepals, giving a star-like flower shape. The anthers are reddish-brown. The flowers are 10 cm (4 in) in diameter and are produced very freely. *Flowering period:* midsummer to late summer; *height:* 3 m (10 ft); *zones:* 3–9.

C. 'Perle d'Azur' The classic blue clematis, raised by Morel in France in 1885, much sought after but not easy to propagate because of its long internodes. The semi-nodding mid to light blue flowers are 10 cm (4 in) across and have a rounded appearance due to the edges and tips of the tepals recurving. The tepals are generally four in number and have a hint of pink towards their base and also on the reverse, which can almost be seen through them as they are quite translucent. The anthers are pale yellow. This is a free-flowering plant, subject to mildew in some locations, flowering all along the stem to its growing tip. It associates very well with roses. *Flowering period:* early summer to early autumn; *height:* 3.5 m (12 ft); *zones:* 3–9. ♈

C. 'Perrin's Pride' This plant was raised in the USA by Steffen Clematis Nursery, New York State, and introduced to Europe by the author in the 1980s. It will produce some large 15 cm (6 in) wide flowers from the previous season's stems in the early summer and then a good crop of later flowers on the current season's stems. It bears well-shaped, well-rounded flowers, the six tepals recurving slightly and bronze-purple in colour. The anthers are greenish-bronze. It needs a light background to show the flowers to best effect. *Flowering period:* early summer to early autumn; *height:* 3 m (10 ft); *zones:* 3–9.

C. 'Pink Fantasy' A very good free-flowering clematis similar in habit to C. 'Hagley Hybrid' and with similar-coloured flowers, introduced from Canada by Jim Fisk in 1975. The pretty 10 cm (4 in) wide flowers have six pink tepals with peachy pink highlights and dusky red

C. 'Prince Charles' is a free-flowering plant that blooms well when grown in a container.

anthers. The deeper central bar is only prominent towards the base of the tepal. Its compact habit makes it a useful pink clematis to grow in a container for later flowering. It is suitable as a cut flower. *Flowering period:* midsummer to early autumn; *height:* 2–2.5 m (6½–8¼ ft); *zones:* 3–9.

C. 'Prince Charles' A compact plant which bears flowers similar to C. 'Perle d'Azur', sometimes also subject to mildew in dry conditions. It was raised by Alister Keay in New Zealand and introduced by Jim Fisk in 1986. The profusely borne mauve-blue 10 cm (4 in) wide flowers change colour in certain light conditions, sometimes to almost a greenish azure blue. They are semi-nodding, with 4–6 pointed tepals twisting slightly, and the anthers are yellowish green – a pretty flower. This clematis is suitable as a cut flower, and for container culture on account of its compact free-flowering habit. *Flowering period:* midsummer to early autumn; *height:* 2–2.5 m (6½–8¼ ft); *zones:* 3–9.

C. 'Rhapsody' This cultivar was raised by Watkinson's Clematis Nursery, Yorkshire, England, in 1992. It is a very pretty free-flowering clematis with stunning sapphire blue tepals which deepen in colour with age. The flowers are 10–12.5 cm (4–5 in) in diameter and have six tepals and creamy-yellow anthers splayed open. It is compact and makes an ideal plant for a container, bringing useful colour to a patio in midsummer. *Flowering period:* early summer to early autumn; *height:* 2.5 m (8¼ ft; *zones:* 3–9.

C. 'Rouge Cardinal' This clematis was raised by Girault in Orléans, France, in 1968. It has a stunning flower colour of velvety crimson with a sheen to the tepal surface, fading as the flower ages. It is a well-rounded 10 cm (4 in) wide flower, the tips of the six tepals recurving, with brownish-red anthers. It is very free-flowering in habit although the plant's structure is rather weak and the foliage is floppy, lacking constitution. *Flowering period:* midsummer to early autumn; *height:* 2.5–3m (8¼–10 ft); *zones:* 3–9.

C. 'Star of India' This useful garden plant introduced by Cripps & Sons in 1867 associates particularly well with roses. It has usually four tepals which are deep purple-blue with a crimson central bar. They are somewhat square in appearance, with rounded edges and blunt tips, and the anthers are greenish-cream. The flowers measure 10 cm (4 in) across and are borne freely along the stem to the growing tip. *Flowering period:* midsummer to late summer; *height:* 3 m (10 ft); *zones:* 3–9. ♕

C. 'Victoria' A splendid old clematis, ideal for clambering around in roses, raised in England in 1867 by Cripps & Sons. The flowers are 10–14 cm (4–5½ in) across and have 4–6 tepals. These are broad and overlapping, deep rosy-mauve in colour with a soft rosy-purple central bar, fading to a light mauve. The anthers are greenish-yellow. It produces its flowers very freely but needs a light background for them to show to best advantage. *Flowering period:* midsummer to late summer; *height:* 3 m (10 ft); *zones:* 3–9.

C. 'Ville de Lyon' A well-known classic clematis, raised by Morel in France in 1899. It is of strong-growing and free-flowering habit, and will produce early flowers from the previous season's ripened stems and a very good crop of summer flowers. Unfortunately the lower foliage burns up by midsummer and the lower part of the plant becomes bare and unsightly, so it must be grown through evergreen shrubs to hide this problem. The 10–12.5 cm (4–5 in) wide flowers are very dramatic and colourful, with bright crimson tepals contrasting with yellow anthers. There are six overlapping tepals which are rounded and blunt-tipped, giving a rounded appearance to the flower. They have a wide deepish-pink central bar, paler than the base colour, which is overlaid by darker veins. *Flowering period:* early summer to early autumn; *height:* 3 m (10 ft); *zones:* 3–9.

C. 'Voluceau' This cultivar was raised in Orléans, France, by Girault in about 1970. It is a very strong-growing, free-flowering plant that will survive coastal conditions. It has petunia-red 10 cm (4 in) wide flowers with contrasting yellow anthers and six slightly twisted tepals. *Flowering period:* early summer to late summer; *height:* 3 m (10 ft); *zones:* 3–9.

VITICELLA TYPES & THEIR CULTIVARS

C. campaniflora (Section Viticella) A deciduous species native to Portugal, similar in habit to C. *viticella*, introduced to the British Isles in 1820. It has slightly glaucous foliage, the leaves divided into many leaflets, and dainty nodding open bell-shaped flowers measuring 2–2.5 cm (¾–1 in). The tepals are white to pale blue, recurving at the tips, and becoming slightly twisted with age. The anthers are creamy green. *Flowering period:* midsummer to early autumn; *height:* 4.5m (15 ft); *zones:* 6–9.

C. c. 'Lisboa' The flowers are larger than the species, up to 5 cm (2 in) across. The four tepals are purple-blue and recurve at the tips, with greenish-yellow anthers. A showy vigorous plant, raised and introduced by Magnus Johnson from seed collected in the Lisbon Botanical Garden. It looks good with large blue-foliage conifers. *Flowering period:* midsummer to early autumn; *height:* 4.5m (14 ft); *zones:* 6–9.

C. viticella (Section Viticella) This deciduous European climber, a native of Italy and Turkey commonly known as the virgin's bower, was introduced to England in the 16th century and in more recent times has given rise to a range of very useful garden plants. The cultivars created in the last 100 years or so, which have small to medium flowers, do not succumb to clematis wilt as do the large-flowered cultivars. The profusely borne nodding flowers of the species are open bell-shaped, 3 cm (1¼ in) across, nodding or semi-nodding, with four usually mauve tepals, and are produced along the flowering stem to the growing tip generally singly or in threes from the leaf axil node on the current season's growth. The length of new growth is normally about 3 m (10 ft), produced in abundance. The leaves are pinnately trifoliate to bifoliate, the leaflets lanceolate to broad ovate, often 2–3-lobed. The species and cultivars are very versatile in the garden and can be grown with all types of trees, shrubs, roses and perennials, either freestanding or as wall-trained plants. They are ideal for growing with or through low growing plants such as low-growing conifers or groundcover plants such as summer- or winter-flowering heathers. They belong to pruning group three and therefore need all the top growth from the previous season to be removed in early spring. The species and cultivars growing on winter-flowering heathers need their top growth removed in mid to late autumn so that the flowers and foliage of the heathers can be enjoyed. The species is very variable in cultivation and it is important to select a good form as plants sold are generally seed-raised; try to buy the plant when it is in flower. *Flowering period:* midsummer until mid-autumn; *height:* 3 m (10 ft); *zones:* 3–9.

C. v. 'Abundance' This very free-flowering cultivar was raised by Jackmans of Woking in the 1930s. The flowers are flat, open, semi-nodding, 5–7.5 cm (2–3 in) across, the tepals being a wine rose and heavily textured, recurving along the margins and the tips. The anthers are yellowish. *Flowering period:* midsummer to early autumn; *height:* 3 m (10 ft); *zones:* 3–9.

C. v. 'Alba Luxurians' This vigorous plant raised by Veitch & Sons in England in about 1900 has slightly glaucous foliage. The flowers are produced on thin pedicels and so tend to flutter in a breeze. The early flowers have a great deal of green on the tepals, sometimes up to half the tepal, making them look unsightly yet still interesting. They are flat, open and nodding, 7.5 cm (3 in) in diameter, the four tepals white at the base beginning green at the tips (in midsummer). The

C. viticella 'Etoile Violette' contributing its abundant flowers to the back of a mixed border.

anthers are purple-black, making an interesting contrast. *Flowering period:* midsummer to early autumn; *height:* 3 m (10 ft); *zones:* 3–9. ♆

C. v. 'Betty Corning' Discovered in the USA by Betty Corning in 1932, this plant is thought to be a cross between *C. crispa* and *C. viticella*. It has retained the scent from *C. crispa* and is a charming clematis, with nodding bell-shaped flowers, 5–6 cm (2–2¼ in) in length. It has four tepals which recurve at the tips, revealing the light pinkish-mauve inner colour, the reverse being a pale pinkish-blue. It has a paler central bar and pale yellow anthers. *Flowering period:* midsummer to mid-autumn; *height:* 2 m (6½ ft); *zones:* 3–9.

C. v. 'Blue Belle' Raised possibly by Jackmans of Woking and lost to cultivation in England but reintroduced by the author from Canada in the 1980s, this is a strong-growing, free-flowering plant. It has 9 cm (3½ in) wide semi-nodding flowers with six tepals of a deep violet-purple and yellow anthers. It is a well-rounded flower similar to C. v. 'Etoile Violette' but larger and slightly darker in colour. It is a most useful clematis for providing large flowers without the risk of clematis wilt. *Flowering period:* midsummer to early autumn; *height:* 3.5 m (12 ft); *zones:* 3–9.

C. v. 'Carmencita' This cultivar raised by Magnus Johnson in Sweden in 1952 has very pretty nodding flowers 6 cm (2¼ in) across with 4–6 carmine tepals with a satin texture and black anthers. It is a free-flowering plant that should be planted so that the flowers can be looked into from below and is therefore ideal for a small tree such as lilac (*Syringa*). *Flowering period:* midsummer to early autumn; *height:* 3.5 m (12 ft); *zones:* 3–9.

C. v. 'Etoile Violette' Raised by Morel in France in 1885, this vigorous very free-flowering plant produces more flowers than C. v. 'Blue Belle' but they are not so large. The 7–8 cm (2¾–3¼ in) nodding, semi-nodding, slightly gappy flowers have 4–6 tepals which recurve at the edge. They are violet-purple with a reddish tint when young, contrasting with yellow anthers. This plant needs a light background to show the flowers off to the best advantage. *Flowering period:* midsummer to early autumn; *height:* 3–4 m (10–13 ft); *zones:* 3–9. ♛

C. v. 'Grandiflora Sanguinea' See C. v. 'Södertälje'.

C. v. 'Kermesina' This free-flowering plant was raised by Lemoine in France in 1883, and is sometimes sold incorrectly under the name of C. v. 'Rubra'. It also has green tips to the tepals in the early part of the flowering season. The semi-nodding flowers are 6 cm (2¼ in) across and generally have four tepals. The colour is a rich deep red, the tepals recurving at the edges and having a white blotch at the base. The anthers are almost black. The flowers look well with a grey background. *Flowering period:* midsummer to early autumn; *height:* 3 m (10 ft); *zones:* 3–9.

C. v. 'Little Nell' A charming small-flowered cultivar raised by Morel in France in about 1915 and introduced by Ernest Markham at Gravetye Manor. The semi-nodding flowers are up to 5 cm (2 in) across with

generally four tepals and are creamy bluish-white. The anthers are greenish-yellow. It looks good scrambling around at ground level or with other blue-flowered plants. *Flowering period:* midsummer to early autumn; *height:* 3 m (10 ft); *zones:* 3–9.

C. v. 'Madame Julia Correvon' This outstanding clematis was raised by Morel in France in 1900, and was almost lost to cultivation until it was found by the plantsman and author Christopher Lloyd and commercial production was started again. The profuse semi-nodding 7 cm (2¾ in) wide flowers have 4–6 tepals which are a vibrant, rich red. The tepals recurve at the tips and as the flower ages they twist, giving a gappy appearance. The tepal reverse is pale pink with a white central bar. The stamens are pale yellow and are splayed open. Because of its reasonably compact habit and free-flowering nature it can be used as a container-grown plant to give added summer colour to the patio. It looks marvellous with roses or grey foliage plants. *Flowering period:* midsummer to early autumn; *height:* 3 m (10 ft); *zones:* 3–9. ♛

C. v. 'Margot Koster' A very free-flowering plant raised in Holland, often criticized for the gappiness of the 10 cm (4 in) semi-nodding flowers which occurs as they age. The 4–6 tepals are a deep mauve-pink. As they mature they recurve on the margins and roll back on themselves, the tips also recurving to give the appearance of a thin-tepalled flower. The anthers are a greenish-yellow. This cultivar looks good with grey foliage plants, blue flowers and roses. *Flowering period:* midsummer to early autumn; *height:* 3.5 m (12 ft); *zones:* 3–9.

C. v. 'Mary Rose' See C. v. 'Purpurea Plena'.

C. v. 'Minuet' Raised by Morel in France and named and introduced by Ernest Markham, this is a cultivar with very pretty flowers. They are semi-nodding, up to 6 cm (2½ in) across, with generally four tepals. These are blunt-tipped, with a base colour of white veined pale purplish-red on the margins. It is ideal for growing into small trees where the flowers can be viewed from below, or on the ground with heathers. *Flowering period:* midsummer to early autumn; *height:* 3 m (10 ft); *zones:* 3–9. ♛

C. *viticella* 'Purpurea Plena Elegans', an old cultivar dating from the 16th century.

C. v. 'Polish Spirit' Raised by Brother Stefan Franczak in Poland and introduced by the author in 1989, this is an outstanding plant with very good foliage – even from the ground upwards it remains green instead of losing its lower leaves in midsummer like most clematis. The 7 cm (2¾ in) wide semi-nodding flowers generally have six tepals which are a rich, very intense purple-blue, with a satin sheen when young. The anthers are blackish red. This plant is too vigorous and dense in habit to grow with other groundcover plants, but is ideal with large shrubs or small trees. *Flowering period:* midsummer to early autumn; *height:* 3–4 m (10–13 ft); *zones:* 3–9.

C. v. 'Purpurea Plena' (syn. C. *v.* 'Mary Rose') This plant is thought to have been cultivated in the 16th century in central Europe, and when reintroduced to commerce by Barry Fretwell he gave it the name 'Mary Rose', although this plant has been known to the author and others in Devon gardens for a number of years, and grown under the original name of 'Purpurea Plena'. The fully double, smoky bluish-mauve, nodding sterile flowers are produced on the new growth and are 5 cm (2 in) in diameter. They are freely produced once the plant is established but need a light background to show them to their best advantage. They are suitable as a cut flower. *Flowering period:* midsummer to early autumn; *height:* 3 m (10 ft); *zones:* 3–9.

C. v. 'Purpurea Plena Elegans' This cultivar, also thought to be from the 16th century or before, is better known than 'Purpurea Plena' and more widely grown. The author has recently produced seedlings with the same flower shape and colour from mixed seed from C. *viticella* cultivars, so it is probably a seedling from a form of the species. This cultivar is more vigorous than the 'Purpurea Plena' and its dusky violet-purple nodding flowers are slightly larger, some 6–7 cm (2¼–2¾ in) in diameter, the outer tepals occasionally green or partly green at the tips. They are fully double with many small tepals and are sterile. This cultivar looks good in small trees and with shrubs with very pale green or grey foliage. It is most useful as a cut flower, picked in long strands for pedestal arrangements. *Flowering period:* midsummer to early autumn; *height:* 3.5 m (12 ft); *zones:* 3–9. ♀

C. v. 'Royal Velours' This cultivar raised by Morel in France in 1914 and introduced by William Robinson and Ernest Markham at Gravetye Manor has stunning deep velvety-purple flowers with a satiny sheen to them and greeny-black anthers. They are semi-nodding with four rounded tepals with recurved tips. Because the flowers are so dark it must be planted against a light background to be effective and looks marvellous with light grey foliage. It is suitable as a cut flower. *Flowering period:* midsummer to early autumn; *height:* 3 m (10 ft); *zones:* 3–9. ♀

C. v. 'Södertälje' (formerly C. *v.* 'Grandiflora Sanguinea') A strong-growing cultivar raised by Magnus Johnson in Sweden in 1952. It has semi-nodding 8 cm (3 ¼ in) wide flowers with 4–6 pinkish-red tepals that recurve at the tip, giving a slightly gappy appearance to the flower, and light green anthers. This plant is well-suited to growing in pine trees. *Flowering period:* midsummer to early autumn; *height:* 3 m (10 ft); *zones:* 3–9.

C. v. 'Tango' This cultivar raised by Barry Fretwell in England in 1986 is similar in habit and flower colour to C. *v.* 'Minuet' but with slightly larger semi-nodding flowers 7.5 cm (3 in) in diameter which hold their colour longer. The tepal colour is greenish-cream with deep mauve pink veins towards the edges and the anthers are dark red. *Flowering period:* midsummer to early autumn; *height:* 3 m (10 ft); *zones:* 3–9.

C. v. 'Venosa Violacea' A very distinctive free-flowering clematis raised by Lemoine in France before 1884, the largest flowered *C. viticella* cultivar. The semi-nodding flowers are 10 cm (4 in) across and generally have six tepals, but occasionally four. It is a very full flower, with boat-shaped tepals that overlap slightly. The central part of the tepal is white, giving way to purple veins that become darker and more intense towards the edges of the tepal. During hot weather, the veins become much closer and cover the whole surface of the tepal. The anthers are black. It makes a good cut flower and in mild climates has a very long flowering season. *Flowering period:* midsummer to mid-autumn; *height:* 3 m (10 ft); *zones:* 3–9. ♆

LATE-FLOWERING SPECIES & THEIR CULTIVARS

The late-flowering species and their cultivars are a very diverse group of clematis, ranging from low-growing herbaceous types to the very rampant tangutica cultivars which can reach some 8–10 m (26–33 ft). They all flower on the current season's stems, producing their flowers in clusters, panicles or groups or along the stems to the growth tip. They belong to pruning group three and therefore require the previous season's stems to be removed down to ground level in early spring. When allowed to grow up into trees, some (for example *C. tangutica*), can be left alone with very little pruning as they would be in the wild. The winter hardiness varies and should be checked against the plant's description and zone rating. Some clematis within this section are scented and this is stated in their description.

C. addisonii (Section Viorna) This charming plant belonging to the Viorna group, a native of the southeastern United States, has glaucous foliage which is sometimes subject to mildew and delightful pitcher-shaped flowers. It is a variable deciduous species with 3 cm (1¼ in) flowers ranging from purple to red with creamy margins to the tepals, which recurve upwards to reveal cream inner tepals. It is of low-growing habit and is ideal for the mixed border. As it is non-clinging it needs support. *Flowering period:* midsummer to early autumn; *height:* 60 cm (2 ft); *zones:* 7–9.

C. aethusifolia (Section Aethusifoliae) This species was introduced to England via France about 1861 and

C. 'Aljonushka' is a non-clinging cultivar with strong foliage and colourful flowers, ideal for the mixed border.

reintroduced to England by Roy Lancaster and the author in 1980. It is a deciduous species from northeastern China with extremely pretty foliage. The leaflets are deeply dissected, pale green and fern-like in appearance. It generally needs to be tied into its host or support. It has delicate 2 cm (¾ in) long bell-like flowers, which are creamy yellow, usually with four tepals which recurve at the tips, and greenish-yellow anthers. The flowers are produced in profusion and have a pleasant daphne scent. They are followed by fluffy seedheads. It does best in a sunny location. *Flowering period:* late summer to early autumn; *height:* 2 m (6½ ft); *zones:* 6–9.

C. akebioides (formerly *C. glauca akebioides*) (Section Meclatis) A deciduous climbing species, native of western China, Sichuan and north Yunnan, with glaucous pinnate leaves, rather thick and fleshy. The 5–7 leaflets are oval to oblong with blunt, rounded, somewhat uneven teeth, occasionally slightly lobed. The yellow nodding bell flowers, with four tepals, are generally tinged or coloured on the top side with greeny bronze or purple. They are 4 cm (1½ in) across, borne closely together in clusters on very short pedicels, and have greenish-brown anthers. A useful garden plant, but only selected clones should be grown as it is a very variable species. *Flowering period:* midsummer to mid-autumn; *height:* 4m (13 ft); *zones:* 4–9.

C. 'Aljonushka' A semi-herbaceous deciduous cultivar from Yalta, Crimea, raised by A. N. Volosenko-Valenis and M. A. Beskaravaingaja in 1963. It is non-clinging in its habit, with *C. integrifolia* as one of its parents, so it needs to be tied into its host or support. The flowers are semi-nodding to nodding, 6–8 cm (2¼–3¼ in) long, having usually four tepals which are rich, slightly mauve pink, with a satin sheen when young, with deep ridges on the reverse and crumpled edges, the tepal tips recurving and twisting as they age. A good colourful mixed border plant, it has strong healthy foliage that is rather coarse in texture and a distinctive habit. *Flowering period:* midsummer to early autumn; *height:* 1–1.5 m (3¼–5 ft); *zones:* 4–9.

C. apiifolia (Section Clematis) A deciduous species native to China and Japan with very little garden value, very free-flowering in its best forms with good seedheads, similar to *C. vitalba* but not so vigorous. The leaves are trifoliate, occasionally pinnate, with leaflets broad ovate to ovate-lanceolate, cordate to tapered at base, deeply incised and often trilobed. The star-like dull white flowers are 2 cm (¾ in) in diameter and are produced in axillary panicles. They are slightly scented and have prominent styles. Collected by the author on the lower slopes of Mount Fuji, Japan, in 1984. *Flowering period:* midsummer to early autumn; *height:* 4 m (13 ft); *zones:* 7.

C. 'Arabella' A very free-flowering deciduous cultivar raised in England by Barry Fretwell in about 1990, *C. integrifolia* being one of its parents. The 7–8 cm (2¼–3¼ in) wide flowers are round in shape and semi-nodding, having 4–6 tepals which are rosy purple, flushed with red. It is a pretty non-clinging plant which can be tied to its host or allowed to scramble through shrubs. *Flowering period:* midsummer to early autumn; *height:* 2 m (6½ ft); *zones:* 4–9.

C. × aromatica A deciduous hybrid between *C. flammula* and *C. integrifolia*, raised in the mid-1800s. It is non-clinging and needs support. Its very dark green leaves are 5–7-pinnate, the leaflets entire and lanceolate, and its 3–4 cm (1¼–1½ in) wide flowers generally have four tepals which are narrow, producing a very gappy star-like flower. The colour is dark violet-purple with yellow anthers. The flowers are strongly scented of vanilla. It needs a light background and looks good with

grey foliage shrubs. *Flowering period:* early summer to early autumn; *height:* 2 m (6½ ft); *zones:* 4–9.

C. 'Blue Boy' A non-clinging deciduous hybrid between *C. viticella* and *C. integrifolia*, raised for its hardiness value by Dr Frank Skinner in Canada in 1947. It is a very free-flowering plant with semi-nodding to nodding 5–7 cm (2–2¾ in) wide flowers, generally four tepals, the tepals being pale blue, recurving at the tips. A good mixed border plant, it can be used to tie on to the uprights of archways or pergolas, or allowed to flop through other shrubs. *Flowering period:* midsummer to early autumn; *height:* 2 m (6½ ft); *zones:* 3–9.

C. brachiata (probably syn. with *C. thunbergii*) (Section Clematis) A vigorous South African deciduous species which is very variable. The leaves are five-foliolate, rarely bipinnate, the leaflets rounded to ovate, coarse-serrate. The semi-nodding to nodding white to creamy green flowers are 2–3 cm (¾–1¼ in) deep and are freely produced in clusters. The four tepals recurve, displaying a large boss of yellow anthers. It is slightly scented. *Flowering period:* late summer to mid-autumn; *height:* 5 m (16½ ft); *zones:* 8–9.

C. brachyura (Section Pterocarpa) A deciduous species native to Korea which appears almost herbaceous in habit. It has bright green trifoliate foliage, the leaflets entire, rounded, occasionally further divided. The flowers are borne low down the plant on stems growing from the leaf axils, each leaf axil bud producing a flower stem with simple to trifoliate leaves with three flowers, each flower stalk (pedicel) having an abortive leaf-like bract. The flowers are 2.5–5 cm (1–2 in) in diameter and are slightly scented; they have four narrow tepals and creamy white anthers, making a star-like flower. A pretty plant, but only for the collector as it does not flower very profusely. *Flowering period:* mid to late summer; *height:* 1–1.5 m (3¼–5 ft); *zones:* 7–9.

C. brevicaudata (Section Clematis) A deciduous species, native to Japan, China and western Mongolia. It is an extremely vigorous climber of little garden value. The leaves are 5–7-foliolate, lower leaflets ternate, entire above, with leaflets ovate-lanceolate, long-acuminate and serrate. The creamy-white star-shaped flowers are 2 cm (¾ in) in diameter, produced in axillary cymes, grouped in large terminal panicles. They are followed by small fluffy seedheads rather similar to those of *C. vitalba*. A plant found by the author growing close to the Great Wall, near Beijing. *Flowering period:* late summer to mid-autumn; *height:* 4–5 m (13–16½ ft); *zones:* 5–9.

C. buchananiana (Section Connatae) A very variable vigorous deciduous climbing species from the Himalayas. The young growth is covered with yellowish to brownish hairs. The leaves are pinnately 5–7-foliolate, the leaflets broad-ovate, cordate at base, coarse-serrate, occasionally lobed. The tubular flowers, which are produced in panicles, are shaped like cowslips, being 3 cm (1¼ in) long. The tepals are a yellow-green to creamy-yellow, recurved at the tips. It is sometimes difficult to establish in cultivation, depending on the altitude at which the clone was collected. *Flowering period:* late summer to mid-autumn; *height:* 4–5 m (13–16½ ft); *zones:* 7–9.

C. chinensis (Section Flammula) A deciduous climber native to central and western China with pinnate leaves, the five leaflets ovate or cordate, usually cordate at the base. A late-flowering plant, so for the most flowers plant in a sunny location. The scented 3–4 cm (1¼–1½ in) wide flowers generally have four tepals which are narrow, making a star-like white flower, and are produced in profusion. *Flowering period:* early autumn; *height:* 4 m (13 ft); *zones:* 8–9.

C. connata (Section Connatae) A deciduous species native to southwest China and the Himalayas, very vigorous and very variable in habit. The leaves are 3–5-foliolate, with paired petiole bases forming a large disc-like shape at the base of each node. The leaflets are ovate, occasionally trilobed. The bell-like 3–4 cm (1¼–1½ in) long flowers have four tepals which are yellowish-green. Some forms open widely, others are closer together, with just the tips recurving, all with creamy-green anthers. It is a very late-flowering plant that should be grown in full sun to obtain a good crop of blooms. *Flowering period:* early to mid-autumn; *height:* 5 m (16½ ft); *zones:* 6–9.

C. crispa (Section Viorna) A deciduous scrambling species from the southeastern part of the USA, found in southern Virginia, extending westwards to southern Missouri and Illinois, as well as eastern Texas and Oklahoma. It has common names such as blue jasmine, marsh clematis, curly clematis and curlflower. The leaves are pinnately 5–7-foliolate, leaflets often trifoliate or lobed, lanceolate to broad ovate, cordate at base and entire. The very pretty flowers are nodding, solitary and terminal, the flowers being pitcher-shaped but the tips of the tepals recurving back on themselves. The flowers are 3–4 cm (1¼–1½ in) in depth, being lavender to purple in colour. The margins of the tepals are almost white, having crispulate edges which give the flower its unusual character. In its native habitat it grows in marshland, sometimes in acid soil, but it grows happily in normal garden soil. *Flowering period:* midsummer to late summer; *height:* 2 m (6½ ft); *zones:* 5–9.

C. douglasii var. scottiae See *C. hirsutissima* var. *scottii*.

C. 'Durandii' An early deciduous cultivar raised in France by Durand Frères in 1874 using *C. integrifolia* and *C.* 'Jackmanii' as the parents. It has simple lanceolate leaves and a non-clinging habit, making it a useful plant for scrambling around with other perennials or groundcover plants. The semi-nodding, flat, open, indigo blue flowers are 8–10 cm (3½–4 in) across, with cream anthers and white filaments which are blue at the base. The 4–6 tepals are deeply ribbed, becoming pointed at the tips. The reverse of each tepal is a deep mid-blue. A gappy but very attractive and interesting flower, suitable as a cut flower. *Flowering period:* midsummer to early autumn; *height:* 1–2 m (3¼–6½ ft); *zones:* 5–9. ♚

C. 'Eriostemon' A non-clinging deciduous plant that is strong-growing and very free-flowering, a useful garden plant for a mixed border, for clothing uprights to archways or pergolas, or growing through climbing roses. It was raised in Holland about 1830 and is thought to be a cross between *C. viticella* and *C. integrifolia*. The purple-blue flowers are semi-nodding, semi-open and are 5–6 cm (2–2¼ in) across, with greenish-cream anthers. The four tepals recurve at the tips and have a satin sheen when young. It can also be grown in a container for summer colour on the patio. *Flowering period:* midsummer to early autumn; *height:* 2 m (6½ ft); *zones:* 3–9.

C. × *fargesioides* 'Summer Snow' (syn. C. × *fargesioides* 'Paul Farges') A cultivar raised by A. N. Volosenko-Valenis and M. A. Beskaravainaja in the Crimea in 1964 by crossing C. *vitalba* and C. *potanini* var. *fargesii*. It is a vigorous deciduous climber used in Estonia and Latvia as a foraging plant for bees and is ideal on large walls or buildings or up into trees. The 4 cm (1½ in) wide slightly scented flowers have 4–6 tepals which are creamy-white and narrow, making a star-like flower with creamy-white anthers. *Flowering period:* midsummer to mid-autumn; *height:* 7 m (23 ft); *zones:* 3–9.

C. *flammula* (Section Flammula) This variable deciduous species is a native of southern Europe, especially along the Mediterranean coastline of Spain and the Balearic Islands, and was introduced into England as long ago as 1590, when it was known as the fragrant virgin's bower because of its strongly almond-scented flowers. The star-like white flowers are produced *en masse* and an established plant can have many hundreds if not over a thousand flowers open at one time. They are 2.5 cm (1 in) across and comprise four tepals which are narrow, with blunt tips, and creamy-white anthers. Some have glaucous leaves, others are almost evergreen; the broader the leaflets, the broader and more well-rounded the flowers. It does best in well-drained soils in a sunny location, and is great in evergreen trees such as hollies (*Ilex*). *Flowering period:* midsummer to mid-autumn; *height:* 4.5 m (15 ft); *zones:* 6–9.

C. *florida* (Section Viticella) This deciduous climbing species from China was found in Hupeh Province by Augustine Henry and near Ichang by Ernest Wilson but now seems lost in the wild or at least has not been seen recently. The type specimen sheet in the Uppsala University Herbarium, collected by Thunberg in 1776, is that of C. *f.* 'Sieboldii' and not C. *florida*. Recent sports reverting to C. *florida* in the author's nursery from C. *f.* 'Plena' and in Ruth Gooch's nursery from C. *f.* 'Sieboldii' are now in cultivation. The leaves are trifoliate, the leaflets lanceolate. The flowers are produced along the stem for 2 m (6½ ft) or so to the growing tip; they are well-rounded with generally six tepals and a good clear white in midsummer but green in the autumn. The anthers are black and the filaments are white at the base becoming purple black, a very dramatic flower. Of one selected cultivar called 'Evison', the flowers are

10–12.5 cm (4–5 in) across. The flower stems (pedicels) have a pair of bracts below the flower, at about halfway down. This form also produces seed which either comes true or reverts to C. *f.* 'Plena'. *Flowering period:* early summer to early autumn outside, until late autumn under glass; *height:* 2–3 m (6½–10 ft); *zones:* 6–9.

C. *f.* PISTACHIO™ 'Evirida' ⊘ This plant was produced from a sport from C. *florida* 'Evison', and resembles it in all aspects except the flower description. It will be introduced in 1999 as an Evison/Poulsen cultivar. It has six tepals which are overlapping, producing a rounded flower 8 cm (3¼ in) across, the tepals being creamy white in summer to creamy green in autumn. The centre of the flower is made up of short stamens with pinkish-grey anthers and there are no styles, these being replaced by a green tuft of aborted stigmas. The plant is extremely free-flowering over a long period and a worthy addition to the florida group. It is best grown through other wall-trained shrubs but is also good for container culture and is suitable as a cut flower. *Flowering period:* early summer to early autumn outside, until late autumn under glass; *height:* 3 m (10 ft); *zones:* 6–9.

C. *f.* 'Plena' This delightful clematis is a sport from C. *f.* 'Sieboldii' and although not well known was apparently introduced at the time the latter was introduced in 1835. It produces full double flowers resembling a rosette, the colour varying from creamy-white in the summer to greenish-white in late autumn. They are 10 cm (4 in) in diameter, with six outer tepals which are overlapping and fall away before the tight central rosette of tepals. The central part of the flower is made up of numerous small tepals with pointed tips. The flowers are sterile, but the plant sometimes reverts to C. *f.* 'Sieboldii'. Because of the rather thin nature of the stems it is best when grown through evergreen shrubs such as ceanothus. It is also ideal for growing in a container for the patio and is suitable as a cut flower, either singly or cut in long strands. A charming plant. *Flowering period:* early summer to early autumn outside, until late autumn under glass; *height:* 2–3 m (6½–10 ft); *zones:* 6–9.

C. *f.* 'Sieboldii' Previously known as C. *f.* 'Bicolor' and C. *f.* 'Sieboldiana', this plant was introduced by Dr Phillipp von Siebold to the Leiden Botanical Garden in Holland and then to the British Isles in 1835. This unusual clematis has a flower that resembles a passion flower and is much sought after. The habit is similar to C. *florida* and C. *f.* 'Plena'. The 10 cm (4 in) diameter flowers have six creamy-white outer tepals in summer, creamy green in autumn, which are overlapping to make a fully rounded flower, especially as the tips of the tepals recurve back. The outer tepals are offset by a dramatic central boss of purple petaloid stamens about 5–6 cm (2–2¼ in) across. These remain for a week or more after the outer tepals have fallen away. The flowers are sterile, but the plants sometimes revert to C. *f.* 'Plena'. It is best grown through other wall-trained shrubs but is also good for container culture and as a cut flower. *Flowering period*: early summer to early autumn outside, until late autumn under glass; *height*: 2–3 m (6½–10 ft); *zones*: 6–9.

C. *fruticosa* (Section Fruticella) An interesting deciduous sub-shrub from Central Asia, Mongolia and China. Its habit is that of a closely branched plant, with lanceolate leaves that are entire or toothed, and generally dark green. The yellow, semi-nodding, semi-open flowers are borne 1–4 per cluster, the tepals recurving at their tips revealing red anthers. They measure 5 cm (2 in) across. A useful mixed border plant. *Flowering period*: midsummer to early autumn; *height*: 60 cm (2 ft); *zones*: 5–9.

C. *fusca* var. *fusca* (Section Viorna) A native of the Kurile Islands, north of Japan, and introduced to England from Asia in 1860, this is a variable deciduous species growing to 1–2 m (3¼–6½ ft), some short forms being self-supporting. The leaves are pinnatisect, the leaflets being stalked. The flowers are most unusual, being covered in thick downy hairs. They are bell-shaped, hanging downwards from the leaf axils, and are 2–3 cm (¾–1¼ in) long. The four tepals are brown, of a thick texture, covered in brown hairs which go right down the flower stalk (pedicel) to the leaf axil node. The inner side of the tepals is cream or occasionally light blue, revealed as the tepals recurve at the tips. A plant of interest for the mixed border or with other shrubs for taller-growing forms. *Flowering period*: mid to late summer; *height*: 1–2 m (3¼–6½ ft); *zones*: 5–9 .

C. *f.* var. *violacea* A variant of the species from China and Korea, mainly growing to 2 m (6½ ft). The flowers, which are large at 3–5 cm (1¼–2 in) across but not so hairy as the

species, are borne in clusters of three in the leaf axil nodes at the growing tip of the current season's growth. They are semi-nodding to nodding and are open bell-shaped, the four thick-textured tepals purple-brown, recurving at the tips to reveal a purple-blue inside and creamy green anthers. The flowers produce very large seedheads which turn orange as they ripen, a very useful asset. A plant for the mixed border, or to be grown through other plants, but a light background is needed to show the flowers to best effect. *Flowering period*: midsummer to mid-autumn; *height*: 2–3 m (6½–10 ft); *zones*: 5–9.

C. *glauca akebioides* See C. *akebioides*.

C. *gouriana* (Section Clematis) A vigorous deciduous climbing species from the Himalayas and China, similar in habit to C. *vitalba*. The leaves are 5–7-foliolate, the leaflets ovate-oblong, long-acuminate, usually subcordate at the base, often entire. The young shoots are pubescent, the mature leaves shiny above. The open, four-tepalled flowers are produced in large panicles and are a creamy-white, 2 cm (¾ in) in diameter, with a large boss of stamens. They are followed by plenty of fluffy seedheads. It is somewhat better as a garden plant than C. *vitalba* as it has larger, more interesting flowers and is not so invasive. *Flowering period*: midsummer to early autumn; *height*: 6–7 m (20–23 ft); *zones*: 6–9.

C. *grata* (Section Clematis) A vigorous deciduous climber, native to the Himalayas, but not of great garden value. The leaves are pubescent, pinnately five-foliolate, the leaflets broad-ovate, coarsely and deeply dentate, sometimes lobed. The creamy white, open, four-tepalled flowers are 2 cm (¾ in) in diameter and are produced in terminal or axillary panicles. This plant is only for the wild-type garden, where it can be grown through trees, and where its 10 m (33 ft) of growth can scramble about. *Flowering period*: midsummer to early autumn; *height*: 10 m (33 ft); *zones*: 5–9.

C. *graveolens* (Section Meclatis) This deciduous climbing species is a native of Pakistan, north-west India, western Nepal and western China. The leaves are bipinnate with 5–7 primary divisions, the leaflets oblong to lanceolate, entire or lobed. The four-tepalled, 5 cm (2 in) wide flowers are yellow with reflexed tips and purplish-brown stamens, the tepals opening and

C. grewiiflora, a tender winter-flowering species from the Himalayas and Burma.

spreading widely apart as they age. The distinctive characteristic of this species is the small notch at the tip of each tepal. *Flowering period:* midsummer to early autumn; *height:* 4 m (13 ft); *zones:* 7–9.

C. g. 'Gravetye Variety' A selected clone of the species with bright green foliage and slightly larger flowers at 6 cm (2¼ in) across. *Flowering period:* midsummer to early autumn; *height:* 4 m (13 ft); *zones:* 7–9.

C. grewiiflora (Section Connatae) This interesting species, native to the Himalayas and Burma, is a strong-growing deciduous climber which I have grown only under glasshouse conditions. Its leaves are pinnate 3–7-foliolate, the leaflets broad-ovate, acute, tapered or cor-

date at the base, usually deeply lobed. The young foliage is thickly pubescent, the stems being covered with yellowish-brown hairs. The nodding flowers have appeared under glass in mid-winter and are broadly bell-shaped, pubescent inside, densely tomentose outside and are produced in panicles. The four tepals are browny-yellow and about 3 cm (1¼ in) long, with reflexed tips. *Flowering period:* late winter to early spring (outdoors), mid-winter (under glass); *height:* 4 m (13 ft); *zones:* 8–9.

C. heracleifolia var. heracleifolia (Section Tubulosae) A native of China, introduced to England in 1837, this variable deciduous species produces flowers in shades of blue and pink. It is an herbaceous sub-shrub with woody basal stems and eventually forms a huge clump of growth. The leaves are large and coarse, and divided into three leaflets which have serrated edges. The flowers are 2 cm (¾ in) long, produced in clusters at the growing tip in the leaf axil buds, and resemble hyacinth flowers, some also possessing a hyacinth scent. The four tepals open fully in some forms and remain closed in others, producing a bell-like tubular flower (it was known originally as *C. tubulosa*); they recurve at the tips, revealing creamy-green anthers. Flower colour can be determined by the foliage colour, light foliage producing pale blue flowers, darker producing dark blue flowers. A good mixed border plant. It is suitable as a cut flower and also has attractive seedheads. *Flowering period:* late summer to mid-autumn; *height:* 1 m (3¼ ft); *zones:* 5–9.

C. h. 'Cote d'Azur' A pale blue selected form, with 2 cm (¾ in) tubular flowers produced in clusters on flower stalks which are up to 15 cm (6 in) in length. The leaflets are not so serrated as in some forms of the species, and it has a slightly more woody base than the species. Introduced by Lemoine et fils, Nancy, France. *Flowering period:* late summer to mid-autumn; *height:* 75 cm (2½ ft); *zones:* 5–9.

C. h. var. davidiana A clone collected by Père David in 1863 near Beijing, with 2 cm (¾ in) pretty pale powdery blue flowers which are sweetly scented. This form does not have a woody base, being more herbaceous in habit. The leaves have serrated edges, and when they become dry in the late autumn they are scented. The flowers are borne tightly in the leaf axil buds and in the terminal buds. A good mixed border plant. *Flowering period:* late summer to mid-autumn; *height:* 90 cm (3 ft); *zones:* 5–9.

C. h. var. *davidiana* **'Wyevale'** A selection raised by Wyevale Nurseries, Hereford, England, in the mid-1950s. It resembles *C. h.* var. *davidiana* but has darker blue flowers, slightly larger at 3 cm (1¼ in), which are strongly scented of hyacinths. *Flowering period:* midsummer to mid-autumn; *height:* 1–1.2m (3¼–4 ft); *zones:* 5–9.

C. h. var. *stans* See *C. stans.*

C. *hirsutissima* **var.** *scottii* (syn. *C. douglasii* var. *scottii*) (Section Viorna) A deciduous non-climbing clone of the species from northwest USA and Canada which is an herbaceous plant with attractive, nodding, bell flowers, introduced by David Douglas in the early 1800s. The lower leaves are simple and the upper are 2–3-pinnate, leaflets oblong, lanceolate or ovate, entire or sometimes sparsely serrate. The young shoots are densely pubescent,

becoming glabrous later, and generally glaucous. The flowers are bell-shaped, up to 4 cm (1½ in) in length. They are solitary and always terminal. The four tepals are mauve blue and are pubescent and thick, reflexed at the tips. The flowers are followed by large fluffy seedheads. A most useful plant for the mixed border, best in a sunny, well-drained site. *Flowering period:* midsummer to early autumn; *height:* 45 cm (18 in); *zones:* 6–9.

C. *hirsutissima* **var.** *scottii* **'Rosea'** (syn. *C. douglasii* var. *scottii* 'Rosea') A very pleasant rose-pink form of the previous plant with 4 cm (1½ in) flowers. *Flowering period:* midsummer to early autumn; *height:* 45 cm (18 in); *zones:* 6–9.

C. 'Huldine' Raised by Morel in France, introduced to the British Isles by William Robinson and Ernest

A very deep red clone of *C. integrifolia* 'Rosea' found in Estonia which is not yet in commerce.

Markham and received an RHS Award of Merit in 1934. This very strong-growing deciduous climber is closely related to the Viticella group. It is said that there are two forms of this cultivar, one of which is shy flowering. The 8 cm (3¼ in) flowers are cup-shaped and held upright, the inner surface pearly white, the usually six tepals producing a rounded flower with yellow anthers. The reverse is most attractive, with three deep reddish-purple bars in the centre of the tepal, becoming paler towards the edges. Seen against the light, the almost translucent tepals show off the three mid-ribs. A long-flowering and rewarding plant, best on large walls or through open trees or large shrubs in sunny positions. *Flowering period:* late summer to late autumn in mild localities; *height:* 5–6 m (16½–20 ft); *zones:* 4–9.

C. integrifolia (Section Viorna) An herbaceous deciduous species introduced to England in 1573 from eastern Europe. This is a very useful perennial with simple elliptic leaves which clasp the stem. It grows to approximately 60 cm (2 ft) but is quite variable. The bell-like flowers, 4 cm (1½ in) deep, have four tepals which recurve outwards, with very pointed tips. The tepal colour also varies from mauve blue to a good deep blue. It is non-clinging and can be allowed to flop around at ground level. *Flowering period:* midsummer to early autumn; *height:* 60 cm (2 ft); *zones:* 4–9.

C. i. 'Alba' There are various forms of the 'white' *C. integrifolia*, some not true white. They are very often grown from seed, the seedlings being most variable and often reverting to the blue form of the species. The form of *C. integrifolia* 'Alba' that I grow was given to me by Magnus Johnson from his collection and has good pure white scented flowers 4 cm (1½ in) deep. To obtain a good scented white clone, purchase this plant when it is in flower and can be checked. *Flowering period:* midsummer to early autumn; *height:* 60 cm (2 ft); *zones:* 4–9.

C. i. 'Pangbourne Pink' Introduced by Dennis Bradshaw in 1992 from his Bushyfield Nursery in Kent, this large-flowered selection of *C. i.* 'Rosea' has a good deep pink flower colour. The flowers are open bell-shaped, 5–6 cm (2–2¼ in) across. Its foliage is also larger than the species. It is a most useful addition to this group. *Flowering period:* midsummer to early autumn; *height:* 60 cm (2 ft); *zones:* 4–9.

C. ladakhiana, a compact member of the Meclatis Section with red spots on the tepals.

C. i. 'Rosea' This too is variable, often grown from seed, so only good selected forms should be used for garden cultivation. It has pale pink or mauve-pink flowers which are 4 cm (1½ in) deep. *Flowering period:* midsummer to early autumn; *height:* 60 cm (2 ft); *zones:* 4–9.

C. × jouiniana 'Praecox' (Section Tubulosae) This cultivar was raised by crossing two very different species, C. *vitalba* and C. *heracleifolia*. It is a most useful garden plant which will scramble around at ground level to cover slabs of concrete or old tree stumps. It has large leaves which are trifoliate, the leaflets dark green with serrated margins. The flowers are 3 cm (1¼ in) across, borne in clusters from the leaf axil buds and the terminal stems, and it branches well, giving a good crop of flowers. They are open with reflexed tepals, generally four, a mixture between bluish-white and mauve, with creamy-white anthers. It can be used to clothe wall areas, where it must be tied to a support. *Flowering period:* midsummer to mid-autumn; *height:* grown on a wall 3 m (10 ft), grown at ground level 50 cm (20 in); *zones:* 3–9.

C. ladakhiana (Section Meclatis) A deciduous climber, native to India and China, which is more compact than most in the Meclatis group, growing to only 3 m (10 ft).

The glaucous leaves are pinnate to almost bipinnate, the leaflets narrow with acuminate tips. The unusual four-tepalled flowers are normally produced in groups of three or seven in the leaf axils and the tepals open to produce a spreading, nodding, open flower 4 cm (1½ in) across. The mature tepals are quite narrow and twisted and have a base colour of yellow to orange-yellow with dark reddish flecks all over the top side of the tepal. The anthers are reddish-brown. A useful plant for a small garden, with attractive silky seedheads when young, becoming fluffy with age. *Flowering period*: midsummer to early autumn; *height*: 3 m (10 ft); *zones*: 6–9.

C. *lasiandra* (Section Connatae) A vigorous deciduous climber, native to central and western China and Japan. The slender stems are angular and glutinous when young. The leaves are ternate or biternate, the leaflets deeply trilobed 7–9-foliolate, the leaflets ovate to lanceolate, irregularly coarse-serrate and generally deep green. The flowers are nodding and produced in groups in axillary cymes; they are bell-shaped, 2 cm (¾ in) long, with reflexed tepals at the apex, and are violet, mauve to white in colour with yellow anthers. Mauve, purple and white forms are found in Sichuan. With such a variable species, a good flowered form must be selected; it is mainly a collector's plant. *Flowering period*: late summer to mid-autumn; *height*: 3–4 m (10–13 ft); *zones*: 6–9.

C. *lasiantha* (Section Lasiantha) This deciduous climbing species is native to California, where it goes into a summer dormancy. The leaves are usually trifoliate, the leaflets broad-ovate, rounded to sub-cordate at base, coarse-serrate to trilobed, teeth rounded. The open flowers are 3 cm (1¼ in) across, sometimes solitary or grouped three or five, with four broad-oblong white tepals and prominent styles. A plant of mainly botanical interest, but useful in a native-plants garden. *Flowering period*: early autumn; *height*: 2–3 m (6–10 ft); *zones*: 8–9.

C. *ligusticifolia* (Section Clematis) A vigorous deciduous climber from western USA and Canada, similar in habit to C. *vitalba*, being rather invasive once established in an area and something of a weed. The leaves are pinnate 5–7-foliolate, leaflets ovate to lanceolate, long acuminate, cuneate at base, coarse-dentate and often trilobed. It has rather coarse, tough foliage. The unisexual star-like white flowers are 3 cm (1¼ in) in diameter with an open boss of stamens and white styles and are borne in panicles. It is not a plant of garden-worthiness, but useful as a woodland plant. *Flowering period*: late summer to mid-autumn; *height*: 7 m (23 ft); *zones*: 5–9.

C. 'Mrs Robert Brydon' (Section Tubulosae) A hybrid between C. *virginiana* and C. *h.* var. *davidiana* raised in North America in 1935 by Robert Brydon, this plant has retained the habit of the former species, growing up to 3 m (10 ft). It produces strong vigorous growth from woody stems and flowers along the growing tips. The foliage is coarse. It should be allowed to scramble at ground level or be tied up into a tree or against a wall where it can look dramatic when in full flower. The flowers are 3 cm (1¼ in) across, the four bluish-white tepals opening fully to produce a gappy flower with cream anthers. The flowers are produced in clusters from the leaf axil buds. It is suitable as a cut flower. *Flowering period*: midsummer to mid-autumn; *height*: 3 m (10 ft); *zones*: 5–9.

C. *orientalis* (Section Meclatis) This deciduous scrambling species has a fascinating small flower and is unlike any other species in the Meclatis group. The true species was reintroduced from Turkey by Dick and Rosalind Banks from Hergest Croft, Herefordshire, England in the early 1980s. It has a large native geographical area from eastern Europe to Turkey, Iran, Afghanistan, the former USSR and western China, and it is consequently quite variable. The leaves are pinnate and glaucous, the leaflets 5–7-lobed or unlobed and rarely toothed, each lanceolate to oblong. The yellow or yellowish-green nodding flowers can be tinged with reddish or purple brown on the outside. They measure 3 cm (1¼ in), with four tepals which open to become spreading then recurve tightly back on themselves, the red filaments and brown anthers becoming visible as the flower matures. They are borne on branched cymes in great numbers and are followed by attractive seedheads which are silky when young and fluffy when mature. This is a very pretty plant when in full flower and worthy of garden use. Although it will come almost true from seed, it should be propagated by cuttings to be sure the good clones are grown. *Flowering period*: midsummer to early autumn; *height*: 2–3 m (6½–10 ft); *zones*: 6–9.

C. pauciflora (Section Lasiantha) This low-growing deciduous species is a native of southwestern USA, especially southern California, where it has a summer dormancy. It has 3–5-foliolate leaves, the leaflets cordate to cunate-obovate, usually tridentate or lobed, glabrous to tomentose. The white, open flowers are borne solitarily or in small panicles and are about 2 cm (¾ in) in diameter. It is a plant best used in a native or woodland garden. *Flowering period:* late summer to early autumn; *height:* 2 m (6½ ft); *zones:* 9–10.

C. peterae (Section Clematis) A deciduous climbing Chinese species with pinnate leaves, the leaflets ovate or elliptic, acuminate, rounded or slightly cordate at the base, entire or dentate. The flat, open flowers are 2 cm (¾ in) across, borne in loose panicles, with white tepals, sometimes creamy white, and prominent styles. A plant for the collector, not of great garden value. *Flowering period:* mid to late summer; *height:* 3 m (10 ft); *zones:* 7–9.

C. PETIT FAUCON™ 'Evisix' ⊘ A deciduous Evison/Poulsen cultivar raised by the author in 1989 as a chance seedling with C. 'Daniel Deronda' being the seed parent, the male parent being either C. *integrifolia* or C. 'Eriostemon'. It has a non-clinging habit and a long flowering period of over three months. Its single elliptic leaves are bronze green in colour when young, becoming green when mature. It flowers most freely from the terminal growth on new growth, producing nodding flowers measuring 7–9 cm (2¾–3½ in) with 4–6 tepals of an intense deep blue. As they open they twist slightly, revealing a stunning orange/yellow boss of stamens. As the flower matures it opens fully, becoming bluer in colour, the stamens becoming creamy white. An ideal plant for the mixed perennial border, for growing with roses or covering the base of uprights to archways or pergolas. *Flowering period:* midsummer to mid-autumn; *height:* 1 m (3¼ ft); *zones:* 4–9.

C. phlebantha (Section Fruticella) A most interesting evergreen species, native to western Nepal, with very glaucous hairy foliage. It is almost self-supporting and grows only to about 60 cm (2 ft), but in optimum growing conditions and given support will reach 1.5 m (5 ft). The leaves are opposite, pinnate, 7- or at times 5–9-foliolate, the petioles lanate, the leaflets sessile or subsessile, acute, broad-cuneate at base, green and sericeous above, thick white lanate beneath. The flat, open flowers are 5 cm (2 in) in diameter, with six white tepals and yellow anthers. A collector's plant and really only suitable for a conservatory or cold glasshouse, except in warm climates. *Flowering period:* mid to late summer; *height:* 60–150cm (2–5 ft); *zones:* 8–9.

C. pitcheri (Section Viorna) A strong-growing, free-flowering deciduous climber from southeastern USA which is almost herbaceous in habit. It is a useful garden plant. The leaves are pinnately 3–7-foliolate, the leaflets ovate 2–3-lobed or trifoliate, rounded or somewhat cordate at the base, occasionally the terminal leaflet reduced to a tendril. The flowers are pitcher-shaped, with four thick tepals which recurve at the tips, the flower length being 3–4 cm (1¼–1½ in). It varies in colour, the clone grown by the author having violet-purple tepals which open slightly at the tips to reveal a green-yellow inside. The flowers produce large spiky seedheads which are most attractive. A useful plant to grow through other wall-trained shrubs, a light background being ideal to display the flowers to their best advantage. *Flowering period:* mid to late summer; *height:* 3.5 m (12 ft); *zones:* 4–9.

C. potaninii var. fargesii (Section Clematis) A deciduous climbing species native to southwestern China which is of good garden value, looking fine growing through large dark evergreen foliage such as that of common yew (*Taxus baccata*). The leaves are bipinnate, the leaflets ovate-acuminate, rounded or tapered at base, irregularly lobed or serrate. The 4 cm (1½ in) wide white flowers have usually six tepals which are broad and blunt-tipped, making a rounded flower but with gaps between the tepals, and yellow anthers. They are borne singly or in bracteolate cymes, followed by attractive small silky seedheads which look pleasing with the late summer flowers. *Flowering period:* midsummer to early autumn; *height:* 3–5 m (10–16½ ft); *zones:* 3–9.

C. ranunculoides (Section Connatae) A variable deciduous species from China, growing as a perennial to about 50 cm (20 in) or as a lax climber to 2–3 m (6½–10 ft). The stems and branches are angular and red in colour, pubescent to subglabrous. The leaves are trifoliate or pinnate five-foliolate, or simple and trilobed; the leaflets are rounded-obovate or ovate, coarse-dentate and pubescent. The pink-purple nodding flowers are bell-shaped, 2–3 cm (¾–1¼ in) deep, borne very late in axillary clusters or groups, and terminal, on stalks (pedicels) which are generally twisted and reddish in colour. The four tepals are very reflexed and ribbed, revealing pinkish anthers and filaments. In selected good forms it is gardenworthy, but only for mild climates on a sunny, well-drained site. *Flowering period:* early to mid-autumn; *height:* 50 cm (20 in) or 2–3 m (6½–10 ft); *zones:* 8–9.

C. recta var. recta (Section Flammula) This herbaceous deciduous species is native to central and southern Europe and was first introduced into England in 1597. A very variable species in leaf form and height, it varies from compact free-flowering clones of 1 m (3¼ ft) in height to tall 2 m (6½ ft) plants of rather loose habit and more sparsely flowered. It is a very useful herbaceous plant for the mixed border where compact clones can be allowed to flop at ground level or be supported by pea-sticks, hazel branches or modern perennial-plant supports. Tall-growing clones need to be used at the back of a mixed border and tied to a strong stake that is deeply and firmly anchored into the soil. The general description of the foliage is as follows: dense branched habit, leaves pinnate 5–7-foliolate, leaflets oval-lanceolate acuminate, cuneate or sometimes cordate, entire, the leaf colour a deep bluish green but can vary to dark green. The flowers are borne in great abundance in terminal panicles, generally having four white, narrow tepals, which produce a star-like flower 3 cm (1¼ in) across, and creamy white anthers. In many clones the flowers are very strongly scented of hawthorn, almost too heavily scented, becoming overwhelming. Some clones have attractive bronzy-red seedheads. There are also semi-double clones becoming available but these are not the old *C. recta* 'Plena' which was recorded to have double flowers. *Flowering period:* midsummer to early autumn; *height:* 1–2 m (3¼–6½ ft); *zones:* 3–9.

C. r. var. purpurea A purple-leaved form of the species, which can be raised from seed. In large batches of seedlings of *C. recta* there can be up to 10 per cent which produce a purple-foliaged plant, but only selected good foliage forms should be given garden space or reproduced. Even with good selected clones the leaves do slowly turn green by the end of the summer, but if the plants are regularly trimmed back during the growing season and not allowed to flower, the effective new growth can be enjoyed several times over the summer. *Flowering period:* midsummer to early autumn; *height:* 1 m (3¼ ft); *zones:* 3–9.

C. rehderiana (Section Connatae) A very vigorous deciduous climbing species from western China, introduced to the British Isles by Ernest Wilson in 1908, with interesting cowslip-like flowers which are slightly scented. The stems are angular. The leaves are pinnately 7–9-foliolate, the leaflets broad-ovate, acute, cordate or rounded at the base, often trilobed, coarse-serrate, and densely covered with hairs. The pendulous flowers, 3 cm (1¼ in) are produced in panicles and are a pale yellow to pale greenish-yellow, especially when young. They hold a lot of pollen. This is a very useful garden plant that needs to be grown on a very large wall or, better still, up into open trees. *Flowering period:* midsummer to mid-autumn; *height:* 7 m (23 ft); *zones:* 6–9.

C. serratifolia (Section Meclatis) A deciduous species from Korea and northeastern China, introduced about 1918, with biternate leaves, leaflets ovate to lanceolate, long-acuminate, oblique at base, sharp-serrate margins, usually a bright green. The nodding, yellow, four-tepalled flowers are 3–4 cm (1¼–1½ in) across, borne solitarily or 2–3 together. The tepals are lanceolate to elliptic and spread open as the flower matures, revealing dark-coloured anthers. They are followed by fluffy seedheads. A good garden plant that can be used as groundcover for its dense habit and free-flowering nature. *Flowering period:* midsummer to mid-autumn; *height:* 3–4 m (10–13 ft); *zones:* 3–9.

C. songarica (Section Fruticella) An erect-growing deciduous sub-shrub with a woody base, native to Mongolia, Korea, southern Siberia and Turkistan. It is a useful garden plant for the mixed border, with blue-green glaucous foliage. The leaves are simple, linear to lanceolate, entire to serrate-dentate, fairly thick, almost fleshy. The 5 cm (2 in) wide flowers are freely produced in large open panicles, solitary, paired or sometimes grouped in threes, in axillary or terminal shoots. They are star-like, with usually four white tepals and white to creamy yellow anthers. They are followed by large silky seedheads. *Flowering period:* midsummer to mid-autumn; *height:* 1.5 m (5 ft); *zones:* 6–9.

C. stans (occasionally classified as *C. heracleifolia stans*) (Section Tubulosae) A deciduous sub-shrub from Japan, growing on stout stems to 1 m (3¼ ft) in height. The leaves are trifoliate, the leaflets broad-ovate, coarse-sharp-serrate and distinctly veined. The tubular flowers are unisexual, 2–3 cm (¾–1¼ in) long, and are produced in terminal panicles in clusters. The flower colour varies, generally being pale lavender blue to very pale blue, and the four tepals reflex at the tips. A useful mixed border plant, normally overshadowed by the brighter and deeper coloured forms of *C. heracleifolia*. It produces attractive silky seedheads. *Flowering period:* midsummer to early autumn; *height:* 1 m (3¼ ft); *zones:* 4–9.

C. tangutica var. tangutica (Section Meclatis) This deciduous climbing species from Mongolia and northwestern China is well known in gardens but is often confused with hybrids between *C. orientalis* and other similar species, or is wrongly named. The true species has bright green leaves which have serrated margins. They are pinnate to bipinnate, the leaflets oblong to lanceolate, sometimes lobed, irregularly dentate, the serrated margins having pointed teeth. The attractive golden-yellow lantern-shaped flowers, 3–4 cm (1¼–1½ in) long, have four tepals which do not open fully as with *C. orientalis*. They are followed by large fluffy seedheads. The mixture of flowers and seedheads make it a most useful garden plant for large wall areas or for growing up into open trees. *Flowering period:* midsummer to late autumn; *height:* 5–6 m (16½–20 ft); *zones:* 4–9.

C. t. 'Aureolin' A cultivar raised in Holland, with larger flowers than the species. The yellow 5 cm (2 in) cowbell-like flowers are followed by large attractive seedheads, which become fluffy with age and are ideal for drying for winter decorations. *Flowering period:* midsummer to mid-autumn; *height:* 2–3 m (6½–10 ft); *zones:* 4–9. ♛

C. t. 'Bill Mackenzie' A very good large-flowered cultivar selected by Bill Mackenzie at the Horticultural College at Waterperry in Oxfordshire, England, in 1968. The flower opens more than the species, becoming open bell-shaped when mature and 6–7 cm (2¼–2¾ in) across. The four yellow tepals are broad, with pointed tips; the filaments are reddish in colour, the anthers brownish-yellow-green. A strong-growing plant, ideal for large walls, open-framed trees or large pergolas. It is the best of all the tall-growing Meclatis group for flowers and seedheads. *Flowering period:* midsummer to late autumn; *height:* 5–6 m (16½–20 ft); *zones:* 4–9. ♛

C. t. 'Burford Variety' Raised at Burford House Garden, England, by John Treasure in the 1970s, as a chance seedling from *C. tangutica*. It is a very good free-flowering cultivar with 4 cm (1½ in) yellow flowers that are more rounded than the species and an excellent display of seedheads. *Flowering period:* midsummer to mid-autumn; *height:* 3–4 m (10–13 ft); *zones:* 4–9.

C. t. 'Helios' A very useful compact cultivar raised in Boskoop, Holland, in 1988, an ideal plant for small gardens. The 4–6 cm (1½–2¼ in) yellow flowers are lantern-like when young, but as they mature the tepals open flat to reveal the reddish-brown-purple filaments and creamy-yellow anthers – a pretty flower which should be more widely grown. The seedheads are large. *Flowering period:* midsummer to mid-autumn; *height:* 1.5 m (5 ft); *zones:* 4–9.

C. t. 'Lambton Park' A large-flowered cultivar, raised in northeast England, with a coconut-like scent. The 5 cm (2 in) wide flowers are cowbell in shape with four thick tepals in a bright buttercup yellow which taper to a point, the edges recurving to reveal the yellowish-green anthers. The large, attractive seedheads are produced freely over a long period. *Flowering period:* early summer to mid-autumn; *height:* 3–4 m (10–13 ft); *zones:* 4–9.

C. t. var. obtusiuscula An interesting subspecies from western Sichuan in China, introduced about 1913 by Ernest Wilson, with young shoots that are more lanuginose-pubescent, leaflets smaller and less serrated. The flowers are more globular in shape at first and are a good rich yellow, opening more widely than the species, generally only 3 cm (1¼ in) long. It is also more compact in habit, and comes almost true from seed as long as there are no other similar species nearby. It is a useful plant for the smaller garden. *Flowering period:* midsummer to mid-autumn; *height:* 3–4 m (10–13 ft); *zones:* 5–9.

C. terniflora (Section Flammula) This Japanese climber is deciduous in cold climates but can be evergreen in mild locations. It was known to North American gardeners as C. *paniculata* or the 'sweet fall scented clematis'. In later years it was renamed *maximowicziana* by taxonomists, now being correctly known as *terniflora*. This plant is well used in North America and has naturalized in some areas, enjoying the hot summers, but sadly it does not flower so well in the British Isles unless the summer is long and hot. British gardeners should plant it in a hot, sunny position to achieve the best crop of flowers. The leaves are pinnately 3–5-foliolate, the leaflets cordate to ovate, entire and usually a very dark green. The hawthorn-scented, star-like flowers are 3 cm (1¼ in) wide, with four narrow white tepals and white anthers. They are produced in great abundance in panicles and are followed by attractive silky seedheads. It is a vigorous plant, ideal for covering fences, archways, pergolas and large wall areas and growing into trees. *Flowering period:* late summer to mid-autumn; *height:* 6 m (20 ft); *zones:* 5–9.

C. t. 'Robusta' An extremely vigorous form of the species, with large leaves which often have a silver stripe down the centre of each leaflet. The leaves are five-foliolate, the leaflets lanceolate to cordate, with pointed tips, entire. The flowers are also larger, being 5 cm (2 in) in diameter, and the white tepals are broader than the species, but still a star-like, gappy flower, with creamy-white anthers and a strong hawthorn scent. It is best grown on large fences or walls or up into trees. It needs a well-drained sunny site to flower well and is probably only suitable to grow in southern England/southern areas of the British Isles, southern Europe and warm areas of the USA and Canada. *Flowering period:* late summer to mid-autumn; *height:* 7 m (23 ft); *zones:* 5–9.

C. texensis (Section Viorna) A most colourful, unusual clematis native to limestone areas of Texas, first introduced into the British Isles in 1880. It is an herbaceous plant, growing from soil level each year, almost perennial in habit. The leaves are glaucous, pinnate, 4–8-foliolate, the leaflets ovate to rounded, occasionally 2–3-lobed, usually cordate at the base, entire, tough-textured. Sometimes the terminal leaflet becomes a tendril. The flowers vary considerably, the outstanding scarlet-red clones being the most sought after. They are

semi-nodding and pitcher-shaped, 3–4cm (1¼–½ in) in length, becoming much narrower towards the mouth, the four very thick tepals having pointed tips that recurve. The inside of the flower is creamy yellow but this is also variable. It is a very hardy clematis, sometimes subject to powdery mildew and very difficult to establish well in gardens, but a useful garden plant. When used in a hybridization programme in the late 1800s, it gave rise to several good garden plants. It was found to be compatible with large-flowered cultivars such as C. 'Jackmanii' and C. 'Star of India'. The cultivars raised are much easier to establish in gardens and produce either nodding or upright miniature tulip-like flowers. *Flowering period:* midsummer to mid-autumn; *height:* 2 m (6½ ft); *zones:* 4–9.

C. t. 'Duchess of Albany' A cultivar raised by Jackmans of Woking in 1890, from crossing C. *texensis* with C. 'Star of India'. This fine clematis has upright miniature tulip-like flowers which are 5–6 cm (2–2¼ in) in length. The four tepals are held closely together, opening enough to reveal the pinkish anthers. The tepals are a satiny deep candy pink on the inside, with a darker central bar. The thick flower stalk (pedicel) gives the flower a long-lasting quality as a cut flower. It is best grown almost at ground level where the flowers can be looked into, though the outside of the flowers does have an attractive pink colouring. A very useful garden plant. *Flowering period:* midsummer to mid-autumn; *height:* 3 m (10 ft); *zones:* 3–9. ♛

C. t. 'Etoile Rose' Raised about 1903 by Lemoine in France using C. *viticella* as a parent; it retains the nodding flower habit of C. *viticella* and C. *texensis*. This is a stunning clematis, producing a mass of nodding to semi-nodding 6 cm (2¼ in) flowers with four tepals. The flowers are deeply textured. The inside base colour is a vibrant, almost pale scarlet pink, the colour becoming paler towards the margins. The outer surface is a deep satiny pink. The margins have serrated edges and reflex at the tips, the tepals opening more fully as they mature to reveal pale yellow anthers. Sometimes this cultivar is subject to powdery mildew and preventative action should be taken early in the season. It is an excellent plant for growing up into small trees with an open framework. *Flowering period:* midsummer to early autumn; *height:* 3 m (10 ft); *zones:* 4–9.

C. *texensis* 'Duchess of Albany' holds its miniature tulip-shaped flowers upright and should be grown at a low level to afford the best view of them.

C. t. 'Gravetye Beauty' Raised by Morel in France about 1900, introduced into England by William Robinson in 1914 and named after his estate, Gravetye Manor. It bears miniature tulip-like flowers which open perhaps a little too much, giving a gappy appearance to the flower as it ages. The 4–6 tepals are a very deep rich red and taper to a point, recurving as the flower matures to reveal reddish-brown anthers. When fully open, the flower measures about 6–8 cm (2¼–3¼ in) across. This cultivar is best grown at ground level through other groundcover plants, or even summer bedding plants,

where its colourful flowers can best be enjoyed. *Flowering period:* midsummer to mid-autumn; *height:* 3 m (10 ft); *zones:* 4–9.

C. t. 'Ladybird Johnson' A fine cultivar raised in 1984 by Barry Fretwell in Devon, England, by crossing C. *texensis* with the large-flowered cultivar C. 'Bees' Jubilee'. The miniature tulip-shaped flowers are 4 cm (1½ in) long, with four deep-textured tepals which are a deep purple-red with a brighter crimson central bar. The tips of the tepals open slightly to reveal the creamy anthers. *Flowering period:* early summer to early autumn; *height:* 3 m (10 ft); *zones:* 4–9.

C. t. 'Pagoda' Raised by John Treasure in Burford House Gardens, England, in the 1970s by crossing C. *viticella* with C. *texensis* 'Etoile Rose'. It retains the vigour of the former and the charm of the latter, having open nodding 6–8 cm (2¼–3¼ in) wide, four-tepalled flowers with recurving tips – a very pretty flower, well named for its flower shape. The outside of the tepals is creamy pink-mauve with a deeper mauve-purple band which tapers to the tip of the tepal, the inside being a pretty creamy pink, deeper at the margins and veined throughout. The anthers are green-cream, and as the flower matures the tepals reflex and open more. A very useful plant for growing on fences, on walls, into small trees or on shrubs with an open framework of branches – the flowers look equally attractive viewed from above or below. *Flowering period:* early summer to late summer; *height:* 3 m (10 ft); *zones:* 4–9.

C. t. 'Sir Trevor Lawrence' Raised by Jackmans of Woking in 1890 by crossing C. *texensis* with C. 'Star of India', this cultivar has a miniature tulip-like flower 5–6 cm (2–2¼ in) in length. The inside of the flower has a pretty colouring to each tepal, margined a dusky purple-red with a central band of scarlet. The tips of the tepals roll back with maturity, revealing a yellow boss of anthers. The outside of the tepals is whitish-pink when in shade and reddish-pink when in full sun, with reddish-pink veins running down the length of the tepal. It is a very good garden plant that should be grown at ground or eye level so that the flowers can be enjoyed to their best advantage. It looks stunning with white summer-flowering heathers. *Flowering period:* midsummer to early autumn; *height:* 3 m (10 ft); *zones:* 4–9.

C. t. 'The Princess of Wales' Another fine Barry Fretwell cultivar, raised in 1984 by crossing C. *texensis* with C. 'Bees' Jubilee'. It has miniature tulip-shaped flowers which are 6 cm (2¼ in) long. The four tepals are a luminous pink with a deep vibrant pink central bar becoming mauve-deep pink as it nears the margin. The outside of the tepals is pale whitish pink at the margins, with a deep pink central band. *Flowering period:* early to late summer, and early autumn; *height:* 2.5m (8¼ ft); *zones:* 4–9.

C. thunbergii See C. *brachiata*.

C. tibetana var. **tibetana** (Section Meclatis) This deciduous climber is native to northern India, with leaves glaucous, leaflets leathery, narrow lanceolate to elliptic or ovate, entire or with 1–3 lobes to the base, rarely toothed. The yellow to greenish-yellow flowers are nodding and open, 4 cm (1½ in) across, and the four tepals have pointed tips which reflex at the ends, opening more as the flowers mature. The flower buds are green and globe-shaped. An interesting garden plant with useful glaucous foliage, it is good through other shrubs, small trees or on fences. It has attractive silky seedheads when young, becoming fluffy when mature. *Flowering period:* midsummer to mid-autumn; *height:* 3–4 m (10–13 ft); *zones:* 6–9.

C. t. var. **vernayi** A native of Nepal and Tibet with glaucous leaves, the leaflets having a few lobes near the base, being of a leathery texture. The leaflets are narrow lanceolate to elliptical or ovate, entire, rarely toothed. The nodding 4–5 cm (1½–2 in) wide, yellow or greenish-yellow flowers are covered with splashes of a rusty bronze or purple-brown on the outside. The tepals are thick and fleshy, being greenish-yellow on the inside, with dark purple stamens. It has attractive silky seedheads when young, becoming fluffy when mature. *Flowering period:* midsummer to early autumn; *height:* 2–3 m (6½–10 ft); *zones:* 6–9.

C. t. var. **vernayi L & S 13342** A form collected by Frank Ludlow and George Sherriff in the Lhasa area of Tibet in about 1947. This differs from other forms of C. *tibetana* in having very thick tepals and is very often called 'the orange peel clematis'. There are many seedlings distributed bearing the name of 'orange peel',

but these must not be confused with this clone. Its foliage is very glaucous, finely cut and most attractive. The four-tepalled flowers are nodding, rather globular when opening. As the flower ages the tepals reflex fully to produce an open bell-shaped flower, 4 cm (1½ in) across, its tepals spreading out open as they mature. The tepals are yellow and have a pointed tip, the thickness being that of lemon rind rather than that of orange peel. A useful garden plant which looks very good with large-leaved rhododendrons. *Flowering period:* midsummer to mid-autumn; *height:* 3 m (10 ft); *zones:* 5–9. ♛

C. × triternata 'Rubromarginata' A deciduous cultivar raised by Cripps & Son in England in 1862 by crossing C. *flammula* with C. *viticella* 'Rubra'. It is a splendid free-flowering plant which is highly scented of hawthorn and not widely grown despite its age as a cultivar. It is vigorous in habit when fully established and produces clouds of narrow, four-tepalled, star-like flowers that are white with wine-red edges, 3–4 cm (1¼–1½ in) across, with creamy anthers. It is useful for growing into small trees or large shrubs, on fences or on large wall areas. *Flowering period:* midsummer to early autumn; *height:* 3–4 m (10–13 ft); *zones:* 5–9. ♛

C. uncinata (Section Flammula) An evergreen climbing species from central China, with blue-green rather glaucous foliage. The leaves are 3–5 divided, each division trifoliate, leaflets ovate to ovate-lanceolate, acute, entire, glabrous. The open star-shaped white flowers are slightly scented, 2.5 cm (1 in) in diameter, with four oblong, narrow tepals and yellow anthers. They are borne in terminal and axillary panicles. An interesting plant for the sheltered garden, in well-drained soil, suitable for walls or at the base of other wall-trained plants. *Flowering period:* mid to late summer; *height:* 2 m (6½ ft); *zones:* 8–9.

C. viorna (Section Viorna) This very pretty variable deciduous species from eastern North America, known as the leather flower or vase vine, is a climbing plant with a woody base or a sub-shrub. The leaves are 5–7-foliolate, the leaflets ovate to elliptic-lanceolate, cordate at the base, entire or somewhat lobed. The flowers are pitcher-shaped, 3–4 cm (1¼–1½ in) deep and pendulous, borne in clusters, and vary from violet to dull purple to pinkish. The four thick tepals recurve at

C. *viorna*, a delightful pitcher-shaped species from eastern North America (shown at 1½ times normal size).

the tips, revealing creamy-yellow margins and yellow anthers. The flowers are followed by very attractive, large, spiky seedheads. The better-coloured forms are most gardenworthy and can be grown through other low-growing groundcover shrubs, where the flowers can be enjoyed at close quarters, or on fences and up into larger shrubs. *Flowering period:* midsummer to early autumn; *height:* 2 m (6½ ft); *zones:* 4–9.

C. *virginiana* (Section Clematis) This vigorous deciduous climber is a native of the eastern parts of the northern USA and Canada. Its local names include woodbine, leather flower, virgin's bower and devil's darning needle. Its young stems are furrowed, subglabrous, the leaves trifoliate, rarely five-foliolate, the leaflets broad-ovate, acuminate, rounded or somewhat cordate at the base, coarse and irregular-serrate. The star-shaped, gappy flowers are 3 cm (1¼ in) wide, borne in axillary panicles, have four narrow white tepals and a boss of stamens which are also white, and are followed by silky seedheads. It is a rampant plant for the woodland or natural garden, ideal for covering large areas, but not a gardenworthy plant. *Flowering period:* late summer to mid-autumn; *height:* 7–8 m (23–26 ft); *zones:* 4–9.

C. *vitalba* (Section Clematis) The only species native to the British Isles, and also native to Europe, Lebanon, Caucasia, northern Iran and Afghanistan, this is a very vigorous, almost unruly, deciduous climber which naturalizes easily. The leaves are pinnately five-foliolate, rarely trifoliate, the leaflets ovate or sub-entire. The creamy white four-tepalled flowers, 3 cm (1¼ in) across, are borne in axillary panicles, being very star-like and gappy, with creamy yellow anthers. It is noted for its extremely attractive seedheads, which are silky when young, becoming fluffy and greyish-brown in colour when mature. They are produced in abundance and are outstanding in late autumn to early winter, especially on frosty mornings. They are excellent for drying for winter decorations. *Flowering period:* late summer to early autumn; *height:* 10 m (33 ft); *zones:* 4–9.

APPENDICES

INTERNATIONAL CLEMATIS REGISTER

Victoria Matthews (International Clematis Registrar)
7350 SW 173rd Street, Miami,
Florida 33157-4835, USA

CLEMATIS SOCIETIES

International Clematis Society (*Secretary:* Fiona Woolfenden)
3, Cuthberts Close, Cheshunt, Waltham Cross EN7 5RB
Tel: 01992 636 524

British Clematis Society (*Secretary:* Richard Stothard)
4 Springfield, Lightwater, Surrey GU18 5XP
Tel: 01276 476387

NATIONAL COLLECTIONS

Raymond Evison
Domarie Vineries, Les Sauvagees, St Sampson,
Guernsey GY2 4FD
Tel: 01481 45942
Over 600 species & cultivars
The nursery is not open to the public.

Treasures of Tenbury Ltd
Burford House Gardens, Tenbury Wells,
Worcestershire WR15 8HQ
Tel: 01584 810777
Species, *C. texensis*, *C. viticella* & herbaceous

Mr M. Oviatt-Ham
Ely House, Green St, Willingham, Cambridgeshire CB4 5JA
Tel: 01954 260481
Atragene Section.

Mr D. Bradshaw
J. Bradshaw & Son, Busheyfields Nursery, Herne Bay,
Kent CT6 7LJ
Tel: 01227 375415
C. montana & *C. chrysocoma*.

Bridgemere Nurseries
Bridgemere, Nr Nantwich, Cheshire CW5 7QB
Tel: 01270 521125
C. orientalis.

Mr & Mrs J. Hudson
The Mill, 21 Mill Lane, Cannington, Bridgwater,
Somerset TA5 2HB
Tel: 01278 652304
C. texensis.

WHERE TO SEE CLEMATIS

British Isles
Hergest Croft Gardens
Nr. Kington, Herefordshire
Tel: 01544 230160

Hidcote Manor Gardens
Hidcote Bartrim, Nr. Chipping Campden, Gloucestershire
Tel: 01386 438333

RHS Garden Hyde Hall
Rettendon, Chelmsford, Essex CM3 8ET
Tel: 01245 400256

RHS Garden Rosemoor
Great Torrington, Devon EX38 8PH
Tel: 01805 624067

RHS Garden Wisley
Woking, Surrey GU23 6QB
Tel: 01483 224234

Sissinghurst Gardens
Sissinghurst Castle, Sissinghurst, Kent
Tel: 01580 712850

Thorncroft Show Garden
The Lings, Reymerston, Norwich NR9 4QG
Tel: 01953 850407

USA
Brooklyn Botanic Garden
1000 Washington Avenue, Brooklyn, New York 11225-1099
Tel: (001) 718 622 4433
Fax: (001) 718 857 2430

Chicago Botanical Gardens
Glencoe, Illinois 60022-04
Tel: (001) 708 835 5440
Fax: (001) 708 835 4484

Canada
Royal Botanic Gardens
PO Box 399, Hamilton, Ontario L8N 3H8
Tel: (001) 905 527 1158
Fax: (001) 905 577 0375

WHERE TO BUY CLEMATIS

British Isles
Pennells Nurseries
Newark Rd., South Hykeham, Lincoln LN6 9NT
Tel: 01522 880044
Fax: 01522 880055

RHS Plant Centre
RHS Garden, Wisley, Woking, Surrey GU23 6QB
Tel: 01483 211113

Treasures of Tenbury Ltd
Burford House Gardens, Tenbury Wells,
Worcestershire WR15 8HQ
Tel: 01584 810777
Fax: 01584 810673

Wycvale Garden Centres plc,
Kings Acre Road, Hereford HR4 0SE
Tel: 0800 413 213 *for details of the nearest Centre*

Sweden
Åkarps Plantskola AB
Mossjagen 17, 23237 Arlor
Tel: (0046) 40 46 33 32
Fax: (0046) 40 46 33 32

Cedergren & Co. Plantskola,
Box 16016, 25016 Raa
Tel: (0046) 42 26 0052/0890
Fax: (0046) 42 26 0890

Italy
Vivaio Anna Peyron
Cascina La Custodia, 10090 Castagneto Po, Turin
Tel: (0039) 11 914 917/8/9
Fax: (0039) 11 912 590

USA
Donahues' Greenhouses Inc.
420 S.W. 10th Street, Faribault, Minnesota 55021
Tel: (001) 507 334 8404
Fax: (001) 507 334 0485

Greer Gardens
1280 Goodpasture Island Road,
Eugene, Oregon 97401

Tel: (001) 800 548 0111
Fax: (001) 541 686 0910

Joy Creek Nursery
20300 N.W. Watson Road, Scappoose,
Oregon 97056
Tel: (001) 503 227 2160
Fax: (001) 503 543 6933

Canada
Adera Nurseries Ltd
1971 Wain Road, R.R.4, Sidney, B.C. V8L 4R4
Tel: (001) 250 656 3445
Fax: (001) 250 656 3486

Linwell Gardens Ltd,
344 Read Road RR No. 6, St Catherines,
Ontario L2R 7K6
Tel: (001) 905 935 0011
Fax: (001) 905 935 1279

South Africa
Keith Kirsten's (Pty) Ltd,
PO Box 1258, Parklands 2121
Tel: (0027) 11 447 2368
Fax: (0027) 11 880 4225

New Zealand
N.Z. Clematis Nurseries
67, Ngaio Street, St Martins, Christchurch
Tel/Fax: (0064) 33 32 58 90

MAIL ORDER SUPPLIERS

British Isles & Europe
Thorncroft Clematis Nurseries
The Lings, Reymerston,
Norwich NR9 4QG
Tel: 01953 850407
Fax: 01953 851788

USA
Wayside Gardens
1 Garden Lane, Hodges, South
Carolina 29695-0001
Tel: (001) 864 941 4512
Fax: (001) 864 941 4502

Canada
Gardenimport Inc.
PO Box 760, Thornhill,
Ontario L3T 4A5
Tel: (001) 905 731 1950
Fax: (001) 905 881 349

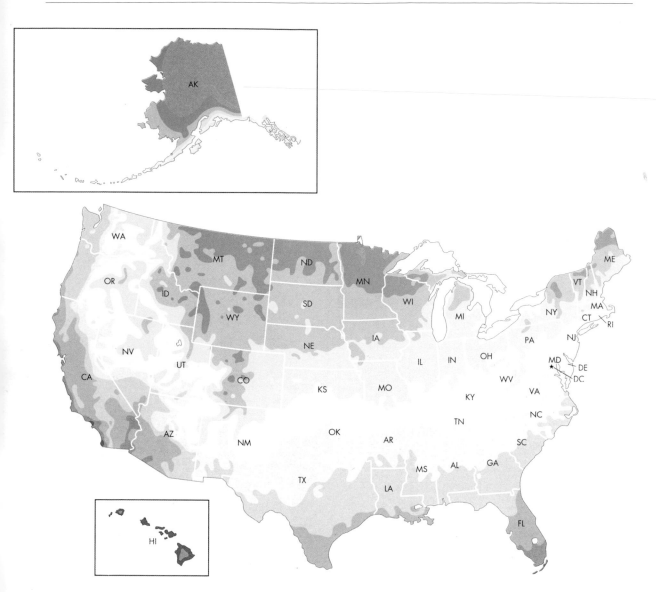

PLANT HARDINESS ZONES

The hardiness zone system developed by the USDA is based on the average annual minimum temperatures for each zone. All plants in the A–Z of Species & Cultivars are rated with a zonal range, the lower zone indicating the coldest temperatures they will reliably survive and the higher one the hottest climate in which they will perform consistently. All areas have their own microclimates which create variations by as much as two zones. Gardeners living outside the USA can deduce the zone in which they live based on their own average minimum winter temperature.

		Fahrenheit	Celsius
Zone 1		below -50°	below -46°
Zone 2		-50° to -40°	-46° to -40°
Zone 3		-40° to -30°	-40° to -34°
Zone 4		-30° to -20°	-34° to -29°
Zone 5		-20° to -10°	-29° to -23°
Zone 6		-10° to 0°	-23° to -18°
Zone 7		0° to 10°	-18° to -12°
Zone 8		10° to 20°	-12° to -7°
Zone 9		20° to 30°	-7° to -1°
Zone 10		30° to 40°	-1° to 4°
Zone 11		above 40°	above 4°

INDEX

Italic page numbers refer to picture captions

Front and back jacket, background photograph:
A selection of the Evison/Poulsen cultivars introduced in the 1990s (clockwise from top left)

C. SUGAR CANDY™ 'Evione'   C. EVENING STAR™ 'Evista'
C. EVENING STAR™ 'Evista'   C. ARCTIC QUEEN™ 'Evitwo'
C. PETIT FAUCON™ 'Evisix'   C. ROYAL VELVET™ 'Evifour'
C. *florida* PISTACHIO™ 'Evirida' C. SUGAR CANDY™ 'Evione'
C. ARCTIC QUEEN™ 'Evitwo'   C. ARCTIC QUEEN™ 'Evitwo'
C. ANNA LOUISE™ 'Evithree'   C. LIBERATION™ 'Evifive'